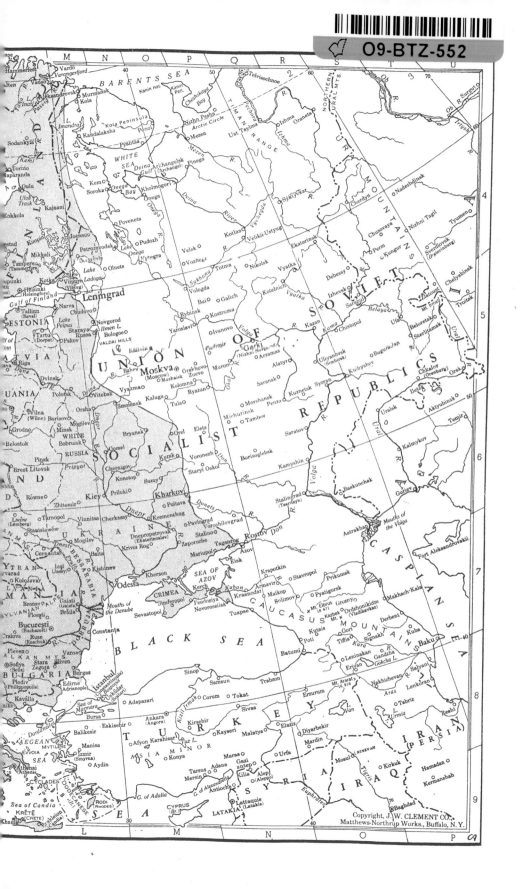

Copyright, J. W. CLEMENT CO.,
Matthews-Northrup Works, Buffalo, N. Y.

THE NAZI
CONSPIRACY

THE NAZI CONSPIRACY

*The Secret Plot to Kill
Roosevelt, Stalin, and Churchill*

Brad Meltzer
and Josh Mensch

FLATIRON
BOOKS
NEW YORK

www.flatironbooks.com

Designed by Donna Sinisgalli Noetzel

Endpaper map courtesy of David Rumsey Map Collection,
www.davidrumsey.com

The Library of Congress Cataloging-in-Publication Data
is available upon request.

ISBN 978-1-250-77726-3 (hardcover)
ISBN 978-1-250-88990-4 (international, sold outside the U.S.,
subject to rights availability)
ISBN 978-1-250-77727-0 (ebook)

Our books may be purchased in bulk for promotional,
educational, or business use. Please contact your local
bookseller or the Macmillan Corporate and Premium Sales
Department at 1-800-221-7945, extension 5442, or by email at
MacmillanSpecialMarkets@macmillan.com.

First U.S. Edition: 2023
First International Edition: 2023

10 9 8 7 6 5 4 3 2

For Professor Tom Collier,
my history professor at the
University of Michigan,
who encouraged me decades ago
to dive into World War II

—B.M.

In memory of my father,
Steven H. Mensch
1943–2021

—J.M.

Contents

A Note on the Text

When quoting from historical sources, we've sometimes corrected or updated the original spelling, capitalization, or punctuation to make the language clearer to modern readers. The wording itself has not changed, unless otherwise indicated in the text or endnotes.

Prologue

—— · ——

Tehran, Iran

November 28, 1943

The President is hiding.

The street is lined with soldiers. There are thousands of them, stretching for blocks on both sides. Most wear Soviet uniforms, some are British or American.

They brandish automatic rifles. In the hot, dry air they're using their weapons and bodies to block the noisy crowds who're trying to push through to get a look at what's happening—or rather, who's coming.

It's a broad avenue, a central thoroughfare through the bustling city of Tehran, the capital of Iran.

Here, in late November 1943, the city is in a heightened state of commotion. Starting today, it'll be the site of one of the most important events over the course of the global war currently sweeping the world. The event was previously kept secret, but has now been revealed to the public. Although Iran is not engaged in the war militarily, it is under Allied control, thus the prevalence of Soviet security forces on hand for the event.

A surge of noise rises from the crowd. Soldiers and onlookers alike turn toward the procession of cars approaching, a mix of military and civilian vehicles. At the center of the motorcade is a long, dark sedan glistening in the bright sun. This is the vehicle the soldiers have been ordered to protect.

Those who can catch a glimpse see a driver in the car's front seat. In the back is a single passenger, a tall, white-haired man in late middle age. The crowds on either side of the avenue crane their necks to get a better look. Intermittently, the passenger is visible through the car's rear windows.

The onlookers lean forward, everyone trying to see the President of the United States, Franklin Delano Roosevelt. Or at least, that's who they *think* is inside.

As the Presidential entourage makes its way through the city, it passes crowded marketplaces and residential buildings. Some residents watch the spectacle through windows or from roofs.

The dark sedan's destination today isn't a secret: The President is traveling to the Soviet embassy, a walled and heavily guarded complex of buildings north of the city center. There, FDR will meet with two fellow world leaders who are his allies in the war: Joseph Stalin, Premier of the Soviet Union; and Winston Churchill, Prime Minister of the United Kingdom.

It will be a summit of world-historical importance: the first time the "Big Three" leaders of the Allied forces in the ongoing war will come together in person. This conference took nearly a year of planning, involving immense geopolitical coordination and complicated security considerations.

Yet amid the grand spectacle, all is not as it seems. Unbeknownst to onlookers and soldiers—and even to many within the procession—the tall gray-haired man in the back seat of this sedan is not, in fact, the President of the United States. Instead, he's a member of the U.S. Secret Service, wearing a bulletproof vest and *pretending* to be the President.

The *real* President isn't even in this motorcade. At this moment, the real FDR is ducked down in the back of a very different vehicle, a small, dirty sedan racing through the backstreets of the city. While the sleek black Presidential limousine is surrounded by armed vehicles and military personnel, the nondescript car transporting the actual President is escorted only by a single fast-moving jeep as it tears through the winding streets.

Why this elaborate deception?

Late the previous night, top Soviet intelligence officials notified U.S. security of an alarming discovery: In this city under Allied control, disguised Nazi agents are on the move. Their mission, according to the Soviets, is to kill Roosevelt. And Churchill. And Stalin. It's an almost unbelievable plot, breathtaking in its audacity. Right here in Tehran, during this momentous conference, Nazi agents will attempt to assassinate the Big Three.

If successful, this plot will have consequences almost impossible to fathom.

For nearly four years now, the Second World War has enveloped the planet. Entire regions of Europe, Asia, and North Africa have been utterly devastated. The suffering and loss of life is nearly incalculable and continues daily. Mass atrocities on civilian populations are almost too numerous to count. Right now, there is no immediate end in sight.

The driving force of the war is a terrifying and appalling ideology that has taken root in several nations, but has reached its most extreme and powerful form in Germany under the Nazi Party.

Built on a twisted form of extreme patriotism, it's fueled by racial hatred, mass propaganda, conspiracy theories, the demonizing of minority groups, and the cult of personality around a narcissistic leader. Under the influence of this ideology—plus the ruthless political party that promotes it—a country that formerly embraced democratic values has turned toward authoritarianism, hatred, and violence. It is Germany and its principal allies, Italy and Japan, who have unleashed this calamitous war.

The clash of world military powers, as vast as it is, is not all that's at stake. As the Nazi regime expands, it's committing mass atrocities that go far beyond the scope of ordinary warfare, targeting peoples it considers "undesirables": the Roma, the mentally ill, Poles, and other Slavic people. Civilian populations, including women and children, are routinely imprisoned, tortured, worked to death, or simply massacred.

Above all, the regime has directed its brutality toward one group that, from the very beginning, it has vilified and blamed: the Jewish people. To solve what they call "the Jewish problem" in Europe, Nazi leaders have, in the course of the war, created an apparatus of mass slaughter so horrific it will take years for the world to fully comprehend.

To fight back, the Allies have planned this long-anticipated meeting of the Big Three—the leaders of the United States, the United Kingdom, and the Soviet Union—knowing that this meeting in Tehran represents the best and perhaps only chance for Allied powers to implement a military strategy to finally cripple Nazi Germany and put an end to the war that has caused such suffering around the world. Planning and executing this strategy will be a mammoth undertaking that will require global military coordination at an unprecedented scale.

Millions of lives depend on the success of this conference. Probably tens of millions.

If the Nazis have their way, these three world leaders won't leave the city alive—and the Allied hopes for victory will die with them.

It's not an exaggeration: The survival of nations is at stake.

And right now, FDR is ducked down, hiding in the back of a speeding car.

PART I

Commander in Chief

1

TWO YEARS EARLIER . . .

The Pacific Ocean

December 7, 1941

The ships have been traveling—secretly—for ten days.

Now, on this quiet Sunday morning, as the first light of dawn winks from the Pacific Ocean, the fleet prepares to change course.

There's no land in sight. Measured against the vast scale of the Pacific, this collection of warships is a tiny blip. But on a human scale, the fleet is enormous: six massive aircraft carriers, two battleships, nine destroyers, three cruisers, eight fuel tankers, and several small support ships. Below the waves are twenty-three accompanying submarines. On each carrier, the flight decks are lined with dozens of planes. In total, tens of thousands of crewmembers are aboard and mobilized.

For most of their ten-day journey, these ships have traveled eastward. Astonishingly, their movement across more than 3,500 miles of water—from a secluded bay on East Asian shores to here in the Central Pacific—has remained undetected by radar systems throughout the ocean. Every aspect of the fleet's journey has been planned and conducted at the highest levels of secrecy.

Now, several hundred miles south of the Aleutian Islands, the fleet commander issues a series of orders to chart a southern course. As the ships begin to move in the new direction, the slower-moving tankers break off from the fleet. The rest accelerate, going from twenty knots to twenty-four knots, a speed that provides momentum suitable for aircraft to launch from carrier decks.

At 6:05 a.m., a green light is waved on the deck of the flagship carrier. It's a signal to launch. One by one, engines roar and warplanes speed across the runway, rising into the dark morning air above the ocean waters. The other carriers simultaneously launch planes of their own.

The aircraft circle above the fleet and begin to maneuver. A total of 183 planes are soon flying south in battle formation, leaving the ships behind.

A reconnaissance plane shoots ahead of the others, disappearing in the clouds. The pilot's job is to scout the sea and air ahead, tuning into nearby radio frequencies to see if there's any indication that either the planes or carriers have been detected.

Ninety minutes later, at roughly 7:40 a.m., the lead pilots can see a sliver of land in the distance. They send a signal to the others: The air fleet remains undetected. Visibility is strong. The coast is clear. Time to attack.

The target? A small island of less than six hundred square miles. It's a place they're not at war with—yet the Japanese air fleet commanders are about to unleash the full destructive power of their fighter planes, bombers, torpedo planes, and dive-bombers.

This is a surprise attack, a preemptive strike intended to inflict maximum shock and devastation.

Within the next two hours, the world will change.

2

———— · ————

Washington, D.C.

It's 8:45 a.m. and President Franklin Delano Roosevelt is still in bed. He wears a sleeping robe and has a tray of food in front of him. This is no leisurely breakfast, however. He's surrounded by paperwork, and a busy telephone sits nearby.

He often starts the day this way, conducting the nation's affairs while under the covers. It's not so easy for the President to move from room to room—since being stricken with polio two decades ago, he's almost entirely without the use of his legs—and he's found that breakfasting and working in bed is often the most efficient way to begin the day.

The President was up late the night before. Well after midnight, he was still on a series of emergency phone calls with members of his national security staff.

Earlier that evening, U.S. Naval Intelligence services intercepted and translated a top secret memo from the Imperial government of Japan in Tokyo to the Japanese ambassadors stationed in Washington, D.C. The memo was in the form of a fourteen-point bulletin, with instructions to the ambassadors to deliver its message to the Americans according to a prepared timeline.

The Navy's intercept contained thirteen of the fourteen written points; the final section supposedly still to come. In methodical fashion, the bulletin outlined the Japanese response to the latest round of American diplomacy, rejecting what it perceives to be the United States' unreasonable demands to stop Japan's expansion into China and various territories in the South Pacific region. In addition, it views the United States' continued sanctions and oil embargo against it as intolerable.

To put it bluntly, ongoing negotiations between the United States and Japan have apparently collapsed.

This deterioration is the last thing the President wants. FDR's primary focus, and the focus of U.S. foreign policy in general, has been on providing aid and supplies to the United Kingdom for its war against Nazi Germany.

Now, with his legs still under the covers, Roosevelt is rereading the thirteen-point bulletin and trying to understand its implications. At roughly 9:30 a.m., a messenger from the Navy Department rushes into the room. He has the fourteenth section, which the Navy just received, decrypted, and translated.

This final paragraph officially states what the previous sections already implied. Japan will declare that since "efforts towards the establishment of peace" have failed, "it is impossible to reach an agreement with further negotiations."

Minutes later, the President receives yet another decrypt, a separate message sent in parallel. This message instructs the Japanese ambassadors to deliver the preceding bulletin to American officials at precisely 1 p.m., with no indication of why this time of day is so important. Even more ominously, the message instructs the ambassadors to destroy all confidential documents within the Japanese embassy and, apparently, to terminate their offices.

This is not good news. Time to get out of bed.

Once up, the President coordinates group phone calls and meetings with key leaders of his foreign policy and national security staff. By midmorning, they've analyzed the documents.

They agree that Japan is probably about to take military action against U.S.-friendly interests in Southeast Asia. Perhaps they'll attack British-controlled Singapore, or Guam, or try to seize the coveted oil fields of the Dutch East Indies. They may even attack the Philippines, an American protectorate.

If so, what should the United States do? Would these actions demand military response?

As his advisors debate options, Roosevelt decides that on this day, the typical Sunday skeleton staff at the White House won't be sufficient. He needs his top people. Soon, the White House operator is making phone calls all around the greater Washington, D.C., area, trying to locate personnel who are out shopping, in church, or with their families.

Among those who receive a call is Grace Tully, Roosevelt's personal secretary, who's relaxing at her apartment in Washington, D.C. "The President wants you right away," the White House operator tells her. "There's a car on the way to pick you up." Tully dresses quickly, "like a fireman" as she later recalls, and runs outside to meet the car.

The growing staff at the White House is tense. A military action somewhere in the South Pacific may be pending. The President's wife, the exceedingly busy Eleanor Roosevelt, had organized a large White House luncheon for supporters that day.

"I was disappointed but not surprised when Franklin sent word a short time before lunch that he did not see how he could possibly join us," she later recalled. As is sometimes the case, she'll play the role of President for the visitors because her husband cannot attend.

Instead, for lunch, the President and his longtime advisor Harry Hopkins huddle with sandwiches over a desk in Roosevelt's White House study. They're strategizing what comes next.

Then, at 1:47 p.m., the President's late lunch with Hopkins is interrupted by a call from Frank Knox, the Secretary of the Navy.

Knox clears his throat as the President gets on the line. Knox's voice is shaking as he says that the Pentagon "picked up a radio from Honolulu from our Commander-in-Chief of our forces there advising . . . that an air raid attack was on and that it was 'no drill.'" It appears, Knox continues after a pause, "like the Japanese have attacked Pearl Harbor."

Pearl Harbor? In Hawaii? That can't be right.

The U.S. naval base on the Hawaiian island of Oahu was thought to be impervious to attack. It's also, based on its location, far from any Japanese interests. So why would Japan possibly attack Hawaii?

Lunch partner Hopkins, one of Roosevelt's most trusted foreign policy advisors, doesn't believe it. "I expressed the belief that there must be some mistake," he records in a memo that day. "Surely Japan would not attack in Honolulu."

But the President has a terrible feeling. He needs to find out what happened.

By this point, Grace Tully is at her desk, frantically managing the Presidential phone lines. Shortly after Knox's call, the White House operator informs her that Admiral Harold Stark, the Chief of Naval Operations, is on the line for the President.

"I could hear the shocked unbelief in Admiral Stark's voice as he talked to me," Tully later recalled. She puts him on with the President, and Stark confirms the incomprehensible news: Japan has attacked Pearl Harbor. The base was entirely unprepared, and the results are catastrophic.

One thing is becoming clear. This will be the worst day of Roosevelt's presidency.

During his time in office, FDR had earned a reputation for unflappability. So while his staff begins to react with "near hysteria" to the news from Hawaii, he remains in control. The President retains "greater outward calm than anybody else," as Tully put it, but "with each new message he shook his head grimly and tightened the expression of his mouth."

Indeed, the terrible news keeps coming. The U.S. naval base was caught totally unaware. Battle stations were mostly unmanned, with ammunition locked in storage rooms and vaults. The ships in the harbor were sitting ducks.

The first wave of Japanese planes set their targets on "battleship row," where the hulking centerpieces of the U.S. Pacific Fleet were docked side by side. The attacking aircraft struck the USS *Oklahoma* first, with strafing guns and a pair of carefully aimed torpedoes. Massive explosions rocked the harbor as the fuel tanks ignited, and the huge vessel soon tilted toward port as water flooded through the damaged hull. Minutes later, the battleship began sinking to the bottom of the harbor, pulling more than four hundred sailors and crew to their deaths.

Within an hour, the entire base was an inferno. Two battleships sank completely, and several other battleships, destroyers, and cruisers were obliterated. The harbor was full of flames and wreckage. A group of Japanese planes also peeled off from the water to strike nearby airfields; the surprise attack decimated what was nearly the Navy's entire fleet of planes on the base.

According to early reports, by the time the attacks ended, well over two thousand American servicemembers or staff were dead. Another thousand were seriously wounded. The average age of sailors on the base was nineteen years old.

Aside from the horrors of the attack itself, the global consequences for what just occurred are momentous. At this moment, Japan is allied with Germany and Italy, nations that are fighting the British in a war that has swept Europe.

Japan's surprise attack on the United States has just altered the global balance of power, but it's difficult to grasp the ramifications.

The West Wing remains in a state of shock and panic. As word spreads through the afternoon, reporters pick up the story and soon the press corps surrounds the White House.

Amid the chaos, at 5 p.m., after a full day of nonstop frantic meetings and phone calls, President Roosevelt slips away to his small personal study adjoining the Oval Office. He's accompanied only by Grace Tully.

Tomorrow he will address both houses of Congress, and now, sitting in this study, he needs to figure out what to say.

For the past few hours, the State Department has been working frantically, preparing a speech for the President's review. It now sits in front of him—fifteen pages long, containing a lengthy history of diplomatic relations with Japan, and a detailed assessment of various military responses to the surprise attack.

Roosevelt tosses the papers aside. He may be addressing Congress, but his real audience is the American people. Rather than deliver a foreign policy lecture, he needs to speak for a nation that he knows was just shocked to the core. His speech should be short, simple, and strong. Every word counts.

With Tully seated nearby at a typewriter, Roosevelt leans back, puffs on a cigarette, and begins to dictate his message.

Tomorrow, President Franklin Delano Roosevelt, Commander in Chief, will address the nation.

3

——— · ———

America tried so hard to stay out of the war.

Like many nations, the United States had recently lost many young soldiers in the First World War. In 1919, after the Versailles Treaty brought U.S. troops home, the overwhelming sentiment in America was isolationism. For the average American, the Great War, which caused so much destruction and pain, accomplished seemingly little.

So why should more young American soldiers be sent across the ocean to fight and die over border disputes between faraway nations? The disillusion and confusion—felt especially by those who fought or lost loved ones—had a profound impact on a generation of Americans.

Then, almost a decade after the Versailles Treaty, the stock market crash of 1929 marked the United States' plunge into a crippling depression. Within a few years, nearly a quarter of U.S. citizens were unemployed, and the nation experienced unprecedented levels of poverty and homelessness.

Franklin Roosevelt was elected President in 1932 with a mission to save the country from permanent ruin. Unlike his predecessor, he took bold, aggressive action by utilizing federal government programs to stimulate growth and create jobs. Increasingly, he saw it as a moral calling to try and eradicate the scourge of poverty and better serve those citizens most in need.

"The test of our progress is not whether we add more to the abundance of those who have much, it is whether we provide enough for those who have too little," he declared. Gradually, the economy recovered.

Unsurprisingly, during this period of isolationism and economic struggle, the nation's military forces were a low priority. In 1939 America's army ranked only nineteenth in the world, below Portugal and just slightly above Bulgaria.

Nevertheless, the U.S. watched with a wary eye as a young German leader named Adolf Hitler rode a new political movement to power. Hitler spoke in apocalyptic terms, and his National Socialist party gradually solidified power by successfully purging domestic enemies. By the early-to-mid-1930s, he was in total control.

The Nazi Party, as it was soon called, trafficked in a rage-filled patriotism that appealed to the fears and prejudices of Germany's rural and working classes. Germany had been stripped of power after its defeat in the First World War, and its economy was then hit hard by the global Depression. These conditions created anxieties that Nazism ruthlessly exploited.

At his huge rallies, Hitler, surrounded by patriotic flags and accompanied by martial music, worked his supporters into a frenzy with bombastic speeches that promised to restore German strength; he spewed anger at "domestic enemies"—immigrants and minorities, mostly—whom he blamed for the nation's problems.

As a solution, Hitler and the Nazi Party demanded a return to "traditional values" and a renewed pride in ethnically "pure" Germans. Along with its racism and xenophobia, Nazism despised intellectuals, urban elites, and progressive ideas like women's liberation. Party leaders sometimes distilled their ideas into a single term, "nationalism," which loosely combined pride in one's country with a fear or hatred of immigrants, nonwhite minorities, and foreign influence. As Hitler declared in 1940, the concept of nationalism was "one strong new idea . . . which would make Germany great again."

Hitler and other party leaders based much of their rhetoric and agenda on a conspiracy theory. They claimed that at the end of the First World War, "globalists" conspired to force Germany's surrender and destroy its economy and culture—and that the Jewish people were behind this conspiracy. By pushing this sinister but purposely vague theory, Nazis could demonize an alleged cabal of wealthy Jews who operated in the shadows, as well as cast blame on the poor and working-class Jewish populations that they claimed were infiltrating European towns and cities to take jobs from honest, hardworking people.

Hatred of Jews and immigrants became a mantra that united the party and rallied its working-class base. "[The Jew] has ruined our race, corrupted our morals, hollowed out our customs and broken our strength," Hitler's Propaganda Minister Joseph Goebbels wrote in a Nazi pamphlet. "As nationalists we oppose the Jews because we see the Hebrews as the eternal enemy of our national honor and our national freedom."

Roosevelt and other world leaders watched as Hitler and the Nazi Party rose to prominence, seized power, and began the systematic persecution of minority groups. In 1935, Germany's new "Nuremberg Laws" encoded white racial supremacy and stripped Jews of citizenship rights. As the Nazis increasingly used violence to eliminate political enemies and brutalize minorities, FDR would declare Nazism the "enemy of all law, all liberty, all morality, all religion."

Meanwhile, Hitler launched an aggressive rearmament program that violated the Versailles Treaty while using the threat of military force to annex nearby territories that he claimed rightfully belonged to "the Fatherland."

Roosevelt thought Nazism was a great danger and often said so. But even after Hitler invaded Poland in September 1939—triggering declarations of war from the United Kingdom and France—the President was beholden to the powerful isolationists in Congress, as well as the public who supported them. During his 1940 Presidential campaign for a third term, Roosevelt played to public sentiment. "I have said this before, and I shall say it again and again. Your boys are not going to be sent into any foreign wars," he promised. He later regretted those words.

Today, we all like to think we'd stand up to the Nazis, but back in 1940, for the most part, ordinary Americans were simply indifferent to European affairs. Even worse, in some quarters of the country, a more sinister component was taking hold.

According to the 1930 U.S. census, roughly seven million people in America were German-born or second-generation German immigrants. While Hitler's rise in their home country appalled many, some German Americans embraced the Nazi ideology of anti-Semitism and white racial superiority, and found that it had traction in the United States. Pro-Nazi organizations like the Christian Front and the German American Bund emerged throughout the northeastern and midwestern states.

These groups tried to spread an Americanized Nazi message that combined conservative social values and flag-waving patriotism with appeals to the anti-Semitism and racism already prevalent throughout the country. Some pro-Nazi groups established clubs and camps for young people—modeled after the Hitler Youth camps in Germany— where American boys and girls in New Jersey, Long Island, and elsewhere learned the Hitler salute and could be seen marching through small towns wearing Nazi armbands.

On February 20, 1939, the German American Bund organized a flagship rally in Madison Square Garden in New York City, with an audience of twenty thousand. Behind the stage was a huge depiction of George Washington flanked by both Nazi swastikas and American flags.

The first speaker of the night declared, to great applause, that "if George Washington were alive today he would be friends with Adolf Hitler!" The night's keynote speech was delivered by the Bund's national leader Fritz Kuhn, who declared that patriotic Americans had a duty to "fight for a Gentile America free of all atheistic Jewish Marxist elements." When at one point a young Jewish man in the audience jumped on the stage to protest the event, Bund members surrounded him, knocked him down, then beat and kicked him in front of the crowd.

It wasn't just grassroots organizations like the Bund that supported Hitler; some prominent Americans were outspoken Nazi sympathizers.

A banner depicting George Washington flanked by both American flags and swastikas at New York City's Madison Square Garden during a February 20, 1939, rally hosted by the pro-Nazi group the German American Bund. The Bund chose the date of the rally to coincide with George Washington's birthday. (Courtesy of Bridgeman Images)

The renowned automaker Henry Ford—founder of the Ford Motor Company and one of the best-known Americans of his day—held overtly anti-Semitic views and was not afraid to express them. In his self-published newspaper *The Dearborn Independent,* Ford wrote a screed with the headline THE INTERNATIONAL JEW: THE WORLD'S PROBLEM. Adolf Hitler himself praised Ford's writing, saying that, "We look to Heinrich Ford as the leader of the growing Fascist movement in America . . . We have just had his anti-Jewish articles translated and published."

Even more influential was the famed American aviator Charles Lindbergh. Celebrated as a national hero, Lindbergh was a pro-German white supremacist who embraced the Nazi's anti-Semitism. Lindbergh said the field of aviation was "one of those priceless possessions which permit the White race to live at all in a pressing sea of Yellow, Black, and Brown."

Lindbergh became a prominent spokesperson for a group called the America First Committee, which urged the United States to stay out of the European war. Rumors even spread that Lindbergh would run for President in 1940 to challenge Roosevelt.

At the same time, some Americans were appalled by the Nazi threat and believed the United States should take a stronger stand against Hitler. Unsurprisingly, the Jewish American community was at the forefront. Having experienced anti-Semitism firsthand, they understood how quickly it could grow and spread.

On November 9, 1938, *Kristallnacht*—the "Night of Broken Glass"—erupted in Germany. That evening, the Nazi Party's domestic paramilitary force known as the SA instigated a nationwide pogrom against Jewish people and riled up German citizens to participate. Armed attackers destroyed 267 synagogues and ransacked hundreds of Jewish hospitals, schools, and businesses. The SA "authorities" beat, arrested, and sometimes killed helpless Jewish civilians as police looked on indifferently.

Kristallnacht would pale in comparison to the greater horrors to come. But it was the first undeniable evidence of Nazi violence that reached the wide international public. Soon, Jewish Americans began pushing for the United States to confront the scourge of Nazism directly and with military force.

This anti-Nazi sentiment was sometimes expressed in creative ways. In 1938, two Jewish comic book creators, Jerry Siegel and Joe Shuster, gave birth to Superman, a character dressed in American colors who used his extraordinary strength to save people in desperate trouble. By 1940, two other working-class Jews, Joe Simon and Jack Kirby, created Captain America as a direct response to Nazism. The first issue, cover dated March 1941, depicted a musclebound red-white-and-blue hero punching out Adolf Hitler. It was an overt political statement at a time when most Americans opposed entry into the war—and it was a fantasy that the United States would stand up and defend the Jewish people and other vulnerable populations from Nazi violence.

The truth, however, was that most Americans simply did not know or care about the threat of Nazism in Europe. They didn't want to get involved in another foreign conflict. Roosevelt couldn't have taken the country to war even he'd wanted to—given public opinion, Congress

In late 1940, two Jewish American comic book creators, Joe Simon and Jack Kirby, created a new superhero named Captain America as an overt political statement encouraging the United States to stand up to Nazi Germany and protect Jewish populations. The first issue, cover dated March 1941—a full nine months before the United States entered the war—depicts the red-white-and-blue hero punching Adolf Hitler. (Courtesy of Captain America, March #1 1941 / Advertising Archives / Bridgeman Images)

wouldn't have authorized it. Even after Hitler conquered most of Central Europe, and after France fell to the Nazis in spring 1940, the United States still hadn't entered the conflict.

Roosevelt did what he could short of committing troops. In March 1941, he signed the landmark "Lend-Lease" bill, authorizing the United States to "loan" armaments and military supplies to the United Kingdom at no cost. The policy was met with internal political resistance—"Lending war equipment is a good deal like lending chewing gum. You don't want it back," the isolationist senator Robert Taft argued—but this program would prove critical to Britain's survival. Still, as of April 1941, a whopping 81 percent of Americans were opposed to the U.S. entering the conflict.

Apparently, it would take an extraordinary event to change their minds. It was coming soon enough.

4

TWO YEARS LATER . . .

Near Qom, Iran

November 1943

The transport plane's cabin is dark, with biting cold air streaming through it. Outside, below cloud level, the sky is black.

Apart from the steady howl of the wind, the most noticeable sound is that of breathing—a steady inhale and exhale from the uniformed men seated around the cabin.

The men—half a dozen of them, maybe more—are sitting on benches on either side of the dark space. They draw breath from military-grade oxygen tanks, each trying to ration their small supply. The plane had recently reached a peak altitude of 18,000 feet, where breathing is near impossible.

Now, finally, the aircraft is descending, having cleared a mountain range. Just as a few of the men might have started panicking for lack of breath, oxygen returns to the cabin.

On the shoulders of the men are red stars—the insignia of the Soviet Union's Red Army. The rifles and pistols they hold are Soviet weapons, and the men's boots and jackets are Soviet uniforms. If these men could spare the oxygen to speak in this dark, windy airplane cabin, they'd speak in Russian.

Each of them also wears a parachute. In several minutes, a sergeant will open the cabin door, and the men will leap out. According to plan, they'll only drop a few seconds before releasing their chutes. After floating down several hundred feet in the black night, they'll land on a flat sandy plain, in the desert outside the city of Qom in Soviet-occupied Iran.

Yet there's something very unusual about these Soviet paratroopers.

The plane that carries them, a Ju 290 cargo craft that doubles as a heavy bomber, is not a Soviet plane but a German one. The pilot is not a Soviet pilot, but a German one. The sergeant who'll open the plane's cargo door is not a Soviet sergeant, but a sergeant of the Luftwaffe, the German air force.

These parachutists may be disguised as Red Army soldiers, but in fact they're Nazi agents. A special division of the SS intelligence services in Berlin trained them and sent them here.

If all goes to plan, once they hit the ground, they won't be recognized as the enemy. And why should they be? They're wielding Soviet weapons and wearing Soviet uniforms with authentic red stars on their shoulders.

From outside the city of Qom, these men have instructions to meet local handlers and load onto trucks that'll take them to the capital city of Tehran.

There, their secret mission begins.

5

---·---

Japan

In the end, it wasn't Nazi Germany that would finally draw the United States to fight in the growing global conflict. It was Japan, a nation on the other side of the globe.

In the 1930s, Japan's military expansion and aggression had no direct strategic connection to the fascist regimes of Germany or Italy. Instead, it was rooted in the complicated history and politics of East Asia. In some ways, Japan's militaristic rise was a direct consequence of the Western colonization of Asian peoples; the countries of Asia learned they must either grow stronger or be taken over and exploited by Europeans.

In the preceding decades, the British, the Dutch, and the French had all forcibly claimed territories in Asia, extracting the natural resources and turning local populations into colonial subjects. Indeed, it was some of these territories in the South Pacific region that Japan sought to wrest from the Europeans and claim for itself.

Yet, while Japan spoke of "liberating" Asian peoples from European control, their actions were those of conquerors. Inspired in part by the rise of Nazi Germany, Japan adopted its own creed of racial superiority, placing the Japanese above all other Asian peoples. This creed then justified Japanese atrocities against Koreans, the Chinese, and other groups they deemed inferior.

By the 1930s, the Japanese annexed and established control over the Korean peninsula. In 1931, Japan invaded the Manchuria region in northern China and established a "puppet state" called Manchukuo. Then, in December 1937, Japan launched a brutal attack on China proper, first conquering the city of Shanghai and then marching to the capital city of Nanjing. In the ensuing "Nanjing Massacre," the Japanese army reportedly slaughtered as many as two hundred thousand Chinese civilians, including children. The rampaging soldiers also engaged in what had become a staple of Japanese conquest: the systemic mass rape of women and girls in occupied territories.

Japan's aggression was met with international criticism, as were the news reports of the civilian massacres. Photographs of Japanese soldiers beheading Chinese prisoners of war had a particular shock value. The desperate Chinese government was forced to move its capital inland to the city of Beijing and pleaded for Western powers to help them defend their people. The United Kingdom and the United States condemned Japan's military aggression.

Japan saw it as a double standard, claiming, with some justification, that white Europeans had done the same to Asian peoples for decades. "The Western powers taught Japan the game of poker but after acquiring most of the chips they pronounced the game immoral and took up contract bridge," as the Japanese Foreign Minister Matsuoka Yosuke put it.

Be that as it may, President Roosevelt's position was clear. He was against colonialism in any form, European or Asian. While he couldn't turn back time and prevent colonial conquests of the past, he could now oppose any nation engaged in hostile military conquest. This position, coupled with the U.S.'s support of China in the region, led Roosevelt to an official policy of deterrence against further Japanese expansion. The U.S. Navy's Pacific Fleet, headquartered in Hawaii—but with bases in the Philippines and elsewhere in the South Pacific—would be that deterrent.

In September 1940, Japan signed the Tripartite Pact with Germany and Italy, formally allying with the European fascists. Although Japan and Germany were on opposite sides of the globe, they shared an animosity toward the United States, the United Kingdom, and the

Soviet Union. When the Japanese General Tomoyuki Yamashita traveled to Berlin to meet Hitler in 1941, he publicly announced that "in the coming age the interests of Japan and Germany would be identical as the two have common spiritual foundations."

Spirituality aside, Japan's pact with Hitler was a strategic gamble. Fully aware that the American public didn't want to get involved in another war, the Japanese hoped its alliance with Nazi Germany would deter the U.S. from interfering with their expansion. Instead, it only raised alarms, convincing America to stand strong against Japanese aggression while imposing tough sanctions, including an oil embargo that could cripple Japanese naval operations.

Even so, Roosevelt never imagined that Japan would provoke a full-scale war with the United States. "It would not do this country any good nor Japan any good, but both of them harm to get into war," he told the Japanese ambassador in Washington, with whom he was friendly. Increasingly preoccupied with the situation in Europe, Roosevelt believed that when it came to Asia, all parties would eventually reach an agreement to avoid a trans-Pacific war.

No surprise, Japan viewed it differently. Their militarist leaders were dead set on continuing Japanese expansion, and they began to believe in the inevitability of a clash with the U.S. Better to strike immediately while they were in a strong position. If they waited for diplomacy, the delay would allow the U.S. to continue to expand its Navy—a process already underway with the Lend-Lease program to the United Kingdom—and Japan would lose the upper hand in the Pacific.

With the element of surprise on their side, Japanese leaders calculated they could debilitate the U.S. naval fleet in one overwhelming strike—and when America saw such Japanese power, they'd back off and stop policing the Pacific for good.

They were wrong. But it explains why, in the summer and fall of 1941, as Japanese diplomats continued their façade of diplomacy, their military leaders were secretly planning one of the most audacious surprise attacks in world history. "Our empire stands at the threshold of glory or oblivion," the Japanese War Minister General Hideki Tojo proclaimed to his fellow generals, aware that striking the United States would be an enormous risk.

On November 26, 1941, Japanese carriers and warships secretly departed from Hitokappu Bay off the northern Japanese coast for the 3,500-mile journey. Ten days later, the ships began their approach to the Hawaiian island of Oahu.

From a military and tactical point of view, the mission would be a stunning success. But the final consequence of the attack would be nearly the opposite of what Japanese leaders hoped.

6

———— · ————

Washington, D.C.

December 8, 1941

WAR! OAHU BOMBED BY JAPANESE PLANES.

So declared the oversized headline in the evening edition of the *Honolulu Star-Bulletin,* hours after the attack. The Honolulu press got the news first, but within minutes, radio broadcasts and other newspapers around the country began filing their stories. By Monday, December 8, every press outlet in the nation was struggling to keep up with the flood of new details.

The attack on Pearl Harbor, it turned out, wasn't a stand-alone event; it was one part of a coordinated Japanese assault across the Pacific, with surprise attacks that same night on Hong Kong, Malaya, the Philippines, Wake Island, and Guam. This was on top of the enormous casualties that German armies were causing throughout Europe.

War was expanding to the west and to the east. People wanted answers.

Why was the U.S. Navy caught so unprepared? What'd this mean for the war in Europe? And above all, how would we respond to this attack on American soil?

At 12:30 p.m. at the East Gate of the White House, President Roosevelt's aides wheel him to the back seat of a waiting car.

Roosevelt's advisors, particularly Secretary of the Treasury Henry Morgenthau, had urged the President to travel in a military vehicle with escorts—better to be safe considering the recent attack. Roosevelt refused, insisting he ride in a convertible with the top down. He's the President of the American people, not some shadowy military dictator who sneaks around.

Shortly after 1 p.m., the car arrives at its destination: the U.S. Capitol, where the full U.S. Senate and House of Representatives are gathered inside. The White House and capital press corps are also swarming, both in and out of the building, everyone waiting for the Commander in Chief.

As the President enters the chamber just before 1:30 p.m., the members of both houses rise for a standing ovation. Roosevelt has many enemies in Congress, but today—at least at this moment—the lawmakers put differences aside and join the unified applause.

When it comes to speeches and other public events, Roosevelt and his handlers have a carefully designed system for him to be wheeled or lifted onto stages and lecterns. Typically, the goal is to hide his infirmity, so he appears before crowds like any other public figure.

Today is different. In full view of everyone present, he makes a point to walk himself, taking several steps to the podium. To do so, he puts all his weight on his arm braces and, with only a companion's hand on his shoulder for balance, drags the dead weight of his own legs along the floor. To pull it off requires intense focus; he could easily stumble or fall to the ground as he has in the past. Given the already heightened emotion, this display of vulnerability and courage has everyone in Congress catching their breath.

Roosevelt makes it to the podium without a fall. Using his arms, he props himself up to his full six-foot-two-inch height. With the eyes of the world on him, the President begins to speak in a clear, methodical tone. There are the words he'd dictated to Grace Tully the day before: "Yesterday, December 7, 1941—a date which will live in infamy—the United States of America was suddenly and deliberately attacked by naval and air forces of the Empire of Japan."

Roosevelt doesn't use any arm movements in his speech. He needs to keep both hands on the podium to support his full weight. As a result, he only uses head movements for emphasis. "The attack yesterday on the Hawaiian Islands has caused severe damage to American naval and military forces," he continues. Then, after a pause, "I regret to tell you that very many American lives have been lost."

It's now a full day after the attack, and some families around the country have already been notified that a loved one perished. In the days ahead, many more will hear the same.

"I believe that I interpret the will of the Congress and of the people when I assert that we will not only defend ourselves to the uttermost but will make it very certain that this form of treachery shall never again endanger us."

This line gets a round of applause, and then a standing ovation. It's a clear signal to Congress what action they must take.

While he's careful in the speech to only refer to Japan, the context of the larger war is impossible to ignore. "Hostilities exist," Roosevelt declares. "There is no blinking at the fact that our people, our territory, and our interests are in grave danger.

"With confidence in our armed forces, with the unbounding determination of our people, we will gain the inevitable triumph—so help us God."

In conclusion, Roosevelt asks, officially, that Congress authorize a state of war "between the United States and the Japanese Empire."

The speech lasts barely six minutes, including breaks for applause. "I do not think there was another occasion in his life when he was so completely representative of the whole people," one senior aide would say, and the speech received praise from every direction.

Within thirty-three minutes after Roosevelt leaves the podium, both Houses of Congress vote on and pass a declaration of war against Japan. The Senate votes 82–0; the House of Representatives votes 388–1.

Many questions remain, but one thing is abundantly clear: The United States of America is now at war.

It's only been a day and a half. As CBS News radio broadcaster Lowell Thomas puts it, "This may have been the most momentous weekend in the history of our country."

If only he knew what was coming.

7

———— • ————

ONE NIGHT EARLIER . . .

Buckinghamshire, United Kingdom

December 7, 1941

News travels fast.

It takes just a few hours for the story of the attack on Pearl Harbor to travel over 7,200 miles from Hawaii and reach this man at a dining table on a different continent.

Sixty-eight years old, he's short and squat, somewhat round in the belly, with wide jowly cheeks and piercing eyes that sit under a perpetually furrowed brow. For two years, he's shouldered the singular task of defending the last corner of Europe—the British Isles—against the aggression and military occupation of Nazi Germany.

He's Winston Churchill, the Prime Minister of the United Kingdom—and for once, tonight, he is speechless.

To friends and enemies alike, Churchill is a force of nature. Words rarely stop pouring from his mouth. His oratory, debating skills, and sharp wit are legendary, as is his appetite for food, drink, and cigars. Despite the unhealthy habits and advancing age, he possesses what seems like an almost inexhaustible energy. He sometimes works straight through the evening, up until dawn, especially if he's been refreshed by his cherished midday bath and brandy.

Churchill was born into a privileged British family and attended the elite Royal Military Academy. After an early career combining

British Prime Minister Winston Churchill, photographed in 1941. From the start of his term in June 1940, almost every moment of Churchill's time in office was devoted to conducting the British war effort against Nazi Germany. (Courtesy of World History Archive / Alamy Stock Photo)

military service with journalism, he became a Member of Parliament at the age of only twenty-six. The boisterous House of Commons proved an ideal training ground for his aggressive debating style. He went on to have a decades-long public career, including military service in World War I, appointments overseas as an officer of the British Empire, and several terms as a cabinet minister. During this period, he also authored several books on history, literature, and other subjects.

By the 1930s, Churchill was in his early sixties and preparing to retire from public life—or so he thought. With the rise of Nazi Germany, he became a vocal critic of Britain's and France's appeasement policy toward Hitler, who was rearming Germany in violation of the

Versailles Treaty and beginning to annex nearby territories. According to Churchill, an appeaser is one who "hopes that if he feeds the crocodile enough, the crocodile will eat him last." He was proven correct when an emboldened Hitler invaded Poland in late 1939, an act that finally took the United Kingdom to war.

Churchill's prescient understanding of the Nazi threat—as well as his military and political experience—made him a natural choice to lead the nation when Prime Minister Neville Chamberlain's term came to an end in early 1940, just as the war was beginning. "I felt as if I were walking with destiny," Churchill would later say, "and that all my past life had been but a preparation for this hour and for this trial."

In his first speech as Prime Minister, delivered to the House of Commons on May 13, 1940—after Hitler and Nazi Germany had already annexed, occupied, or conquered nations like Czechoslovakia, Poland, Norway, the Netherlands, Belgium, and others, often committing brutal atrocities along the way—Churchill summarized his mission:

> You ask, what is our policy? I can say: It is to wage war, by sea, land and air, with all our might and with all the strength that God can give us; to wage war against a monstrous tyranny, never surpassed in the dark, lamentable catalogue of human crime. That is our policy. You ask, what is our aim? I can answer in one word: It is victory, victory at all costs, victory in spite of all terror . . . for without victory, there is no survival.

As for his own role, he said, simply, "I have nothing to offer but blood, toil, tears and sweat." Almost instantly, Churchill came to embody the British war effort.

The problem was, he was presiding over a disaster. Just five days after he became Prime Minister, France surrendered to Nazi forces. German tanks rolled into Paris. Up to that point, France was supposed to have the largest military in the world. The Germans crushed it with ease.

In the face of such strength, the smaller nations of mainland Europe had to surrender to Germany or risk annihilation. Mussolini's Italy quickly joined the war on Germany's side, creating a bulwark around the Mediterranean. Hitler seized resources, treasure, and armaments from conquered territories, further increasing Germany's might.

Only the British remained. The English Channel, guarded by the Royal Navy and the Royal Air Force, was all that protected the British Isles from the swarm of Nazi ground forces. The United Kingdom's overseas allies—Canada, Australia, and a few others—offered support but couldn't contribute much.

In June 1940, the Luftwaffe, Germany's vaunted air force, launched an aerial campaign to conquer the United Kingdom. Their bombers aimed for British cities, targeting civilians to inflict maximum suffering and force surrender. Barely a month into Churchill's term as Prime Minister, Britain's very existence was in doubt.

His great hope—and the United Kingdom's salvation, he believed—was that the United States of America would enter the war. He desperately wanted, and needed, a strategic partner. He'd come to respect President Roosevelt, and he thought FDR understood the Nazi threat. But despite Churchill's insistent begging and pleading—and Churchill could be *very* insistent—Roosevelt would not or could not bring America into the war.

For nearly two years, all Churchill could do was hope that something—anything—would change America's mind.

Now, tonight, when the news of Japan's attack on Hawaii finally reaches him, Churchill is sitting at his dining table in Chequers, a country retreat outside London designated for the Prime Minister. He's in the middle of a dinner meeting with several military advisors, as well as two American diplomats. The radio plays in the background.

The BBC radio announcer reads the special report—the Japanese Imperial Navy bombed Pearl Harbor. At first, Churchill and his aides are confused. The designation "Pearl Harbor" isn't well known outside the U.S. Some at the table think the announcer said "Pearl River," which they assume must be a river in China. The two Americans know exactly what the announcer means, but they're still confused by the news, and initially hesitant to interject and correct their hosts.

In true British fashion, the truth is finally revealed by the butler. Entering the room after hearing the broadcast in the servants' quarters, he reports that the Japanese have in fact bombed the U.S. naval base in Hawaii.

The room is stunned. Even Churchill, for the moment, doesn't speak.

The United Kingdom's role in the war had recently become even more complicated when, in June 1941, while Germany and the British were still engaged in ongoing aerial battles over the English Channel, Hitler shocked the world yet again by invading the Soviet Union.

To launch this invasion—Operation Barbarossa, as they called it—Germany amassed one of the largest fighting forces in human history. With ruthless speed, the Wehrmacht infantry and tank divisions stormed eastward across the vast expanse of Eastern Europe while the Luftwaffe rained destruction from above. The German forces left an appalling loss of life in their wake. Within a few months, the massive German front had traversed hundreds of miles and Nazi troops were approaching Leningrad and Moscow.

When the invasion first began, Churchill pledged his support to the USSR, promising whatever aid he could give. He urged every ally to do the same.

The problem was, forging an alliance with the Soviet Union was a complicated business. For starters, the Soviet Union was a communist country, and therefore anathema to what the United Kingdom stood for. To ally with the Soviet regime meant overcoming their vast differences in political, economic, and moral outlook. In a speech to Parliament, Churchill made clear, however, that this is precisely what the United Kingdom must do:

> No one has been a more consistent opponent of Communism than I have for the last twenty-five years . . . I will unsay no word that I have spoken about it. But all this fades away before the spectacle which is now unfolding . . . Any man or state who fights on against Nazidom will have our aid. It follows, therefore, that we shall give whatever help we can to Russia and the Russian people.

More troubling was the fact that only two years earlier, the Soviets had in fact been collaborating with Hitler. With its own agenda of territorial expansion, the Soviet Union joined the Germans in the brutal conquest of Poland in 1939 and participated in the resulting atrocities. The Soviet Union had, quite literally, started the war on the side of Nazi Germany. Only when Hitler suddenly broke his alliance and invaded their nation did the Soviet Union have any problem with the Nazi agenda. For this reason alone, the Soviets were an untrustworthy partner.

Finally, by allying with the Soviet Union, Churchill would now have to personally deal with the man who famously controlled the country with an iron fist: Joseph Stalin.

Unlike previous communist leaders, who were motivated at least in part by economic justice, Stalin had proven himself to be an authoritarian despot motivated only by raw power. Like Hitler, Stalin had routinely used murder and violence to eliminate political rivals. Like Hitler, Stalin had committed mass atrocities against minority groups in his own country. Stalin's nickname, "The Man of Steel," arose from his personal ruthlessness.

Now, he and Churchill are on the same side.

For the Prime Minister, the war effort plus this uneasy relationship with Stalin is pushing him to the brink. He desperately needs help; he needs a partner. For two years now, since the war began, he's yearned and prayed for the United States to be that partner.

So as they sit at the dinner table at Chequers, it's Churchill who reacts first to the butler's announcement. Standing up from the table, he throws down his napkin and rushes out of the room. A few others, including the American ambassador to the United Kingdom, John Winant, run after him.

As Churchill enters the study next door, he feels an overwhelming need to act. Something must be done—but what? Send ships to the South Pacific?

It's Winant who steadies him. They can't conduct foreign policy based on a radio segment. Winant suggests they first call Washington, D.C., together and confirm what happened. Moments later, Winant is dialing the White House. President Roosevelt is on the line.

Churchill takes the receiver. "Mr. President, what's this about Japan?" he asks.

"Yes, the Japanese attacked Pearl Harbor," Roosevelt replies. Then, after a pause, the President speaks the most transformative words Churchill has heard since the start of the war: "I guess we're in the same boat now."

In the same boat. It looks like the United States is joining the war.

The call doesn't last long. Churchill is careful not to display happiness in front of the Americans who are with him; after all, the U.S. just suffered a tragedy. But after two years with his nation on the verge of extinction, Churchill is now flooded, as he later put it, with "the greatest joy." He's reminded of a remark he once heard from a Foreign Minister, that the U.S. is like "a gigantic boiler. Once the fire is lighted under it there is no limit to the power it can generate."

After a few hours of meetings and phone calls, Churchill collapses for the night. "Being saturated and satiated with emotion," he later wrote, "I went to bed and slept the sleep of the saved and thankful."

Still, it is premature to celebrate. The next day, President Roosevelt will ask for and receive from Congress a declaration of war only against Japan. He doesn't request the same against Germany or Italy, and if he did, Congress would probably not grant it.

In fact, when it comes to the U.S. going to war against Germany, that's a decision that won't be made by Winston Churchill, Franklin Roosevelt, or even the U.S. Congress. It will be made by a very different person, several thousand miles away.

8

———— • ————

Rastenburg, Prussia

December 7, 1941

Someone has to tell the Führer.

It happens at the *Wolfsschanze*—"The Wolf's Lair"—a secluded fortress in a remote forest in East Prussia—now Poland—roughly 150 miles north of Warsaw. Six months ago, after the invasion of Russia, the Nazi leadership built this secret enclave so top officials could be closer to the Eastern front.

Here, over a thousand miles from where the British Prime Minister is dining at Chequers—on the very opposite end of the European continent—the news of Japan's attack on Pearl Harbor likewise comes as a complete surprise.

It's probably only a matter of minutes after Churchill heard the news that Nazi officials at the Wolf's Lair learn of the attack. Now comes the potentially harder part: An officer on the press staff must personally deliver the news to the leader of the Reich, the Führer, Adolf Hitler.

Hitler's personal office and quarters are at the center of the Wolf's Lair. The entire complex is fortified and heavily guarded, intended to be impenetrable should enemies ever discover its whereabouts. The Lair is typically staffed by nearly a thousand soldiers and other employees. Among those thousand are fifteen women, all German, whose sole duty is to sample each portion of Hitler's meals before he eats it. If an enemy has successfully poisoned his food, one of these women will die rather than the Führer.

Lately, rather than operating from Berlin, Hitler has been spending more time at this remote lair in the Prussian forest. He's obsessed with the day-to-day operations of the German armies on the Russian front, and being here allows greater focus.

Hitler's decision to invade the Soviet Union earlier in the year was his greatest gamble and, he believes, his masterstroke. Conquering the inferior Slavic people, eliminating the scourge of communism, securing the rich resources in the USSR, and punishing the large Jewish populations of the East are essential components in his grand design.

On the Eastern front, however, all has not gone according to Hitler's plan. Given how quickly German armies had swept through central and Western Europe in 1940, crushing every resistance they encountered, Hitler imagined that the Soviet Union would also crumble with ease. At first the Wehrmacht performed as expected, with millions of troops and tanks advancing many hundred of miles over the summer and decimating everything in their path, including any divisions of the Soviet army that tried to repel it.

Yet after this spectacular beginning, the mission began to stall. German troops were becoming exhausted, and for military leaders, the task of keeping millions of soldiers fed and equipped over the vast Soviet terrain was logistically overwhelming. Meanwhile, Stalin, after recovering from the initial shock of Hitler's betrayal, regrouped the Red Army and transformed his nation to a war footing. As tired German troops finally neared Leningrad and Moscow, they encountered a stiffer and better-organized Soviet resistance.

Just as the German offensive was beginning to falter, it also encountered the toughest enemy of all: "General Frost"—Russia's long, brutally cold winter that has historically defeated invading armies. In November, temperatures plummeted, and arctic winds began sweeping across the vast frozen tundra.

Hitler had been so sure that he would secure victory over the Soviets by early fall, he and his military leaders simply failed to equip the millions of German soldiers in infantry and tank divisions with proper winter gear. Soon, the exposed troops were dying of frostbite before they even encountered the enemy. Then, on December 5, as Soviet generals sensed weakness, they launched a surprise counterattack against the German divisions moving toward Moscow. Much to Hitler's fury, the battered German troops retreated from the Soviet line.

Now, with the winter hitting full force, Hitler has no choice but to pull his armies back to defensive positions. Most troops will remain in Russia for the winter—the Germans have conquered much of its western territory—but a renewed offensive against the major cities now must wait until spring. This, of course, gives Stalin more time to prepare a defense.

Germany still has the superior army. But this is the first real setback for Nazi forces since the war began. It's the chink in their armor. Now Hitler's worried that once the news reaches Berlin, morale in Germany will suffer. Most importantly, the setback makes him look weak—and for the mighty Führer, nothing is worse than that.

Hitler, therefore, is in a foul mood on the night of December 7.

It's only two days after the Soviet counteroffensive. When he first hears the news about Pearl Harbor, Hitler is just as surprised as Churchill and Roosevelt. Because of the absolute secrecy required for the surprise attack, Japan hadn't notified their own allies of the plan. The news arrives, as one Nazi official later described it, like "a bolt from the blue."

At the Wolf's Lair, some Nazi leaders are initially worried. With the setback in Russia, the last thing they need is the United States potentially entering the war.

But there is one person who sees it as great news: Adolf Hitler.

Hitler "slapped his thighs with delight as news of the report was brought to him," according to one Nazi official's account. After two days of gloom and rage, the Führer is suddenly animated again. Pearl Harbor brings new energy, a change of momentum, and a welcome diversion from Russia. Everything about the war would be different now. "It was as if a heavy burden had been lifted," one onlooker described, "as with the greatest excitement he explained the new world order to everyone around him." It also played into Hitler's grandiose narratives of a great conflict of civilizations, with himself at the center.

For the Nazi officials there, Hitler's enthusiasm is contagious. Or at least, everyone is required to follow along. That night, the Wolf's Lair is "caught up in an ecstasy of rejoicing," and Nazi Foreign Minister Joachim von Ribbentrop is soon "jumping for joy about the Japanese attack on the United States."

By chance, Hitler is already scheduled, three days from now, to deliver a major speech to the Reichstag, the German parliamentary body. The timing couldn't be better. The speech will provide the perfect forum for the Führer to divert the world's attention from his setback on the Eastern front, and instead seize the global narrative in the aftermath of Pearl Harbor.

The next morning, December 8, the Führer travels roughly 450 miles from East Prussia to his formal government offices in Berlin. Here, he immediately meets Joseph Goebbels, his Minister of Propaganda, to begin working on the coming speech. They decide to delay the speech one day, until December 11, to allow more time to prepare.

Some of Hitler's ministers in Berlin, like the military leaders at the Wolf's Lair, urge caution when it comes to responding to Pearl Harbor. With Germany's armed forces already extended to the east in the Soviet Union, and still battling with Great Britain to the west, the last thing they need is another enemy, in this case, the United States. Perhaps Hitler's strategy, they suggest, should be to support Japan in its conflict with the Americans, but not provoke direct conflict between the U.S. and Germany. Thus far the United States has only declared war on Japan, and perhaps it's best to keep it that way.

Hitler angrily rejects any such idea. For starters, he doesn't fear the United States. Compared to the proud white European powers, America is, he believes, fundamentally weak. The United States had betrayed its original white racial heritage to become a mongrel nation full of lesser races. As Hitler's ally Benito Mussolini of Italy put it dismissively, America is a "country of Negroes and Jews."

Beyond military factors, Hitler also believes, as a matter of course, he must always project strength. He must always be the aggressor and dictate events. "A great power doesn't let itself have war declared on it—it declares war itself," as von Ribbentrop put it, echoing the Führer's thinking. Without consulting or even informing his military leaders, Hitler instructs his Foreign Ministry in Berlin to start drawing up a formal declaration of war against the United States while he and Goebbels work on their speech.

On December 11 at 3 p.m., three days after Franklin Roosevelt addressed the U.S. Congress, Adolf Hitler enters the Kroll Opera House in Berlin, where the 865 members of the Reichstag are seated. Because Hitler has already purged or arrested any members of the Reichstag who dared publicly oppose him, today he'll be speaking to the faithful. The speech will not only be broadcast all over Germany, but around the globe.

Cries of "*Sieg Heil*" fill the room. The Führer approaches a grandiose podium with a massive Nazi symbol hanging behind it. From here, Adolf Hitler begins to speak.

He starts with an update on the war effort, extolling the successes of the German army on the Eastern front. When he talks about their casualty numbers, he gives figures that are inaccurate. One of Hitler's leadership tactics, reflected in the messaging of the Nazi propaganda program, is to ignore the truth and say only what is flattering to himself and the Nazi regime. If the facts are unflattering, he simply lies. Those lies will be amplified by his propaganda apparatus, while the truth will be buried or forgotten.

While discussing the war in Russia, Hitler makes no mention of the Soviet counteroffensive on the Eastern front; he makes no mention that German forces have failed in the principal goal of capturing Moscow before winter, or that the offensive must now be delayed until spring. He speaks no words on behalf of the many German soldiers who, because of his miscalculations, are now starving and freezing or already captured by the Red Army.

As Hitler immediately recognized, better to divert attention from the dismal news in Russia—especially when he's got a new narrative to spin.

And so, midway through the speech, Hitler's tone shifts as he snidely mentions "that man who . . . likes to make his chats from the fireside."

On December 11, 1941, four days after the Japanese attack on Pearl Harbor, Adolf Hitler addresses the Reichstag at the Kroll Opera House in Berlin. His speech will forever alter the course of the war. (© SZ Photo / Bridgeman Images)

He knows they'll understand—everyone knows about Franklin Roosevelt's weekly "fireside chats." Hitler proceeds to attack Roosevelt's character and abilities, referring to his "ignorance" and "narrow intellect." He insults Roosevelt's wife, First Lady Eleanor Roosevelt, for recent remarks she made against the Nazi Party.

He then goes into a policy rant, saying that Roosevelt, since taking office, "had increased the State Debt of his country to an enormous extent, had decreased the value of the dollar," and "had brought about a further disintegration of economic life." Regarding Roosevelt's signature economic program, Hitler claims, "Roosevelt's New Deal legislation was all wrong: it was actually the biggest failure ever experienced by one man."

Of course, neither Hitler nor the members of the Reichstag particularly care about Roosevelt's domestic economic policies. This is just a lead-up for the main event.

Hitler's voice becomes darker and more sinister. Roosevelt's economic failure, he says, "is not surprising if one bears in mind that the men he had called to support him, or rather, the men who had called him, belonged to the Jewish element." Here's where the applause starts to come. "The full diabolical meanness of Jewry rallied round this man," Hitler continues, his voice rising, "and he stretched out his hands."

Now Hitler arrives at his grand narrative. Roosevelt, he declares, is like Churchill—part of the "Anglo-Saxon-Jewish-Capitalist World." They are the globalists. And the Jews, as Hitler describes it, are "all for disintegration and never for order." President Roosevelt is part of the great conspiracy. He's being controlled by the "Eternal Jew," who poses a threat to the traditional values of white people in Germany and in all of Europe. The German people must stand behind their Führer and fight against these foreigners and Jews.

After the long buildup and massive applause, Hitler makes it official: Germany will declare war on the United States of America. "Our enemies must not deceive themselves," he insists, triumphantly. "In the two thousand years of German history known to us, our people have never been more united than today."

With this declaration, the global stage is irrevocably set. Nazi Germany, Italy, and Japan are at war with the United Kingdom, the Soviet Union, and the United States.

The Reichstag address, from Hitler's point of view, accomplished his objectives. He distracted German public attention from the recent military setbacks against the Soviets; he projected strength and seized the global initiative by declaring war against the United States before the United States could declare war on Germany; and he vilified America as part of the cabal of Jewish globalists who were out to destroy the German people.

Through the course of the speech, Hitler referred to Roosevelt by name over three dozen times. It's no accident—he needs to create a clear enemy. On top of that, Hitler enjoys making things personal. While his vast armies rain death and suffering across the world, he sees himself as engaged in a personal battle against the world leaders who stand in the way of Germany's grand mission.

Churchill. Stalin. Roosevelt. These are Hitler's enemies. In the great battle of wills, he believes he must prevail.

Hitler's personal fixation on the Big Three will guide some of Nazi Germany's most fateful decision-making. In fact, nearly two years from this moment, it will lead to what could be one of the most ambitious assassination plots in history.

PART II

Storm and Ruin

9

---·---

Tehran, Iran

January 1943

He knows how to blend in.

On a typical day in Tehran, the marketplaces are buzzing with customers, the cafés and shops doing brisk business as a mix of cars, bicycles, and pedestrians crowd the narrow streets. In this city and in this country, unlike in many other places in the world, life appears not so different from how it did three or four years ago, before the start of the war. With some exceptions, most of the visible uniforms are yellow—the color worn by officers of the local Iranian security forces.

But like many other nations, Iran couldn't choose to be neutral in the war. It shares a northern border with Russia, and right now it's under Allied control. Tehran, the capital city, is monitored by a combination of Soviet, British, and American forces.

That's why this slender man in his late twenties—who sometimes visits Tehran's cafés and marketplaces—must keep a very low profile. In fact, he needs to wear a disguise.

His name is Franz Mayr. But only a small handful of people in the city know this name. For everyone else he uses an alias. Why so much secrecy?

Franz Mayr is a Nazi—a detail he wants no one to know.

Why's he here?

Four years earlier, in his midtwenties, Mayr was a recent law school graduate living in Potsdam, Germany, and working in a bureaucratic position as an industrial secretary. When the war began, he was eager, like many other young German men, to join the Nazi cause.

He initially trained as a military signals operator, but Mayr's superiors soon transferred him to an arena better suited to his cerebral abilities: intelligence. Soon, he joined the Sicherheitsdienst, or SD, the Nazi intelligence organization. Unlike Germany's traditional military intelligence agency, the Abwehr—which had a decades-long history and operated with some autonomy—the SD was an organ of the Nazi Party and answered only to Adolf Hitler.

Within the entry-level ranks of the SD, Mayr befriended another young recruit named Roman Gamotha. Without giving the decision much thought, the two signed up together for "Middle East duty," unaware of what this meant or where it would take them. In a very short time—a matter of weeks—the two received an assignment to travel to the neutral nation of Iran, assume aliases there, and operate in the country on behalf of Germany.

In other words, they would be Nazi spies.

Mayr and Gamotha received little training in advance. As a British intelligence file later described the two young agents' mission:

> [T]he S.D. were unable to give them any accurate information about the country. Nor did they receive any training in intelligence work, W/T [wireless transmitters] or sabotage methods . . . They were given no contacts, no definite assignments, nor were there any courier arrangements. [The] head of Section VI merely told them first to get to Persia and there to become acquainted with the country.[1] Instructions would follow.

---

1 Many Europeans and Americans at the time incorrectly referred to the nation of Iran as "Persia." The preference of the Iranian government was for "Iran," and that is the terminology we will use in this text. The term "Persian" should refer to the ethnic group that has traditionally comprised the majority of the region's population, but that term was also frequently misused by Westerners to refer to any Iranian of non-Western descent. In both cases, we will use the terms correctly in our text, but

Those instructions actually never arrived. The two agents made their way to the capital city of Tehran and connected with the German embassy. Obtaining fake jobs as cover, they had the autonomy to work as agents-at-large in the city.

Despite their unfamiliarity with the language and local customs, life was initially not too hard for the spies, because the country and its government were pro-German at the start of the war. The country's leader, a strongman named Reza Shah, looked up to Hitler during the 1930s and was eager to learn from and adopt elements of Nazism.

Hitler responded favorably to Reza Shah's fawning attention and sought to cement a relationship. At one point, Hitler amended the Nuremberg Laws—the infamous Nazi "race laws" in Germany that codified white supremacy and anti-Semitism—to include "Persian peoples" as sort of honorary members of the superior Aryan race.

Hitler's true motivations were almost certainly less about his admiration for Iranians and more about how he could benefit from the relationship. For one, Iran had oil, and Hitler needed oil to feed his growing war machine. Secondly, the geography of Iran provided many strategic benefits, including trade routes that ran from the Persian Gulf to the Caspian Sea.

It was this latter quality—Iran's geographic position in the war—that would suddenly transform spies Mayr and Gamotha's lives in Tehran.

Once Hitler attacked the Soviet Union in June 1941, one of the Allies' top priorities was to take arms and supplies from the United States and the United Kingdom and deliver them to the Soviet Union for their defense against the massive Nazi invasion. The United States and Britain quickly saw that the Trans-Iranian Railway running through Iran was the best route to get supplies to the Soviet army.

The Allies wasted little time. In August 1941, a mix of Soviet and British forces crossed into Iran from the north and east, quickly forcing a surrender of the pro-German government.

At that, Hitler's strongman friend Reza Shah fled the country and

---

when quoting contemporaneous sources will use whatever language was employed by the writer or speaker at the time.

was replaced by his son, Mohammad Reza Pahlavi, who unlike his father was willing to cooperate with the Allies. The Soviets, British, and Americans now controlled Iran, meaning U.S. and British arms were now flowing through the country, straight to the Soviet Union.

For the two young German spies, everything changed. Suddenly they were in enemy territory. If they were outed as Nazi agents, they would be arrested or killed. And since the Allies had cut off communication channels between Iran and Germany, the spies had no way to contact their superiors in Berlin.

"The situation inside the country is getting worse and worse," Mayr wrote in his diary on June 28, 1942. "Yesterday radio and newspaper gave warnings again not to give shelter to anyone belonging to the Axis powers. The state police threatened severe punishment for this."

The duo received no signals whatsoever from home; their handlers in Berlin had apparently forgotten about them or assumed they were dead. As Mayr put it, they were living "the life of an enemy in the midst of the enemy" where there was "danger every hour and every minute of every day and every night."

In this environment, Mayr's partner Gamotha decided to abandon their "Middle East duty." After the Allied invasion, he fled Tehran, planning to escape over the border to neutral Turkey.

Mayr, though, refused to flee. During his time in Iran, he'd slowly built up a network of German sympathizers. In a city now under British, Soviet, and American control, he'd turned some of the locals into a pro-Nazi resistance movement, prepared to rise up against the Allies when the opportunity arose. One of his closest confidants was a man named Vaziri, the son of the head of Tehran's police force. Through Vaziri, Mayr had learned how to bribe local officials to get things done.

Indeed, Mayr had come to see himself as a seasoned operative in the region. He learned the language and, according to his diary, believed he understood the people and the culture.

Slowly but surely I begin to know how to treat Persians. I know their tricks, their intrigues, in which they are richer than any other people. Rightly treated, these people are prepared for any risks, trouble, or even sacrifices . . . Perhaps one has to learn first to suffer the lies—little and big which even the best friend is capable of telling to be able to get on with the people.

For most of 1942, Mayr shuffled between safehouses, adopting different aliases and wearing various disguises, always on the move. For several months, he lived outside Tehran in the attic of a German sympathizer's home—that is, until British officials raided the house. Fortunately for Mayr, he wasn't there during the raid, though the British seized his papers and diary. At that point, he knew the British were on to him.

Yet through these ups and downs, Mayr never wavered from his mission. He remained a dedicated German agent, devoted to the cause.

Still, it wasn't just his loyalty to the Führer that kept him in Tehran. There was another reason he stayed, and it had nothing to do with politics.

Franz Mayr, the Nazi spy, was in love.

Mayr first met Lili Sanjari shortly after he arrived in Tehran. She was nineteen years old at the time, working for the trading firm where Mayr and Gamotha had been given cover jobs. Sanjari was the daughter of a prosperous Iranian family that had once briefly lived in Germany; some of Sanjari's childhood years had been spent in Berlin. Perhaps this connection to Mayr's homeland is what drew them together.

When the Allies took over and Mayr was forced to go underground, the relationship went underground with it. Sanjari could only see him in secret, and they spent long periods apart, since any connection with Mayr would put both her and her family at risk. One letter from Sanjari to Mayr, seized by the British during the attic raid, describes their circumstances while he's in hiding.

I should so much like to come to you . . . Unfortunately I can't travel alone as the roads are too dangerous, otherwise I would have been with you long since. Please don't be angry that I haven't written more this time but I am being pressed . . . I still have a few minutes left to be able to tell you that I long for you and I love you very much. Today more than yesterday and certainly less than tomorrow. I should so much like to see you.

At the start of the year 1943, life is complicated for Franz Mayr. He's juggling multiple disguises and aliases as an undercover agent in a foreign city controlled by the enemy. One false move and he'd be arrested or worse. All the while, he's carrying on a clandestine love affair with a woman from a prominent family whose lives he's putting in danger.

But in fact, Mayr's complications are only beginning. There are details about Lili Sanjari that even Mayr doesn't know. And global events are underway that will soon change his life in Tehran in ways he can't imagine.

10

———— · ————

Casablanca, Morocco

January 24, 1943

The press conference was a complete surprise.

Yet here they are, a few dozen reporters representing the wire services, newspapers, and military press agencies in the world, seated on folding chairs or kneeling in the grass on a sunny green lawn surrounded by bushes and bright tropical flowers.

They're gathered in the garden villa of the luxurious Anfa Hotel, just outside Casablanca in the North African country of Morocco. The picturesque setting is deceptive, considering what lies just outside the hotel grounds. "The entire area for blocks around was full of troops, anti-aircraft equipment and barbed wire," *The New York Times* explained.

For the past ten days, the Anfa Hotel has served as the site of a conference between the American and British heads of state and their accompanying staffs. This concluding press conference was announced at the last minute. Everything about the summit has been a closely guarded secret. Only now, with the proceedings over, can the participants reveal what just transpired.

On the lawn facing the reporters are two side-by-side white leather armchairs. In one of these chairs is the President of the

Winston Churchill and Franklin Roosevelt (seated, left) address reporters in the garden of the Anfa Hotel at the conclusion of a ten-day summit meeting in Casablanca, Morocco, in January 1943. During the press conference, the two leaders will summarize Allied military strategy for the coming year. (Courtesy of the Library of Congress.)

United States, Franklin Delano Roosevelt. "He wore a gray business suit and a black tie," according to an Associated Press reporter seated a few feet away, "and as usual was smoking a cigarette in a long holder."

Behind Roosevelt and around him, mostly standing, are members of his senior military staff. Then, a moment later, "Prime Minister Churchill walked out with a cigar in his mouth" and took his seat in the other white chair.

They sit side by side, two leaders of the great Allied war effort.

The event is unprecedented in more ways than one. Roosevelt's journey to Morocco was the first time a U.S. President had ever traveled by plane while in office. It's also the first time a sitting U.S. President has ever visited the continent of Africa. Shortly after his arrival, Roosevelt took a jeep to inspect the American troops stationed nearby as they prepared for combat. It was the first time since the Civil War that a U.S. President had visited American troops on the front lines during wartime.

Yet all of these so-called "firsts" pale in comparison to the central mission of the trip, which is now finally being revealed: a meeting between Allied heads of state and their staffs to assess the immense war now engulfing the world and to agree on a military strategy for the coming year.

As the press conference begins, Roosevelt speaks first.

"I think it can be said that the studies during the past week or ten days are unprecedented in history," the President declares to the gathered correspondents. "The Chiefs of Staffs have been in intimate touch; they have lived in the same hotel. Each man has become a definite personal friend of his opposite number on the other side."

In fact, that's not quite true. The members of the American and British staffs often bickered, complaining about their counterparts during the long sessions, where disagreements big and small had to be hammered out amid no shortage of conflicting opinion. Still, the President and the Prime Minister, along with their staffs, know that the world is watching. They must appear completely united.

"These conferences have discussed, I think for the first time in history, the whole global picture," Roosevelt continues. "It isn't just one front, just one ocean, or one continent—it is literally the whole world; and that is why the Prime Minister and I feel that the conference is unique in the fact that it has this global aspect."

The Allied nations, FDR says, "have reaffirmed the determination to maintain the initiative against the Axis powers in every part of the world." Nodding toward Churchill next to him, the President continues, "I think we have all had it in our hearts and our heads before, but I don't think that it has ever been put down on paper by the Prime Minister and myself, and that is the determination that peace can come to the world only by the total elimination of German and Japanese war power."

Looking down at his prepared remarks, the President further clarifies the last point. "The elimination of German, Japanese, and Italian war power means the unconditional surrender by Germany, Italy, and Japan."

These words—"unconditional surrender"—cause a stir among the correspondents. They look at the President in surprise, their pens scribbling furiously.

Unconditional surrender represents a significant change of wartime strategy. It means that the Allies will refuse to negotiate peace terms with Germany, Italy, or Japan. There will be no compromise to end the war, even if the enemy is willing to offer one—which means, for both sides, it's either total victory or total defeat. The victor dictates the terms.

The press aren't the only ones surprised at Roosevelt's word choice. "I was standing nearby and when the President made that remark the Prime Minister snapped his head toward the President," U.S. Army Captain John L. McCrea would later recount, "giving the impression . . . that the phrase came as a surprise to him." Other eyewitnesses also notice Churchill's seemingly shocked reaction.

Records of the conference show that "unconditional surrender" was discussed and agreed upon in the sessions, so Churchill wouldn't have been surprised that Roosevelt believed in such a policy. What does surprise him, though, is that FDR just said the words in front of the world press. Behind closed doors, there was no plan to go public, and Churchill later revealed that he would probably not have chosen to do so.

With Churchill looking on, Roosevelt continues, stating that this policy "does not mean the destruction of the population of Germany, Italy, or Japan, but it does mean the destruction of the philosophies in those countries which are based on conquest and the subjugation of other people."

After a few more statements the President finishes. It's Churchill's turn. Now, in real time, in front of dozens of reporters, he has to decide whether to back up Roosevelt's language.

"Well," the Prime Minister begins, "one thing I should like to say, and that is—I think I can say it with full confidence—nothing that may occur in this war will ever come between me and the President. He and I are in this as friends and partners, and we work together."

For Churchill, this personal solidarity with Roosevelt has always been clear.

Within days after Pearl Harbor and Germany's declaration of war against the United States, the British Prime Minister and his military leadership boarded a cross-Atlantic steamer bound for Washington, D.C., to formally establish the military alliance between the two nations. Both leaders held joint press conferences, and on December 26, 1941, Churchill became one of the few foreign leaders to address the United States Congress.

Churchill was warmly and even rapturously received by the American press and public. In his speech to Congress, Churchill warned that "the forces ranged against us are enormous." But if the nations worked together, he continued, "sure I am that this day, now, we are the masters of our fate. That the task which has been set us is not above our strength. That its pangs and toils are not beyond our endurance. As long as we have faith in our cause, and an unconquerable willpower, salvation will not be denied us."

His speech ended with an almost mystical assertion of the bond between the two countries. "I avow my hope and faith, sure and inviolate, that in the days to come the British and American peoples will, for their own safety and for the good of all, walk together in majesty, in justice and in peace."

In addition to the public presentations, this visit was an opportunity for the two leaders to get to know one another personally. They'd worked together before, of course, but this would be Churchill's first stay as a guest at the White House.

Roosevelt liked to run a calm, orderly White House. Churchill's arrival was like a tornado.

Upon arriving in the East Wing, the Prime Minister demanded the staff change his room, and made elaborate requests for workspaces for his staff. His voice could be heard booming through the corridors. The White House butler Alonzo Fields later recalled how Churchill immediately pulled him aside.

"Now Fields," Churchill harangued him, "we want to leave here as friends, right? . . . I must have a tumbler of sherry in my room before breakfast, a couple of glasses of scotch and soda before lunch, and French champagne and well-aged brandy before I go to sleep at night."

Fields did his best to honor Churchill's requests, but trying to determine when the Prime Minister would go to sleep at night was near impossible, since the Prime Minister kept no regular schedule and often corralled his or the President's staffs into spontaneous late-night meetings and policy sessions that would last until sunrise.

The visit was full of surprises for the President too. One day in the late morning, when Roosevelt's aide Harry Hopkins wheeled him to Churchill's quarters to discuss a matter of policy that had come up, they were startled to walk in on the Prime Minister, as Hopkins described it, "stark naked and gleaming pink from his bath." To cut through the embarrassment, Churchill smiled and declared to his hosts that "the Prime Minister of the United Kingdom has nothing to hide from the President of the United States."

Despite their different temperaments, the two leaders formed an immediate friendship. Both were confident and optimistic men who worked extremely hard, valued camaraderie, and liked to mix laughter into their duties as head of state. Quickly dispensing with formalities, they spoke to one another frankly. Above all, their bond was a shared sense of duty: They would do anything and everything in their power—together—to defeat Nazism and win this war.

At the time, Churchill's White House visit was planned to be a week but—like a dinner guest who stays too long—he extended it to over three weeks. In the end, Roosevelt, not to mention the White House staff, were exhausted. Yet this first in-person meeting of the minds, a visit that Churchill nicknamed the Arcadia Conference, was only the beginning of their wartime partnership. Throughout 1942, the two leaders were in constant communication—and in public always presented a united front.

Now, almost one year later, here in Casablanca, Churchill's public and private friendship with Roosevelt is no doubt central in his mind as he speaks to the reporters gathered on the sun-dappled lawn of the Anfa Hotel.

He begins by summarizing the military operations on the war's different fronts, then responds to public impatience that the war is taking longer than anticipated. "Even when there is some delay there is design and purpose," the Prime Minister explains, describing some of the vast logistical difficulties of transporting troops and equipment around the globe.

Now, as Churchill continues, he must make his decision. Will he repeat Roosevelt's language? The United States and the United Kingdom, he states, will continue to prosecute the war with "unconquerable will." He pauses for a moment, and then continues, "until we have procured the *unconditional surrender* of the criminal forces who plunged the world into storm and ruin."

Churchill has chosen to back up the President. By repeating Roosevelt's statement, Churchill is putting aside whatever reservations he may've had. If there's public criticism, they'll face it together.

Of all the news that comes out of the conference in Casablanca, it's these two words—"unconditional surrender"—that will make headlines around the world. The summit itself will sometimes be referred to as the "unconditional surrender" conference.

This new policy means, technically, that the Allies will never negotiate for peace with the belligerent nations. Both FDR and Churchill have seen the horrors that the Axis powers have unleashed over the past year—and based on how the war is going, they know what's coming.

11

———— · ————

"Storm and Ruin."

Those are the words that Winston Churchill used to describe the state of the world at the start of 1943, in the middle of the ongoing war.

Indeed, the twelve months following the attack on Pearl Harbor—the calendar year of 1942—was the year in which the growing conflicts in Europe and Asia would explode into a global conflagration of unprecedented scale and catastrophic destruction.

After the Americans officially joined the war, the Allied side consisted of the United States, Great Britain, and the Soviet Union, along with partners China, Canada, Australia, South Africa, and several smaller nations.

On the other side, Nazi Germany controlled all of continental Europe and had secured or bullied their way into getting military help from not just Italy, but Romania, Hungary, Finland, Slovakia, Yugoslavia, Bulgaria, and the Independent State of Croatia. Germany's ally Italy, supported by German troops, created a bulwark in southern Europe along the Mediterranean Sea.

Japan, in a spectacular display of naval and aerial prowess in the months following Pearl Harbor, quickly conquered Guam, Hong

Kong, the Philippines, the Dutch East Indies, Malaya, Singapore, Burma, and other Pacific nations or former European territories.

Despite its vastness and complexity, the global war at the start of 1943 can be roughly divided into three major theaters of operation.

On the Pacific front, the Japanese are fighting the United States—along with U.S. allies Australia and New Zealand—in the struggle for control of the South Pacific region encompassing dozens of countries and countless islands.

On the Southern front, also sometimes called the Mediterranean or North African front, British, American, and Canadian forces are battling with Italians and Germans for control over the Mediterranean region. This theater is not as bloody as the others in terms of loss of life, but it's politically complex, involving multiple nations and former colonial territories with divided governments and shifting allegiances.

Finally, there's the Eastern front.

No other arena of the war—or of any war, before or since—can compare to the apocalyptic destruction and mass suffering caused by Nazi Germany's full-scale invasion of the Soviet Union.

The invasion is defined partly by military strategy: Hitler believes, probably correctly, that if his armies can conquer the Soviet Union, then Nazi Germany will simply be unstoppable. The war, at that point, will be won.

But Operation Barbarossa, as the Germans call the invasion, is premised on something else, too. In Nazi ideology, the Slavic peoples, including Poles and Russians, are inferior, even subhuman. The Soviets are also communists, whom Hitler despises and who were the Nazi Party's great political rivals in their fight to control Germany. Finally, the Soviet Union has a large population of Jewish people—the enemy that Nazi conspiracy theories blame for corrupting and trying to destroy all that is good and sacred for the proud German people.

That's what it comes down to. Communists and Jews. According to the Nazis, these are Germany's enemies—and because the "Eastern hordes" are subhuman, their lives are expendable.

The result was an invasion of indescribable brutality and horror.

When the Nazi armies began their offensive on Soviet lands, Wehrmacht commanders often used the overwhelming tactic of the

Kesselschlacht, or "cauldron battle." The German ground forces would approach a village, town, or city head-on from the west, attacking with blazing artillery and complemented by a Luftwaffe air assault from above. The fast-moving Panzer tank divisions then closed in from the north and south, creating a "cauldron" in the middle that incinerated soldiers, civilians, homes, animals, or vehicles caught within it. It was a harshly effective tactic that showed no regard for loss of life.

The only escape was usually to the east, farther into the Soviet Union, letting the German armies press forward relentlessly.

As they razed towns and villages and slaughtered civilians, the invading Nazi armies intentionally destroyed every farm, food supply, and irrigation system, unleashing a devastating famine across the countryside. This was one part of the Nazi "Hunger Plan"—an attempt to starve to death as much of the civilian population as possible.

The residents who managed to escape before the Panzers arrived faced a different kind of hell. Masses of people, many of them peasants, grabbed whatever meager belongings they could carry and fled by foot or on carts, on dirt roads or through fields or swamps.

One writer traveling by train described what he saw out the window:

The whole field was covered with people who were lying, sitting, swarming. They had bundles, knapsacks, suitcases, children and handcarts. I had never seen such huge quantities of household things that people took with them when leaving home in haste. There were probably tens of thousands of people in this field . . . The field got up, started moving, advanced towards the railway, towards the train, started knocking on the walls and windows of carriages. It seemed capable of tipping the train off the rails. The train moved on . . .

The Soviet Union had no means of handling this flood of people with no access to food, water, shelter, or medical care. Add that to the roaming packs of children, orphaned by war, vulnerable to sickness and famine. There was no solution to this humanitarian catastrophe, and many perished as refugees in their own country.

The Soviet army fighting the invaders faced their own brutal conditions. Soviet forces were often ill-fed, ill-equipped, and poorly trained. Medical treatment was so scarce, many injured soldiers were just left on battlefields to die. Soviet military leaders sometimes sent badly armed infantry troops to almost certain death simply to slow down the enemy advance and buy time for the defense. The Red Army commanders had instructions to execute any of their own soldiers who retreated or attempted to flee from battle.

For common Soviet soldiers, conditions were sometimes so miserable—or the prospect of death or enemy capture so certain— that some young men resorted to the gruesome tactic of shooting themselves through the left hand, pretending the wound was from the enemy, in the hope they would be sent home from the front.

Once commanders discovered this trick, they instructed field hospitals to report any soldiers bearing the telltale bullet wound through the left hand—and the soldiers were executed or sent to prison camps. One army field doctor took pity on these young men, and when he encountered the left hand wound he would, as an act of mercy, amputate the soldier's entire left arm so the hand wound would not be discovered. It was a harsh reality: Living with one arm was better than dying in a Soviet prison or being shot in the head.

As the war on the Eastern front continued through 1942, the Soviet casualty numbers were simply staggering. In the *Kesselschlacht* cauldron battle in Kyiv alone, over seven hundred thousand Soviet soldiers and civilians were killed or captured—and most of those that were captured died as POWs or in labor camps. Several other battles throughout the Soviet Union in 1941 and 1942 had casualties in the hundreds of thousands, and dozens of "smaller" battles had casualties of fifty thousand or more.

The German army also suffered brutal losses during the first two years of fighting in the Soviet Union, with a rough average of sixty thousand German casualties per month from the middle of 1941 to the end of 1942. By any normal standard of war, those are massive numbers—but in comparison, the Soviets lost nearly *ten times* that number during the same period. And while the Axis losses came from soldiers dying in battle, the Soviet losses included huge numbers of innocent civilians, including women and children.

Perhaps one event best illustrates the sheer scale of suffering and loss endured by innocent Soviet civilians.

The Siege of Leningrad.

In late 1941, the Wehrmacht's Army Group North—the northern-most of the three main prongs of the German offensive, led by several tank, artillery, and infantry divisions and supported by the Luftwaffe from above—had cut a swath through the Baltic states, advancing to the outskirts of Leningrad, formerly known as St. Petersburg, the Soviet Union's second-largest city with 3.5 million people.

Rather than march to the urban center and force a surrender, where they'd have to deal with the complicated capture or imprisonment of the remaining population, the German army encircled the city, cutting off the food supply to eliminate the population. Hitler laid out this strategy in a directive to Army Group North commanders:

> The Führer is determined to erase the city of Petersburg from the face of the earth . . . Following the city's encirclement, requests for surrender negotiations shall be denied, since the problem of relocating and feeding the population cannot and should not be solved by us. In this war for our very existence, we can have no interest in maintaining even a part of this very large urban population.

In other words, the explicit goal was to kill, by starvation, every person in the city. Nothing the Soviets could do, including the city's full surrender, would stop it.

As the Nazi forces began to encircle the city, the Soviets began a desperate evacuation of roughly one million inhabitants, including over four hundred thousand children. While some of these evacuees escaped south or east, many were killed at the hands of the encircling armies or soon died from hunger or exposure to the elements. And when the "iron band" of the Nazi siege was locked in place, approximately 1.7 million citizens remained in Leningrad with no hope for escape.

What ensued over the next year was, by some estimates, the greatest loss of life ever to occur in a modern city. The famine was instant and continued month after month. German planes bombed city warehouses that contained extra food, leaving nothing for the population. City officials instituted a rationing program to hand out remaining scraps of bread, but the daily ration was tiny and the bread was often stale and mixed with sawdust.

Over time, the starving population was forced to eat horses, dogs, cats, and eventually rats, insects, and other vermin. When these sources were exhausted, people tried to eat leather, wood, glue, and other raw materials. As disease and malnourishment ravaged the city, corpses piled up in the streets. Since removing the bodies required exertion that burned valuable calories, the city mandated that bodies not be moved.

In the midst of this absolute desperation, some citizens resorted to the unthinkable. Soviet security forces arrested over two thousand residents for the crime of cannibalism. Tragically, many of those arrested were mothers who, having run out of options, would resort to anything to feed their emaciated children who were dying in their arms.

In early 1942, at the peak of the siege, roughly one hundred thousand city inhabitants died per month from famine or disease. In the spring and summer, Soviet fighters managed to open gaps in the encirclement, allowing for the occasional flow of food supplies into the city. This cut the death rate somewhat, but as the winter of 1943 approached, the conditions in the city remained appalling. By the time the siege was over, an estimated nine hundred thousand residents had died within city limits.

While Leningrad starved, the Nazi armies pounded Soviet cities and villages elsewhere in the country with relentless ferocity.

Yet somehow, by the end of 1942, after eighteen months of devastation, the Soviet Union was still standing. After the near calamity of almost losing Moscow at the end of 1941, Stalin created an impenetrable military barrier around the capital, forcing the Germans to try to bring down the USSR by other means.

Hitler, it soon became clear, had made a key strategic miscalculation. He'd assumed that the Soviet Union would fall quickly. "We have only to kick in the door and the whole rotten edifice will come crashing down," the Führer had predicted to his commanders. Nations like Norway, Belgium, Denmark, and even France had capitulated almost immediately after experiencing a taste of the Wehrmacht's fearsome power. Yet the Soviet Union was not like Norway, Belgium, Denmark, or France. It was prepared to withstand the German army's most crushing blows, at almost any human cost, and still keep fighting back.

Over the long months, Soviet army officers gained more experience, and their troops became better trained. In addition, the United States was supplying the Soviets with an increasing flow of planes, trucks, weapons, food, and raw materials. While the Red Army continued to suffer massive casualties, every month thousands of Soviet teenagers reached military age and could join the fighting forces to replace the fallen. And while Nazi forces had to transport fresh troops thousands of miles from Germany to reach the Eastern front, the Soviet Union could bring its newest recruits to the front lines almost instantly.

Still, in the fall of 1942 the German ground forces in the east remained the most powerful fighting force in the world. For the coming winter, Hitler began preparing for a massive offensive in southern Russia, with the goal of taking the medium-sized but industrial city of Stalingrad. The city was the link to the southern oil fields, and Hitler believed that if Nazi forces could occupy and hold it, he could finally cripple the Red Army. The fact that the city had Stalin's name in it gave the assault an additional symbolic meaning.

For this offensive against a single modest city, the Wehrmacht engaged a force of over one million soldiers, including troops from Italy, Romania, and Hungary. The infantry was supported by 1,000 tanks, over 2,000 aircraft, and over 13,000 pieces of artillery.

For the city's defense, the Soviets fielded a force of close to 1.2 million soldiers, supported by a total of 1,200 tanks, 1,400 aircraft, and 15,000 artillery pieces. Rather than evacuate the city's roughly four hundred thousand residents, the Soviet army put every able-bodied citizen to work building fortifications, digging trenches, and planting tank mines.

By the end of 1942, as Franklin Roosevelt and Winston Churchill were preparing for their war conference in Casablanca, many parts of the world were in the throes of apocalyptic destruction. Civilians were being starved in Leningrad and slaughtered in China; Nazi armies were killing POWs by the millions; native populations were being wiped off the planet; countless towns, villages, and cities were being decimated; famine and disease were spreading through countries already devastated by war; and German forces were about to embark on a military campaign in southern Russia that would prove to be the bloodiest in human history.

These were the stakes of the war. In Franklin Roosevelt's mind, the Axis powers had started this conflict—and bore responsibility for it. It was against this backdrop of worldwide cataclysm that the President declared that "unconditional surrender" was the only option.

Unconditional surrender meant Nazi Germany and Imperial Japan could not be negotiated with. They had already broken every promise, violated every treaty, and committed unthinkable war crimes. To use Hitler's own words, the Axis powers had embarked on a "war of extermination," with no regard for human life.

At the start of 1943, it was clear that a very long war still loomed ahead, one that would be measured in years, not months.

The only way for the Allied powers to end the catastrophe was to band together, devise a unified plan, and fight with every ounce of strength they had.

It would take complete solidarity between the Allied nations—but as Franklin Roosevelt was about to learn, solidarity, even in the face of such enormous devastation, wasn't nearly as easy as it seemed.

12

Tehran, Iran

January 1943

Nazi spy Franz Mayr has a new mission.

Not *new,* exactly . . . but a *revived* mission, with a fresh sense of purpose.

While the Allied heads of state are meeting on the world stage in Casablanca, Mayr is at work on a smaller scale—on a project that he believes could make a real difference in the direction of the war.

Mayr's recent surge of energy has come from an unexpected place. At some point in the past two months—the exact date is not known— Mayr heard a radio broadcast in Tehran that changed his circumstances completely. On the surface, the broadcast was unremarkable: a routine news update from a station in German-controlled territory in Europe, featuring an announcer reading a script that provided a predictably slanted take on recent events in the war.

What Mayr knows, however, is that the broadcast wasn't routine at all. The announcer had repeated certain words and phrases in a manner that were intended for him and him alone.

The plan started back in the fall, when Mayr had heard that Allied forces controlling the city had allowed some Japanese diplomats into Tehran. Through his connections, Mayr gained access to the diplomats and passed them a note that he requested they bring back to Tokyo, and then forward to Berlin.

The note briefly explained his circumstances and provided information about contacts in nearby Turkey who could help him safely pass future messages. His note also included a request for additional money and supplies . . . and a map with coordinates for a safe drop zone outside Tehran where German planes could potentially parachute persons and equipment.

Finally, Mayr's note contained instructions to Berlin to alter a particular future radio broadcast in a specific way—using a repeated phrase—that would notify Mayr that his spymasters back home had received his message.

The odds of this scheme working were so unlikely that when Mayr heard the broadcast with exactly the repeated phrase he suggested, it seemed nothing short of a miracle. What's more, it indicated that powerful people in Berlin not only still knew who he was but were apparently willing to revive his seemingly forgotten mission.

Still, he has questions. Is there some new reason why his superiors in Berlin have taken a sudden interest in Iran? Is there a plan afoot that might soon include him? Or, with the war now focused on southern Russia, have they finally realized the strategic value of the Iran region, and are now ready to offer him greater resources and support?

If nothing else, the signal clearly means that they plan on communicating with him more in the future—and hopefully, providing him a means to communicate with them in return.

For the first time in nearly two years, Mayr is no longer abandoned and alone. His grand vision—establishing a secret underground pro-German network in Tehran that's strong enough to rise up, overthrow Allied control, and deliver Iran back to the Nazis—now seems like a true possibility.

To Mayr, though, this plan was never far-fetched. Hitler himself had clearly expressed interest in Iran's oil fields and told his close advisors that "by the end of 1943, we will pitch our tents in Tehran . . . Then the oil wells will at last be dry as far as the English are concerned."

Now, here it was—1943—and Franz Mayr is ready to help the

Führer obtain this goal. He just needed the right help and resources. Then he'd be the hero—the one turning Iran's capital city back to the Fatherland. Finally, based on the remarkable radio broadcast he recently heard, help was on the way.

Mayr has shared the incredible story of the coded radio message to only a few of his closest allies in the city. Among them, of course, is his girlfriend, Lili Sanjari.

In truth, Sanjari has been much more than Mayr's girlfriend. During his many months in Iran, he'd relied on Sanjari and her family connections to cultivate much of his underground network. And because Sanjari was local—and a native speaker—he frequently sent her as a "cut out" to meet and give messages to his Iranian contacts so that he could keep his own identity and whereabouts a secret.

Remarkably, given Mayr's circumstances, the couple has been together for over two years. Sanjari had stayed with him despite the dangers and difficulties of his secret life as an undercover spy.

No doubt, there have been downsides. Just before the Allied occupation shut off Mayr's contact with Germany, he'd sent a formal request to his handlers in Berlin that he be able to marry Sanjari. As a member of the Nazi Party, he needed permission to wed any non-German.

His superiors turned down his request. She was a native Iranian, and therefore could not be trusted.

The answer from Berlin disappointed the young couple. And at some point in late 1942—perhaps out of frustration at Mayr's inability to marry her, or possibly for other reasons of her own—Sanjari, unbeknownst to Mayr, began to stray.

She was an avid pianist and music lover—which explains why she began frequenting a nightclub in town that featured a Western-style brass dance band. Here, she began a secret relationship with a musician in the band, a twenty-three-year-old American GI named Robert Merrick. When the young couple weren't partying at the club, they would sometimes meet for clandestine trysts in rented rooms that Sanjari paid for.

Needless to say, her Nazi lover had no idea.

But just as there are things that Franz Mayr doesn't know about

Lili Sanjari, there are also things that Lili Sanjari doesn't know about Robert Merrick.

Merrick, in addition to playing in a band and working as a lowly Army transport clerk, is also serving as an informant to the U.S. Counter Intelligence Corps (CIC), the Army's intelligence division that operates in Tehran.

So when Sanjari began confiding to Merrick about her years-long relationship with Nazi spy Franz Mayr, Merrick conveyed everything he learned to his CIC contacts, including Major E. P. Barry of the U.S. Provost Marshal's office. From there, Major Barry would send the information directly to Joe Spencer, the head of the British intelligence office in Tehran. The British, who were closely monitoring Nazi activity in the region, told the Americans to urge Merrick to continue the relationship so that they could learn as much as possible about Mayr. So that's exactly what Merrick continued to do.

Unfortunately for Mayr, he continually confided nearly every detail of his work to Sanjari. She knew where he'd stayed, what secret aliases he'd used, and, perhaps most importantly, she knew the identities of the key players in the elaborate network of Nazi supporters that Mayr had worked so hard to cultivate.

In short, Sanjari knew almost everything about Mayr's Nazi operation.

Of course, that meant Robert Merrick, the twenty-three-year-old American GI and informant, knew almost all of it too. And whatever Merrick knew, so too did the head of British intelligence in Tehran.

What no one could anticipate, though, was that in a matter of months, Tehran will be at the very center of the geopolitical landscape.

So for Franz Mayr, 1943 is about to be a very interesting year.

13

Washington, D.C.

January 30, 1943

It was "the most unprecedented and momentous meeting of the century."

So declared the front pages of American newspapers in the wake of the Casablanca Conference. The intricate war planning that occurred at the conference remained mostly secret, but the elaborate public theater of the summit, complete with photographs of Roosevelt visiting Allied troops near the front lines, was a media sensation.

A few of Roosevelt's enemies in Congress publicly questioned the wisdom of the "unconditional surrender" comment. Yet these voices were few and far between. For the most part, both within the United States and throughout the Allied world, the response to the conference was extremely positive.

So, as Roosevelt arrives back on American shores on January 30, 1943, he has every reason to feel that the whole complicated undertaking was a success.

Still, no matter how much praise he receives from the press or from colleagues, there's one aspect of the summit in Casablanca that remains, in Roosevelt's mind, a failure; or, at least, a serious disappointment.

Stalin wasn't there.

From Roosevelt's perspective, it's tough to claim that the conference represented a unified war strategy when the country that has been doing the great majority of the actual fighting against Nazi Germany—the Soviet Union—was not represented.

More important, Roosevelt didn't want it to be this way.

In June 1941, when Hitler first launched his surprise invasion of the Soviet Union, Roosevelt immediately expanded the American Lend-Lease program to provide goods and armaments to the Soviet Union. Establishing these supply routes required detailed coordination between the U.S. and Soviet governments. That communication only increased when the United States formally entered the war in December 1941.

As Roosevelt saw it, the U.S. had to play an essential role in managing the Soviet relationship within the Allied alliance. The United Kingdom's relationship with the Soviets had been stormy before the war, and Churchill had been a longtime public critic of communism and of Stalin's regime. Sure, after Hitler invaded the Soviet Union, the Prime Minister publicly supported Stalin, but the long decades of distrust were not easy to overcome. Churchill didn't help matters by initially promising the Soviets military support that the British could not fulfill.

Roosevelt believed he had to take the lead with Stalin. "I know you will not mind my being brutally frank," he wrote to Churchill in March 1942, "when I tell you that I think that I can personally handle Stalin better than either your Foreign Office or my State Department. Stalin hates the guts of all your top people. He thinks he likes me better, and I hope he will continue to do so."

In May 1942, Roosevelt invited Soviet Foreign Minister Vyacheslav Molotov to meet in person and plan strategy. According to the White House logs, the staff used the alias "Mr. Brown" for Molotov—so they could keep the trip secret until he returned to Moscow.

Stalin appreciated the diplomacy, and even more so, the American military supplies.

But there was something else the Soviet Premier wanted, even more than planes and goods. What Stalin really wanted was for his two Allied partners to launch a joint attack against Hitler's armies from the west, preferably directly across the English Channel into occupied France.

Stalin believed that this strategy, and this strategy alone, would force Hitler to redirect enough of his armies away from the Eastern front, giving the Soviets a chance to seize the advantage over the Wehrmacht and push them back into Germany.

For that reason, Stalin was deeply disappointed when, in early 1942, his two Allies made it clear they would not launch any such "cross-Channel attack" for the rest of the calendar year. Some American military leaders had pushed for such a plan, but Churchill was unwilling to embark upon anything so risky. Simply put, Churchill believed that the British and American forces weren't yet up for the task. The German defense in Western Europe was simply too strong.

Stalin's frustration with their decision lasted all year, creating an ongoing rift in the partnership. All summer and fall, as the Red Army and the Soviet people continued to sacrifice so mightily to fight Nazi Germany, the British and Americans only engaged against Axis troops along the faraway southern Mediterranean—mostly to challenge Italy's position—in a front of the war that Stalin considered, in his words, a "distraction."

In Stalin's view, the Nazis would succeed or fail in Russia—and right now, it was only the Soviets who were doing the fighting and dying against Hitler's armies.

For that reason, as winter approached, Stalin was growing increasingly impatient.

Roosevelt knew this. So in late 1942, when he and Churchill first came up with the idea of the Casablanca Conference, Roosevelt's plan was that all three leaders would take part and make it easier to come to terms on key strategic concerns.

On December 2, he wrote Stalin directly:

The more I consider our mutual military situation and the necessity for reaching early strategic decisions, the more persuaded I am that you, Churchill and I should have [a] meeting . . . My suggestion would be that we meet secretly in some secure place in Africa that is convenient to all three of us . . . I hope that you will consider this proposal favorably because I can see no other way of reaching the vital strategic decisions which should be made soon by all three of us together.

Roosevelt added, on an almost personal note, that "my most compelling reason is that I am very anxious to have a talk with you." Roosevelt had never met Stalin in person, and he wanted to forge a personal working relationship.

Stalin received Roosevelt's message on December 5, and the next day wrote back:

> I welcome the idea of a meeting between the three heads of the Governments to establish a common strategy. To my great regret, however, I shall be unable to leave the Soviet Union. This is so crucial a moment that I cannot absent myself even for a single day. Just now major military operations—part of our winter campaign—are under way, nor will they be relaxed in January.

Roosevelt could hardly object. At that moment, the Soviet Union had millions of Red Army soldiers deployed, fighting Nazi troops on Russian soil.

If Stalin couldn't meet in December or January, Roosevelt would press him for a later date. He and Churchill would wait. On December 8, a day after receiving Stalin's message, Roosevelt responded:

> I am deeply disappointed you feel you cannot get away for a conference in January. There are many matters of vital importance to be discussed between us . . . I fully realize your strenuous situation now and in the immediate future and the necessity of your presence close to the fighting front. Therefore I want to suggest that we set a tentative date for meeting in North Africa about March 1.

For almost a week, the President heard nothing back. Finally, in a message dated December 14, Stalin replied:

> I, too, express deep regret at not being able to leave the Soviet Union in the immediate future, or even in early March. Front affairs simply will not let me do so. Indeed, they necessitate my continuous presence.

I do not know as yet what were the specific matters that you, Mr. President, and Mr. Churchill wanted discussed at our joint conference. Could we not discuss them by correspondence until we have an opportunity to meet? I think we shall not differ.

Stalin was shutting down hope for any group conference in the immediate future.

Frustrated, Roosevelt closed the matter with a curt reply: "I am very sorry arrangements for a conference could not be made but I can well understand your position."

Roosevelt and Churchill had no choice but to proceed without Stalin. The so-called great Allied war summit occurred without the participation of the nation that was doing most of the fighting against Hitler.

Sure, the Casablanca Conference received good press. But upon his return to the United States, Roosevelt is determined that before the end of 1943 there must be another in-person summit between all *three* major powers—the United States, the United Kingdom, and the Soviet Union. He thinks it will be essential to the war effort—in this global war of enormous magnitude and complexity, the nations' leaders need to agree upon and map out a grand strategy.

Shortly after the U.S. entered the war, the world press began to refer to Roosevelt, Churchill, and Stalin as "The Big Three."

Now, for Roosevelt, the mission is clear: If he can bring together the Big Three—face-to-face—they can work through differences, agree upon a military and political strategy, and present to the world a united front against Nazi Germany and the Axis powers.

Only if the three leaders come together in person, he believes, can they put an end to the unspeakable horrors of the global war.

It's an audacious idea—one that requires secrecy and new levels of security. Certainly, there are risks to bringing everyone under one roof. If something goes wrong, it would be catastrophic.

14

---·---

Germany

In the mid-1920s, in the early days of Nazism, Hitler knew he needed better security.

This was back when the National Socialist Party was still a small but forceful political organization on the rise. Because the organization was controversial, party leaders realized that a dedicated security force was necessary to protect its members. There were many early iterations, but in 1925, the party formed what would later become the key component of the Nazi Party's security force: the Schutzstaffel, or "Protection Squadrons," more commonly known as the SS.

Originally designated as Hitler's personal bodyguards, the SS quickly expanded. They became a familiar sight at Nazi events, with their early trademark black uniforms, matching black boots, and swastika armbands.

Under the leadership of the organization's eventual mastermind Heinrich Himmler, the SS developed a complicated military-like command structure and an elaborate array of ever-changing positions, titles, uniforms, and insignias. As the Nazi Party gradually rose to power in Germany, the SS rose with it, ballooning in size from 280 men in 1929 to 52,000 in 1933.

By this time, the SS had its own police department—the

Gestapo—and a constantly expanding paramilitary force, the Waffen-SS.

In its recruitment efforts, the SS prized two essential qualities above all: absolute fealty to Hitler and the Nazi Party—the official SS motto was "Loyalty is my Honor"—and white racial purity.

To ensure the latter, the SS conducted elaborate background checks on prospective members and employees, and only those who met codified racial standards were eligible. As Himmler described it, "like a nursery gardener trying to reproduce a good old strain which has been adulterated and debased; we started from the principles of plant selection and then proceeded quite unashamedly to weed out the men whom we did not think we could use for the build-up of the SS."

In 1931, while the Nazi Party was engaged in a power struggle with communists and other rival political parties over future control of the German state, Himmler made a critical decision: The SS should have a dedicated intelligence service. With this capacity, the Nazi Party would be able to spy on its political enemies, particularly communists, track the movements of opposing parties, and monitor dissenters within its own ranks. The SS could also then track Jewish populations in every region of the country.

Building this dedicated intelligence apparatus from scratch was an ambitious undertaking. To pull it off, Himmler needed the right person in charge.

It didn't take long. His name was Reinhard Heydrich.

Heydrich had been raised in a cultured, prosperous family in Halle an der Saale, about twenty miles outside Leipzig. His father was an opera singer who ran a music conservatory; young Reinhard was a gifted violinist and his parents wanted him to pursue music. Instead, he pursued fascist politics.

While in his teens, he joined an anti-Semitic fraternal club and a local pre-Nazi paramilitary group to do battle with communist party organizers in the region. In 1922, following his eighteenth birthday, he joined the German navy, and after several promotions became an officer of naval intelligence.

But it wasn't until 1931 that Heydrich found his true calling—

after leaving the navy, he joined the rising Nazi Party. Himmler was looking for someone to create and build a dedicated intelligence service under the umbrella of the SS. Upon interviewing Heydrich, Himmler was so impressed, he hired him immediately.

Heydrich got to work and, over the course of two years, built the Sicherheitsdienst, or SD, from scratch. When Hitler became chancellor of Germany in January of 1933, the SD was elevated from political party apparatus to state-run agency that answered to the national leader.

As head of the SD, Heydrich established himself as one of the most ruthless and ambitious Nazi officials. He was arrogant and manipulative, and excelled at the hypercompetitive backstabbing politics of the Reich.

Using the powers of the Nazi intelligence service, he quickly built dossiers on his colleagues and their families so he had leverage over everyone, including his superiors. Hitler and Himmler approved of Heydrich's relentless ambition, and in 1934, Himmler handed him dual control of the Gestapo, the much-feared SS secret police force. After that, Heydrich was elevated to be chief of the Reich Security Main Office, an umbrella organization that controlled all the SS security forces, including the SD, the Gestapo, and the "criminal police," known as the Kriminalpolizei, or Kripo.

After an in-person meeting with Heydrich, a young SD recruit named Walter Schellenberg said, "I walked out of his office overwhelmed by the strength of his personality to an extent that I have never experienced before or since."

Schellenberg was in awe of Heydrich, who soon became his mentor. "This man was the hidden pivot around which the Nazi regime revolved," the young recruit would later describe. "He was far superior to all his political colleagues and controlled them as he controlled the vast intelligence machine of the SD . . . Heydrich was, in fact, the puppet-master of the Third Reich."

Not surprisingly for someone able to accumulate so much power within the Reich, Heydrich was a fervent believer in the most virulent Nazi racist ideology. He was an avowed white supremacist and believed all nonwhite peoples to be biologically and culturally deficient.

Reinhard Heydrich was one of the most powerful leaders in Hitler's Reich. He created and led the SD, the Nazi intelligence services, after which he became chief of the Reich Security Main Office. When the war began, Heydrich personally oversaw the creation of the Einsatzgruppen—the mobile SS death squads that committed mass murders of civilians in Eastern Europe throughout the war. (Courtesy of World History Archive / Alamy Stock Photo)

A lifelong anti-Semite, he referred to Jewish people as "the eternal subhumans." Like Hitler, Heydrich attributed Germany's economic struggles to the presence of Jews in the country and throughout Europe. He believed that the vast apparatus of the Nazi SS—of which his SD and Gestapo were components—should be the "the offensive force which could initiate the final battle against the Jews."

In no time, Heydrich initiated the battle. With the blessing of Himmler and Hitler, Heydrich used his immense powers to institute a reign of terror against the Jewish people of Germany. "Untouched by any pangs of conscience and assisted by an ice-cold intellect, he could carry injustice to the point of extreme cruelty," as Schellenberg described it. Between the SD and the Gestapo, Heydrich's SS apparatus could arrest Jews, deport Jews, imprison Jews, interrogate Jews, and, eventually, kill Jews.

As terrifying as the SS was to the Jewish people of Germany in the 1930s, it was later in the war that Heydrich's "extreme cruelty"—and the cruelty of the regime he served—would take on horrific new dimensions.

15

There was an actual game plan.

It began with Germany's invasion of Poland in 1939. Reinhard Heydrich—head of the Nazi intelligence service known as the SD—came up with the concept of the Einsatzgruppen, or "Operation Groups," that would serve as a paramilitary wing of the SS in defeated territory.

After the Wehrmacht—the German army proper—had defeated a town or city, an Einsatzgruppe unit would immediately follow to secure the newly occupied territory. What "securing" generally entailed was rounding up and then arresting or massacring any civilians considered "enemies of the Reich."

For the Poland invasion, Heydrich's SD created a list of sixty thousand Polish citizens considered a "danger" to the Reich, including any known or suspected communists, professors, partisans, or Polish nationalists. The Einsatzgruppe units, furnished with these lists, would track down these enemies and arrest or shoot them on sight.

And of course, the Einsatzgruppen targeted the Jewish people. While the Nazis considered all Poles to be inferior and did not hesitate to slaughter those civilians considered hostile to the Reich, the Jews were in a special, more dangerous category. During the razing of

Eastern Europe, SS commanders began lifting restrictions on which alleged enemy populations should be killed. Jewish populations in particular need no longer be accused of any particular crime; simply being Jewish was crime enough.

With the invasion of the Soviet Union in 1941, the work of the Einsatzgruppen expanded and became more systematized. They were mobile death squads. The SS frequently recruited local collaborators to aid in the slaughter, so in places like Romania, Lithuania, Latvia, and Belarus, the Einsatzgruppen would enlist the help of local anti-Semitic or anti-communist organizations to carry out massacres of Jews, Roma, suspected communists, and others.

But mostly, the Einsatzgruppen acted alone. In many conquered villages, the group leaders simply rounded up the civilians in the town square and shot them one by one. For larger towns and cities, the process was more complicated. There, the Einsatzgruppen would corral all of the civilians identified as enemies—including communists, Jewish people, and other ethnicities, depending on the region—into large groups at a checkpoint in the town.

These victims, who were often poor, didn't speak German, and did not yet understand the fate awaiting them, were forced to hand over all personal belongings. SS soldiers would then march them a few miles outside the town to a predetermined location, usually an open field or clearing in a forest, where a mass grave had already been dug.

Here, the SS soldiers would shoot them one by one in front of the group, and throw the bodies in the grave. Entire families would be huddled together in terror, screaming for mercy, only to watch as one family member after another was slaughtered before their eyes. Because there were often many hundreds or thousands of victims, a massacre for a given town or city could take several hours or more.

One of the largest and most horrific massacres committed by the Einsatzgruppen was in Ukraine on September 29 and 30, 1941. Mobile SS units marched a total of 33,771 victims from the capital city of Kyiv to a ravine called Babi Yar and created one of history's most appalling mass graves. The physical act of shooting this many people one by one was so time consuming, it took two full days of soldiers working in shifts around the clock to complete the act.

The rules for how these massacres were carried out sometimes varied, or were left to the discretion of local SS commanders.

In the Ukrainian village of Bila Tserkva for example, an SS mobile unit gathered and killed several hundred Jewish civilians, but declined to kill a group of ninety Jewish children age six or younger. Instead they left the children in an unsupervised, empty building on the outskirts of the village without food or water. A few days later the soldiers of nearby Wehrmacht platoon heard their crying, and the platoon's Catholic chaplain discovered the children in filthy conditions, undernourished and covered in excrement. Together with a staff officer, the chaplain tried to request food and protection for the children.

The request was denied. Instead, local SS commanders ordered that the children be shot and killed, just as their parents were. The staff officer who had tried to help the children was ordered to participate in the slaughter.

The children's "wailing," the staff officer later recalled, "was indescribable. I shall never forget the scene throughout my life. I find it very hard to bear. I particularly remember a small fair-haired girl who took me by the hand. She too was shot later . . . Many children were hit four or five times before they died."

Scenes such as these took place repeatedly, throughout Eastern Europe and the Soviet Union, during the long course of the war.

As the war evolved, the greatest difficulty the Einsatzgruppen faced was that they couldn't kill captured Jewish people fast enough. Massacres required armed personnel and ammunition, both precious resources.

In addition, Nazi commanders started seeing the negative toll on the soldiers asked to carry out repeated mass executions of innocent civilian men, women, and children. While many SS members had no problem participating in these massacres and even relished it, some who were tasked to kill young children reported nightmares and psychological distress.

As a result, Heydrich and other leaders began experimenting with new methods to achieve the same objectives. Throughout the summer of 1941, Einsatzgruppen began utilizing "gas vans" as a less resource-intensive alternative. After capturing Jewish people and other alleged criminals in a conquered town or village, the SS would load their victims into the backs of diesel cargo trucks. The trucks were specially designed so that their exhaust emissions were redirected back into the cargo hold where the victims were carried.

By the time a truck arrived at a pre-dug mass grave, the hundreds of closely packed passengers were asphyxiated. Some mothers in the cargo holds would save their infants or small children by wrapping their own bodies around them. When the SS soldiers tasked to unload the corpses discovered these still-breathing babies, they would quickly crush the infant skulls against trees or with rifle butts.

Even these more efficient gas vans proved inadequate to handle the sheer quantity of persons the SS forces were sent to massacre. The conquered territories were too vast, the villages too many, and the SS soldiers, trucks, and rifles too few to cover the expansive Jewish population spread all over Eastern Europe.

In total the SS mobile death squads murdered several hundred thousand Jewish civilians in Eastern Europe and the Soviet Union in the first two years of the war, but this was still a small fraction of the total Jewish population of the region. The SS system of mass murder was still too inconsistent. Millions of captured Jews remained imprisoned in various SS prison camps or labor camps—or had been sent to one of several German-controlled Jewish "ghettos" in Poland to await their fate at the hands of the Nazi government.

By the end of 1941, SS leaders decided that they needed a more centralized strategy to solve the "Jewish problem" across the entire European continent.

To formalize a plan, all they needed was a meeting place.

16

---•---

Fort Benning, Georgia

April 15, 1943

It's no ordinary train.

Army officers and personnel gather outside the Post Train Depot at Fort Benning, Georgia, to get a glimpse of the locomotive as it pulls into the station. This military base outside of Columbus, Georgia, is bustling at its wartime peak, with nearly eighty thousand enlisted soldiers training for duty, in addition to officers and staff.

On most days, Fort Benning runs according to strict routine. Today will be different.

As the train pulls in, the exterior looks the same as it does on most days. However, the rearmost car looks different from the rest. In fact, it's not like any other train car anywhere.

It's called the *Ferdinand Magellan,* and for the last few years it has had one purpose, to transport the President of the United States, Franklin Delano Roosevelt.

The *Magellan,* also referred to in government circles as "U.S. Car No. 1," weighs 285,000 pounds, making it at the time the heaviest railcar ever built in the United States. The extra weight comes mostly from the half-inch thick nickel-and-steel protective armor that encases all four sides as well as its roof. It also has bulletproof windows and two escape hatches through which the wheelchaired President can be propelled in case of emergency.

Two days ago, on April 13, the train departed from Washington, D.C., and is now making the second of many stops on a circuitous, two-week, 7,600-mile cross-country tour. Most of the stops will be at military training facilities—like here at Fort Benning—so the President can meet officers, observe troops, and see war training up close. He'll also make several stops at plants and factories around the country that are producing warplanes, weapons, and other military supplies.

While technically an "inspection tour," this elaborate journey is just as much about raising morale, generating headlines, and improving wartime public relations. Across several states, the President will give speeches, attend receptions, and be received by saluting soldiers and cheering crowds.

While there may be plenty of cheering *outside* the train, inside there's a President who is dead serious, especially after the news he's just received.

While preparing for the long railroad trip, Roosevelt had insisted that he remain in contact with his military advisors in Washington, D.C., and also wished to receive the Navy's daily intercepts of enemy communications without delay. A special train car had been outfitted to facilitate these Presidential requests.

Twice a day during the journey, a naval assistant named William Rigdon walks the length of the train to bring the daily decrypts to the President. "The communications car housed a diesel powered radio transmitting and receiving station," Rigdon would later explain, "that kept the President in constant touch with the Map Room at the White House . . . This car was just behind the engine. The *Magellan* was at the rear. Between the two I walked many miles taking messages to the President and picking up those he wished to send."

Many of the naval decrypts that Rigdon delivered to the President were trivial. But on April 14—the day before pulling into Fort Benning—the *Magellan* has just received a top secret decrypt of a radio transmission from Japan that now demands immediate attention.

The message, decoded and translated from Japanese, begins like this:

From Solomon Defense Force to Air Group #204, Air Flotilla #26. On April 18 C in C Combined Fleet will visit RXZ, R, and RXP in accordance following schedule 1. Depart RR at 0600 in a medium attack plane escorted by 6 fighters. Arrive RXZ at 0800.

Translated from military code-speak, here's what it means. Admiral Isoroku Yamamoto, the Commander in Chief of the Combined Fleet of the Japanese navy—the most revered military leader in Japan, and the mastermind behind the attack on Pearl Harbor—is scheduled to fly on April 18 from Rabaul to the Balalae Airfield on an island near Bougainville in the Solomon Islands, as part of his own inspection tour of Japanese troops and installations in the region.

What makes this intelligence so remarkable? For one thing, because Admiral Yamamoto almost never leaves the safety of his command center aboard the Japanese navy's closely guarded grand battleship the *Musashi*.

Secondly, Yamamoto's means of air travel—"a medium attack plane escorted by 6 fighters"—will leave him unusually exposed. A well-planned strike could take down his plane. The Japanese clearly planned Yamamoto's trip with absolute confidence that the Americans could not possibly learn about it.

But U.S. Naval Intelligence *did* learn about it. After intercepting the Japanese navy's radio transmissions, they successfully cracked the supposedly unbreakable Japanese code, and have deciphered the Admiral's itinerary.

"We've hit the jackpot," the U.S. watch officer of the decoding team in Hawaii declared upon first laying eyes on the translated decryption. "This is our chance to get Yamamoto."

The revelation was quickly passed up the military chain of command, from Naval Headquarters, to the Pentagon, to the Map Room of the White House. Finally, it arrives on the *Ferdinand Magellan*.

President Roosevelt has a chance to eliminate—to assassinate—

Japan's most brilliant and revered military leader. He may never get the chance again.

At this point in time, over a million U.S. troops are deployed in the Pacific theater, fighting a savage war. Over the past year, although the United States has slowly gained an advantage over the Japanese Imperial Navy, it has come at enormous cost, and Japanese military leaders show no sign of yielding. Their war machine remains vast, their troops remain committed, and their goal is to fight to the end.

For this reason, any advantage the United States can gain may bring victory a little closer, and therefore save thousands of Allied lives in the Pacific.

The U.S. naval commanders have confirmed that the intelligence about Admiral Yamamoto is reliable. They're also sure the strike is doable. If Roosevelt wants to take out the Admiral, he has the capability.

The only question is: *Should* he?

A year ago, in the early spring of 1942, President Roosevelt faced a similarly difficult decision. After a series of Japanese victories that followed Pearl Harbor, American morale was low. Military leaders proposed to the President a daring idea: While bloody battles were raging all over the South Pacific, the U.S. Navy could quietly launch a few medium-range B-25 bombers from an aircraft carrier just outside the perimeter of Imperial Navy control. These bombers, specially modified to increase fuel capacity, could make it all the way to Japan. If the B-25s could elude enemy radar, they could penetrate Japanese airspace, drop a few payloads over Tokyo, then have just enough fuel to make it to Chinese airfields over the border.

No bombing raid of such huge distance had ever been attempted before, and military leaders believed Japan would be caught completely off guard. The raid would accomplish very little militarily, but the symbolism of American bombs falling on Japan's capital city would be a major morale boost for the Americans.

Roosevelt gave the go-ahead, and the result was the famed "Doolittle Raid," led by forty-five-year-old Jimmy Doolittle. A total of sixteen B-25s with five-person crews flew 650 miles undetected before crossing into Japan and through the skies over Tokyo.

The planes bombed some planned targets, mostly industrial and military installations, and then headed for China. The B-25s made it out of Japan unharmed but ran out of fuel before they could reach the Chinese airfields. One diverted to land in Russia, while the crews of the other fifteen parachuted into Chinese territory before their planes crashed. A few died in the drops or were captured by roaming Japanese troops on the ground, but the vast majority made it to the safety of Chinese villages, where they were sheltered and fed before eventually returning to their home country.

Just as Roosevelt had hoped, the raid generated jubilant headlines in the United States.

The Doolittle raiders were instant war heroes, and those who made it home were lavished with parades and ceremonies. Doolittle himself was awarded the Congressional Medal of Honor. Practically overnight, Hollywood movies were in the works.

The airmen who didn't make it home—three were executed by a Japanese tribunal, and eight were held in POW camps until after the war—were made into heroic martyrs. The raid did negligible damage to Tokyo, but at a low point in the war, it was a morale boost for Americans, putting a dent in Japan's aura of invincibility.

There was, however, a terrible price to be paid.

Japan was, as expected, humiliated. As planned, the Doolittle Raid made a statement, but now the Japanese had to make a statement in return. They were already engaged in battles against U.S. troops throughout the Pacific islands, so there was little they could do to retaliate against the Americans. But they could make a show of retaliation against someone else: the Chinese, whose airfields the Americans used for the raids, and whose civilians had given aid to the crash-landed American pilots.

Japanese forces swept into China's undefended civilian coastal provinces where the Americans had been given comfort. What happened next was a horrific bloodbath.

"They shot any man, woman, child, cow, hog, or just about anything that moved," one Catholic missionary who was living in the town of Ihwang recorded in his diary. "They raped any woman from the ages of 10–65, and before burning the town they thoroughly looted it . . .

None of the humans shot were buried either, but were left to lay on the ground to rot, along with the hogs and cows."

Japanese soldiers raided dozens of towns, villages, and cities throughout the region. When troops entered Nancheng, a city of fifty thousand residents, they simply annihilated it. All men were killed, and the women and girls were "raped time after time by Japan's Imperial troops and are now ravaged by venereal disease."

Following orders from superiors, the Japanese raiders destroyed every hospital in the region and intentionally poisoned the water supply with deadly contaminants, causing massive outbreaks of cholera, malaria, and dysentery with no medical facilities to treat the stricken.

In total, the Japanese retaliation killed an estimated 200,000 to 250,000 defenseless Chinese civilians.

Sure, the Doolittle Raid gave Americans something to cheer about, but was a morale boost worth the sacrifice of more than two hundred thousand innocent lives?

It was a question Roosevelt faced firsthand when Chinese leader General Chiang Kai-shek wrote to him directly. Citing the 250,000 deaths, he told FDR, "These Japanese troops slaughtered every man, woman and child in those areas. Let me repeat—these Japanese troops slaughtered every man, woman and child in those areas."

For decades, American accounts of the Doolittle Raid made little or no mention of the horrific civilian losses suffered by the Chinese as a result of it. That part certainly didn't make it into the Hollywood movies.

Today, historians continue to debate whether the Doolittle Raid was of significant value to the overall war effort. Some argue that the raid caused Japan to alter its naval strategy in a manner that led to decisive Japanese losses; others contend that the raid had little tangible impact beyond the positive headlines in America.

What's undeniable is that our Chinese allies endured horrific atrocities—and that in a war so vast, a single decision can have massive consequences difficult to foresee.

For FDR, a secret air strike to kill Admiral Yamamoto could lead to a similarly unpredictable result.

There are other concerns that Roosevelt also must weigh. For one, the strike against Yamamoto would alert the Japanese that the U.S. has been intercepting and decrypting its secret communications. The Japanese would be forced to change their codes and implement a new system. Should the U.S. yield an ongoing intelligence advantage just to take down one senior officer?

Finally, there's the question of morality. Traditionally, the United States had frowned on targeted assassinations as a tool of battle. Should the U.S., a beacon of democracy, really be in the grim business of intentionally murdering enemy leaders?

The fact is, by this point, assassinations were already part of the fabric of the war—on both sides of the conflict.

Just days before Roosevelt left on his train ride, anti-Nazi partisans within Germany attempted to assassinate Adolf Hitler by planting a suitcase bomb on a train Hitler was planning to board. A few weeks before that, a different group of German activists also attempted to assassinate Hitler, again with a bomb, while the Führer was conducting a tour of a munitions factory.

Although the recent attempts on Hitler's life were made by individuals, elsewhere in the war, military and government entities utilized assassination as official strategy.

On November 17, 1941, British Commandos attempted to eliminate Field Marshal Erwin Rommel, Germany's top general on the Mediterranean front, by storming a building where informants believed he was working.

Later in the war, in 1944, a British Special Operations team will develop a plan to parachute snipers into the Bavarian Alps to assassinate Hitler while he visits his secluded personal villa. Despite months of preparation, British Special Ops will encounter insurmountable logistical difficulties and choose to abandon the mission.

One of the war's more troubling incidents occurs on June 1, 1943, when the two pilots and thirteen passengers aboard a commercial British airplane—flying from neutral Lisbon, Portugal, to Bristol, England—look out their windows to see a handful of German fighter planes. The Luftwaffe, with no warning or provocation, shoot the British aircraft out of the sky, killing everyone on board.

Why would the German air force shoot down an unarmed civilian passenger plane flying from neutral territory? A theory quickly emerges that the Germans believed that, based on faulty intelligence, Prime Minister Winston Churchill was on the flight.

Churchill was scheduled to travel from Portugal to England on the same day, and German spies spotted a man at the Lisbon airport who bore a striking resemblance to the Prime Minister—complete with cigar and trademark hat, accompanied by aides who resembled Churchill's staff. The German spies called in the target, and when the plane took off, the Luftwaffe trailed the aircraft and shot it out of the sky.

The man who looked like Churchill was, in fact, a British film producer with no connection to the government. One of his traveling companions was famed British film actor Leslie Howard, who died with every other person on the plane.

Needless to say, the incident caused an international furor. Although no proof of motive was ever established, many people believed that the Nazis were attempting to kill the British Prime Minister.

One of those who believed it was Winston Churchill himself. "The brutality of the Germans was only matched by the stupidity of their agents," he later wrote about the incident. "It is difficult to understand how anyone could imagine that with all the resources of Great Britain at my disposal I should have booked a passage in an unarmed and unescorted plane from Lisbon and flown home in broad daylight."

The fact is, in a war where the global stakes are so high, assassination is an irresistible tool. The possibility that the entire course of the war could be changed with a single bomb or bullet is simply too powerful to ignore.

To this day, there's no definitive record of how exactly Roosevelt processed the information he received about Yamamoto. Nor is there a clear record of who he discussed it with or how the final order was given. There is only the order he gave. According to one account, after Roosevelt received the intelligence on the *Ferdinand Magellan,* he simply stated two words: "Get Yamamoto."

From there, the strike was on.

17

ONE YEAR EARLIER . . .

Wannsee, Germany

January 1942

They picked Wannsee, a locality on the outskirts of Berlin.

They even sent out invitations—like it was a normal business meeting.

On November 29, 1941, roughly five months after the Nazi invasion of Russia, Reinhard Heydrich invited key SS agency leaders to this high-level ministerial conference. Included in the invitation was a copy of a letter from Hitler confidante and Nazi leader Hermann Goering, ordering and authorizing Heydrich to devise, on behalf of the Führer, a "total solution to the Jewish question." The goal of this conference was to formalize this "solution" under Heydrich's leadership.

The conference was held on January 20, 1942, in an ornate meeting room in what is now the Havel Institute in Wannsee. It's a leafy district southwest of the city, centered around two small lakes along the Havel River.

Among the fifteen Reich leaders in attendance at the conference were Heinrich Müller, who had taken over the Gestapo from Heydrich, and Adolf Eichmann, head of the "Jewish Affairs" department of the Reich Security Main Office.

Heydrich took charge of the meeting. In his opening presentation he read a prepared paper outlining in dry bureaucratic language a program by which every Jewish population in Europe should be first exploited as slave labor, and then simply murdered:

> In the course of the final solution the Jews are to be allocated for appropriate labor in the East. Able-bodied Jews, separated according to sex, will be taken in large work columns to these areas for work on roads, in the course of which action doubtless a large portion will be eliminated by natural causes. The possible final remnant will, since it will undoubtedly consist of the most resistant portion, have to be treated accordingly, because it is the product of natural selection and would, if released, act as the seed of a new Jewish revival.

In other words, Jews would first be worked to death, and any remaining would be slaughtered. Because the Einsatzgruppen were not sufficient to accomplish this, alternate means would be necessary.

In advance of the meeting, Heydrich had asked Eichmann to calculate the Jewish population in every European nation, including current and former Soviet territories, and encompassing all areas both inside and outside of German control. Eichmann prepared a written breakdown of population numbers and shared the document with the group.

With these figures, Nazi planners could begin to formulate a logistical strategy for how to round up, secure, and transport all Jewish populations to labor camps where they could be worked to death before being killed. It would be a vast and complex operation, but here at the Wannsee Conference were the beginnings of the plan.

Eichmann's study concluded that there were currently roughly eleven million Jewish persons on the European continent.

This was the Final Solution: to murder eleven million Jewish men, women, and children.

Among the many horrors to emerge from the conference was the fact that not a single attendee—including some government ministers who predated the Nazi rise and were not themselves members of the SS—raised the slightest objection to the program.

There was no debate. It's possible that every attendee already knew

```
                        - 6 -
```

L a n d	Zahl
A. Altreich	131.800
Ostmark	43.700
Ostgebiete	420.000
Generalgouvernement	2.284.000
Bialystok	400.000
Protektorat Böhmen und Mähren	74.200
Estland - judenfrei -	
Lettland	3.500
Litauen	34.000
Belgien	43.000
Dänemark	5.600
Frankreich / Besetztes Gebiet	165.000
Unbesetztes Gebiet	700.000
Griechenland	69.600
Niederlande	160.800
Norwegen	1.300
B. Bulgarien	48.000
England	330.000
Finnland	2.300
Irland	4.000
Italien einschl. Sardinien	58.000
Albanien	200
Kroatien	40.000
Portugal	3.000
Rumänien einschl. Bessarabien	342.000
Schweden	8.000
Schweiz	18.000
Serbien	10.000
Slowakei	88.000
Spanien	6.000
Türkei (europ. Teil)	55.500
Ungarn	742.800
UdSSR	5.000.000
Ukraine 2.994.684	
Weißrußland aus-	
schl. Bialystok 446.484	
Zusammen: über	11.000.000

In advance of the January 1942 Wannsee Conference, Nazi SD leader Reinhard Heydrich asked Adolf Eichmann, head of the "Jewish Affairs" department of the Reich Security Main Office, to tabulate a list (above) estimating the total Jewish population of Europe by country or territory. Eichmann's list would help Nazi leaders formulate the genocidal Final Solution to what they called the "Jewish problem" in Europe. (Courtesy of House of the Wannsee Conference)

that Nazi forces were massacring Jewish populations in large numbers. Even so, the implementation of genocide as official government policy was a new idea—and still no one objected. The only disagreements were about which of the large government entities should control various parts of the process.

The ongoing Einsatzgruppen massacres had already involved the participation of tens of thousands of soldiers, workers, and local officials. Now, the entire German government and many sectors of private industry would mobilize toward the explicit goal of mass murder. The vast logistics of the operation would require the participation of hundreds of thousands of individuals, workers, and functionaries from every sphere of society.

They all went along with it.

Perhaps most important, the effort could not succeed without at least the tacit consent of the German public. Hitler and other Nazi leaders knew that without public support, the war effort would crumble. And although ordinary German citizens were not privy to the minutes of the Wannsee Conference, only the most willfully ignorant could fail to know the horrors the Nazi regime was inflicting upon innocent Jewish populations. The public, for the most part, continued to support the regime's atrocities.

As the Wannsee Conference adjourned, the attendees relaxed and chatted. Heydrich took a seat in front of the room's elegant fireplace and treated himself to a cognac.

His moment of relaxation wouldn't last. In the following days, weeks, and months, he threw himself into the planning and implementation of the grand Nazi strategy. Under the leadership of Heydrich, Eichmann, and others, dozens of SS "prison camps" and "labor camps" throughout Poland and Eastern Europe—places already filled with unspeakable suffering—would soon evolve into something else: genocidal death camps.

Implementing the Final Solution was the culmination of Heydrich's ambition. But his leadership would come to a premature end. Among his responsibilities, he'd been put in control of the German-occupied region of the former Czechoslovakia. It would be his undoing.

In May 1942, while traveling in an open convertible car through the Prague streets, two Czech resistance fighters jumped in front of the vehicle with guns raised. The gunmen didn't get a shot off, but one of them was able to toss a bomb at the car, which exploded on impact, severely wounding Heydrich. He would die days later in the hospital.

He was the target of an extraordinary assassination plot. The two gunmen had parachuted into the city from a plane that came from London, England. The assassins were part of a Czech resistance movement supported by the British intelligence services. The Royal Air Force had flown the plane, and British intelligence had helped them piece together Heydrich's car route so they could strike at the right time and place.

Back in Berlin, Heydrich received a hero's public funeral. One of the Nazi Party's brightest stars was gone. Heinrich Himmler gave the eulogy, and Hitler himself ceremoniously placed Heydrich's many medals on the funeral pillow.

In private, however, the Führer was furious that Heydrich had exposed himself to danger by driving in an open car. After the funeral, Hitler fumed:

> Since it is opportunity which makes not only the thief but also the assassin, such heroic gestures as driving in an open, unarmoured vehicle or walking about the streets unguarded are just damned stupidity, which serves the Fatherland not one whit. That a man as irreplaceable as Heydrich should expose himself to unnecessary danger, I can only condemn as stupid and idiotic.

If Hitler was angry at Heydrich's carelessness, he was absolutely enraged at the enemies of the Reich who had eliminated such an invaluable asset. The SS tracked down the assassins, who were hiding in a church in Prague, but the two men killed themselves before they could be captured.

It wasn't enough for Hitler, who demanded greater retribution. When German intelligence suggested that the assassins were linked to the Czech villages of Lezaky and Lidice, the Nazis had their targets.

On orders from Hitler and Himmler, SS units completely razed the tiny village of Lezaky, slaughtering every resident. In the slightly larger village of Lidice, the SS rounded up and killed all males over the age of sixteen, a total of 199 men. The SS put Lidice's women and children on trains to death camps in Poland; at the camps, Lidice's roughly two hundred women were worked to death, and the village's eighty-one children, aged one to fifteen, were sent to the gas chambers.

The German intelligence turned out to be false—there was no link between the assassins and those villages—but that hardly mattered to Nazi leaders. Their goal was for public retribution against anyone who dared strike at the regime.

As for Heydrich's assassination, it didn't impede the progress of the Nazi genocidal program, though it did shake up the SS bureaucracy. Among the ripple effects, it advanced the career of Heydrich's young protégé, Walter Schellenberg.

At the time, Schellenberg had no idea how the dominos of history would fall—or how, a year later in early 1943, his newest mission would intersect with heads of state Joseph Stalin, Winston Churchill, and Franklin Delano Roosevelt.

What Schellenberg does know for sure is what his mentor Heydrich taught him: that an SS leader must be willing to do anything—absolutely anything—to serve the Führer.

18

ONE YEAR LATER . . .

Wannsee, Germany

March 19, 1943

The champagne is flowing in Wannsee.

A dozen or more uniformed men are gathered in a spacious and elegantly appointed room just after nightfall. The neighborhood, just outside Berlin, is home to several government buildings, and this is one of them.

The guests of honor are six young men, mostly in their twenties. For the past several weeks, they've undertaken an intensive training regimen, and in a few days they will embark on a top secret mission. These men will face considerable danger, and their superiors have thrown this small party to honor their bravery and celebrate their impending departure.

The men have trained in several facilities in several locations, sometimes apart and sometimes together. They've received lessons in sabotage, in explosives, in wireless communication, and in specialized weapons. They've learned, perhaps most critically, how to parachute. It's a skill they'll need immediately, because they'll soon be dropped from a plane into an unfamiliar and hostile place: the nation of Iran.

Also present at this event is Walter Schellenberg, who watches the others with careful eyes. He wears an SS uniform of the rank *Oberführer,* with an insignia of an oak leaf on each lapel. Reinhard

Heydrich's former protégé is now the head of the Nazi Party's foreign intelligence service.

At one point, Schellenberg was in the running to take Heydrich's place as the head of the Reich Security Main Office. Instead, after his mentor's assassination, they assigned him to take over that office's Section 6, making him the chief of foreign intelligence for the SD. Although it isn't quite the pinnacle of Nazi leadership, this senior post puts him among the upper echelon. He often meets in person with Himmler, and sometimes directly with Hitler.

Now, this young striver's new leadership position brings new opportunities. Today, it even brings him back to Wannsee, to the exact same building—and possibly the exact same room—where his mentor chaired his infamous Wannsee Conference.

Walter Schellenberg was the leader of Section 6 of the Reich Security Main Office, putting him in charge of foreign intelligence for Nazi Germany. In this position, he oversaw all intelligence and counterintelligence operations in nations or territories outside of German control. (Courtesy of Sueddeutsche Zeitung Photo / Alamy Stock Photo)

On this day, when Schellenberg arrives and the small celebration begins, there's a new covert foreign mission, one that seems relatively small. Certainly, nothing of the magnitude of that earlier historic meeting.

Although Schellenberg will oversee this mission from Berlin, its origins predate his leadership. He recently learned that back in 1940, near the start of the war, the SD had sent two agents to Iran to establish a network in the region and lay the groundwork for future Nazi control.

When the British and Soviets occupied Iran in 1941, they severed communications between Tehran and Berlin, and SD officials assumed the two agents were captured or killed. With so many other pressing matters around the world, the agency simply gave up on them and made no further effort on their behalf. When Schellenberg took over the foreign intelligence office, the Iran mission had been largely forgotten.

Then, just a few months ago, at roughly the time Schellenberg assumed leadership, Section 6 office received a "bolt from the blue"—a message from Franz Mayr, one of the agents who was sent to Iran so long ago.

Miraculously, Mayr wasn't dead—and had not been captured. He'd somehow survived the occupation. And not only had he survived, he'd been operating in Tehran for the past two years and had established a robust underground network of German sympathizers and collaborators in the city.

Mayr's message was received at a time when the Iranian region had assumed critical importance. On the Eastern front, Nazi forces were engaged in massive operations—including the battle for Stalingrad—in the southern section of Russia, close to the Iranian border. Soviet forces were receiving supplies from the United States and Britain via the railroad that ran straight through Iran from the Persian Gulf.

With this surprise message from Franz Mayr—this "bolt from the blue"—Schellenberg and his colleagues saw one of the best things that anyone can hope to find in a fight: an opportunity.

In his communication, Mayr had sent requests for money, supplies, and wireless transmitters. He had provided Berlin directions and coordinates for safe drop zones in the tribal regions outside Tehran where the Allies conducted little oversight.

Mayr's plans for Tehran appeared to be political—he was interested in fomenting dissent in Iran against the Allied occupiers, making Iran ripe for a Nazi takeover—but Schellenberg had something else in mind. Sabotage.

With Mayr's network already in place on the ground, and using the coordinates he had provided, the SD in Berlin could air-drop weapons, explosives, and trained men to destroy or at least disrupt the railroad line used to deliver arms to the Soviets.

And so, the current mission was born. They named it Operation Franz, after the brave spy who had been left for dead only to reemerge two years later, still risking his life for the Fatherland in a hostile country.

If Operation Franz could succeed, so the leadership of the SD believed, Nazi forces in Russia would gain an advantage over the Red Army, and perhaps a decisive one. Disrupting a major railroad that runs through the Allied-controlled country would be no easy task, but given the stakes for the German war effort, the SD would be foolish not to try.

Schellenberg could use a victory. Both his organization and its rival, the Abwehr—Germany's longstanding military intelligence agency—had experienced a recent failure, and an embarrassing one.

Almost two months ago, when Franklin Roosevelt and Winston Churchill held their press conference, the world press ran fawning stories about the U.S.–British summit in Casablanca. The problem was, the Nazi leadership were taken by complete surprise that the event had occurred in Morocco. German intelligence had failed in advance to learn the exact dates or location of the conference.

Not only had they failed, they were humiliated. When the Allies were planning the conference, German intelligence had indeed intercepted decrypted secret communications between the U.S. and the British that contained the word "Casablanca" in relation to a proposed summit. But the analysts completely misunderstood the meaning. Because "casa blanca" translates to "white house" in Spanish, the Germans concluded that the conference was to occur at the White

House in Washington, D.C. It was only when Nazi leaders saw the international news coverage at the end of the summit that they realized their mistake.

Hitler was furious at the mishap. Although Schellenberg's foreign intelligence office was not singled out for blame, his organization had failed completely to predict the correct date or location.

And so, tonight's party with champagne.

Also in attendance is Schellenberg's immediate superior, Ernst Kaltenbrunner, the head of the Reich Security Main Office. In appearance and demeanor, the two men could not be more different. Schellenberg is thin and well spoken, with a boyish face; Kaltenbrunner is six-four and broad-shouldered, with coarse features and a booming voice. One colleague described Kaltenbrunner as a "tough callous ox." Unlike Schellenberg, who was studying law at university when party officials recruited him to be part of the organization's elite, Kaltenbrunner got his start in working-class Austria in the Nazi Party's early street-brawling days.

The two high-ranking officials aren't just different on the outside. In fact, they despise each other. "From the first moment he made me feel quite sick," Schellenberg later said of Kaltenbrunner, describing his superior's "very bad teeth," his "hands of an old gorilla," and his "small, penetrating eyes . . . like the eyes of a viper seeking to petrify its prey."

Schellenberg is also appalled by Kaltenbrunner's excessive drinking, something that Schellenberg sees as a weakness of character. He himself always sticks to a "quota of one or two glasses of wine" to remain in firm control.

It's during occasions like this that Schellenberg's mind sometimes drifts to his former superior—not just his superior, but his personal role model. Unlike Kaltenbrunner, Reinhard Heydrich, the founder of the SD, shared Schellenberg's cultivated manners and refined taste.

Of course, Heydrich also had enormous ambition—and became a legend in the Reich.

Perhaps one day soon, Schellenberg will have a chance to fill the shoes of his mentor. Perhaps he, too, will have a chance at greatness.

19

Qom, Iran

April 15, 1943

The weapons hit the ground with a thud.

They're in a heavy sealed crate that kicks up dirt and sand on impact. The desert is otherwise quiet under the moonless night sky until, several seconds later, there's another thud a few dozen yards away. This time, it's not a crate but a human being that lands, followed by an open parachute.

The weapons crate and the paratrooper were connected by a cord and dropped from a plane. The crate had its own small parachute that the paratrooper could open remotely just before pulling his own chute. The supplies therefore remained attached by rope to the parachutist, but didn't pull him down unnaturally fast. It's an ingenious system that was recently designed by an aviation engineer back in Berlin.

Within the next several minutes, five other crates attached to five other parachutists also hit the ground, one by one, at semiregular distances from the first. If anyone were in the vicinity of these drops, they would soon hear voices in the dark, calling out in German, as the parachutists try to locate one another. Eventually, the band of six take stock of their position.

At first, the landing seems successful, with all six men uninjured and most, if not all, of their gear intact. But the men realize—perhaps that night or perhaps by the first light of morning after a few hours of sleep under tents—that something is amiss.

According to their compasses and the visual position of a nearby mountain range, they're not where they're supposed to be. Instead, they're several dozen miles south from where they intended to land, which puts them farther than they'd like from their first destination, the city of Tehran.

What went wrong? The men aren't sure. The coordinates of the drop zone were sent to Berlin in a message from Franz Mayr, a spy in Tehran after whom their mission was named. He's the man they're supposed to find in the city. Perhaps Mayr's maps were faulty, or perhaps the pilot made an error. Whatever the reason, the group must adapt.

Five of the six paratroopers are young men, still in their twenties. But one of them, Karl Korel, is more seasoned. At thirty-eight, he's the veteran, and unlike the others, he's been to Iran before and can speak Farsi.

Although he's not technically in charge of the mission—he was originally brought on as a translator—he quickly assumes a leadership role. It's up to Korel to get them out of this potentially dangerous situation, stuck in an isolated desert far on the outskirts of the capital of Iran.

After some deliberation, Korel determines that the full group of six shouldn't make the trek across the desert. There's too much to carry; they'll quickly run out of water. Instead, he'll cross the desert by himself, traveling light, while the others camp with the gear in the nearby foothills. If he can make it to Tehran, he'll locate Mayr and then return with trucks or camels to retrieve everyone else. It's not an ideal plan, but there aren't many options.

Within forty-eight hours of their landing, Karl Korel embarks upon what he knows will be a long, difficult trek across a forbidding landscape. At any point, if local authorities in this Allied-controlled country discover him and hand him to the British or the Soviets, a terrible fate awaits. The rest of the group has no choice but to wait in the desert, try to conserve water, and hope for the best.

A few nights prior, these agents of the SD were in Berlin, drinking champagne in an elegant room in Wannsee. Tonight, they're more than two thousand miles away from home in an Iranian desert—and their adventure is just beginning.

20

·

Washington, D.C.

April 29, 1943

When the *Ferdinand Magellan* pulls into Union Station in Washington, D.C., after two full weeks on the road, one person is probably more relieved than anyone else.

It's the man who keeps the President safe.

His name is Mike Reilly. As head of the White House Secret Service, he leads a team of agents who follow the President everywhere. For Reilly, a long cross-country journey by the President is an exercise in nonstop stress and anxiety—because from Reilly's point of view, the President's every stop, every speech, every public appearance in a new town or city contains the potential for disaster.

Roosevelt and Reilly are an odd pair, to be sure, but they've formed an unusually tight bond. Roosevelt is a northeastern aristocrat who attended the finest schools and grew up with every privilege; Reilly is a brawny working-class former high school football player from Montana who was, as Reilly later described himself, "an Irishman who sometimes had more muscle than brain."

Interestingly, it's Roosevelt's physical condition that gives their relationship a special intensity—and a special intimacy. At a time when little or nothing was done in public or commercial spaces to accommodate the needs of the differently abled, Reilly is the one who makes sure that there are ramps for Roosevelt's wheelchair, and that the President's sleeping quarters and bathrooms are equally accommodating.

Sometimes, the broad-shouldered Reilly has to gently lift and carry the President up or down stairs, or through spaces inaccessible to a wheelchair.

What Reilly may lack in intellectual sophistication, he makes up for in loyalty and resourcefulness. He was in his midtwenties when he first joined the Secret Service, and through hard work and diligence quickly rose through the ranks.

On the day after Pearl Harbor, December 8, 1941, he was promoted, at age thirty-two, to replace his aging superior as the Supervising Secret Service Agent at the White House.

Even when it's not wartime, the most obvious concern for the Secret Service is stopping those who intend to do the President harm.

Mike Reilly (left) was put in charge of the Secret Service at the White House the day after the Japanese attack on Pearl Harbor. From that moment he was almost always by Roosevelt's side. The responsibility for keeping an unusually frail President safe during a time of war gave Reilly "shivers in the daytime and nightmares in bed." (Courtesy of Bettmann / Getty Images)

"The big bugaboo of presidential protection is assassination," as Reilly put it. "Traditionally American presidents are shot, but they could be bombed, poisoned, stabbed, or murdered in a train wreck. Our job was to prevent any of these." When a war begins, the circle of potential enemies expands from the usual deranged individuals and domestic extremists to foreign enemy agents, saboteurs, and assassins.

It was Reilly who, upon first taking charge, envisioned and created a separate dedicated location for all incoming White House mail and packages, so that a trained team could screen every parcel for bombs and explosives.

It was Reilly who, when food arrived from all over the world intended as gifts to Roosevelt, came up with a system to send samples to a special office of the Food and Drug Administration where they were tested for poison.

And it was Reilly who, before the President made his historic plane flight to Casablanca earlier in the year, personally oversaw the design of a specially modified Presidential aircraft that would provide extra safety measures and accommodate Roosevelt's disability. As a result, it was also Reilly who then had to travel in advance to every one of the layovers along the President's cross-continental journey, inspecting every airfield, tarmac, car route, and hotel.

For Mike Reilly, however, the real stress didn't come from hidden killers—it came from something far more mundane: the dangers posed by travel. "I could outwit a regiment of Axis assassins and it would mean nothing if the President's special train ran through a switch or hit a split rail," as he later put it.

Whether FDR was traveling by car, rail, boat, or plane, there were always a thousand details and safety measures to worry about. During long trips, the responsibility and pressure to keep this unusually vulnerable President safe gave Reilly "shivers in the daytime and nightmares in bed."

So on April 29, when the *Ferdinand Magellan* returns to Washington, D.C., and the President safely makes his way back to the White House after a two-week journey around the country, including a brief stayover in Mexico, Mike Reilly is relieved to put the shivers and nightmares behind him. Finally, a moment to relax.

Yet what Mike Reilly doesn't know—and what almost everyone else in the Presidential orbit doesn't know either—is that Franklin Roosevelt had spent the middle of that train journey anxiously awaiting top secret communications from his senior naval commanders. The subject? Operation Vengeance. The plan to kill Admiral Yamamoto.

Most likely, the secret news that Roosevelt was awaiting arrived while he was crossing the plains of Oklahoma. On April 18, a squadron of sixteen P-38 U.S. fighter planes had located and trailed two Japanese bombers that, escorted by nine fighters, had just launched from Kukum Field on Guadalcanal in the Solomon Islands.

Sure enough, Admiral Yamamoto was in one of the bombers, on his way to a scheduled tour of Bougainville. With the element of surprise on their side, the U.S. planes moved in on the air squadron, dispatched the Japanese fighters, and then circled in on their target.

One of the P-38s swung behind Yamamoto's plane, and the U.S. gunners unleashed a volley of bullets. The Admiral's bomber started spewing black smoke, and within minutes, the plane crashed into the jungle below.

Admiral Isoroku Yamamoto (in white) gives what will be his final salute to Japanese naval pilots in the Solomon Islands. Targeted killings of high-ranking officials—in other words, assassinations—were common practice during the Second World War. (Courtesy of Wikimedia Commons)

A day later, on April 19, a Japanese search-and-rescue party found the crashed plane with Yamamoto's body nearby.

Unlike the Doolittle Raid, U.S. officials kept the Yamamoto strike under wraps. It was a clandestine operation and they wanted to keep it that way. The Japanese also did their best to keep it a secret, knowing that the loss of the revered Admiral would cripple public morale in Japan.

The Japanese navy waited a full month to announce Yamamoto's death and never revealed what they knew: that it was the result of a premeditated strike on the part of the Americans, and that U.S. intelligence had decrypted the Japanese navy's supposedly unbreakable codes.

Japan's official statement, repeated in newspapers around the world on May 21, was simply that Yamamoto had "engaged in combat with the enemy and met a gallant death on a war plane." In the weeks between Yamamoto's death and Japan's official announcement, only a few people in the world knew what really happened.

Roosevelt, for his part, kept the incident completely under wraps. His first public comments about it would be at another White House press conference shortly after Japan's official announcement. Toward the end of the briefing, a reporter asked Roosevelt:

Q: Mr. President, would you care to comment on the death of the Japanese admiral?
THE PRESIDENT: (pause) He's dead?

Q: The Japanese radio announced it.
Q: Yamamoto.
Q: Killed in action while directing operations in an airplane.
THE PRESIDENT: Gosh! (laughter)

Roosevelt feigns surprise, pretending he's learning about the strike right there, but his tone is a wink to reporters that he knows more than he's letting on.

If there's some smugness in Roosevelt's delivery, it's because he's proud of what his military accomplished. U.S. Naval Intelligence had decrypted a series of codes that the Japanese believed to be unbreakable. The mission itself was a success, and as a result, one of Imperial Japan's most brilliant and respected military leaders—the mastermind behind Pearl Harbor—has been permanently removed.

Still, President Roosevelt can't rest easy. Nor can his Secret Service chief, Mike Reilly.

America's enemies are *also* capable of intercepting communications and breaking secret codes—and as Roosevelt and Reilly will soon learn, assassination plots can go in both directions.

21

Tehran, Iran

Late April 1943

He needs a lucky break.

After the midnight parachute drop, Nazi paratrooper Karl Korel has crossed the desert and is now finally in Tehran.

The entire mission has so far been difficult. The parachute drop went off course, the trek across the desert was dangerous, and now he is walking into an Allied-occupied city alone, with no support, no protection, and no means of communication with either his team in the desert or his handlers in Berlin.

His goal, at this point, is near impossible: to locate, in this teeming city of three-quarters of a million people, a single person—the Nazi SD agent Franz Mayr. Without any additional information, this is already a tall order, but there is also another problem.

Mayr is in hiding. He's probably wearing a disguise, certainly doesn't use his real name, and could be in a basement or back room almost anywhere in the sprawling metropolis.

In his quest to find Mayr, Korel only has a few things going for him. Unlike everyone else on his team, he can speak and read some Farsi. He's been in Tehran before, back in 1941, before the Allies seized control. And during that previous visit, Korel actually met Franz Mayr, as well as some others in Mayr's circle.

It's this latter fact—that Korel had met a few of Mayr's acquaintances—that will make the difference.

While Korel is wandering around downtown, probably somewhat aimlessly, looking for clues in cafés and markets, he happens to spot an older woman who looks familiar.

It's a stroke of luck almost too good to be believed.

As Korel gets closer, he confirms it's the mother of Lili Sanjari, Franz Mayr's lover in Tehran. Mayr was already in a relationship with Sanjari when Korel had met him back in 1941. Sanjari was from a prominent family, and Korel had also met her parents.

In addition, paratrooper Korel also knew that just before the Allied invasion of Iran, when all communication between Iran and Germany was cut off, Mayr had sent a request to marry Sanjari. Although it was denied, it showed that the relationship was serious. At the very least, Korel can hope that they might still be together.

The question is, how safe is it to approach Sanjari's mother out of the blue? For all Korel knows, the Sanjari family switched their loyalty to the Allied side once the Soviets, British, and Americans took control of the region.

If so, this woman could lead Korel straight to an Allied prison. Still, the task of finding Mayr in this city is otherwise so daunting, he probably feels like he hasn't got much choice.

Amazingly, Korel's luck holds. After he introduces himself, the elder Sanjari agrees to help. She confirms that Franz Mayr and her daughter *are* still together and, even better, she knows Lili's whereabouts. All Korel has to do is follow.

That is how, on roughly April 15, 1943, Berlin's Operation Franz connects with Franz Mayr, the loyal Nazi spy who'd been in hiding in Tehran for two years.

There is no record of exactly where the elder Sanjari led Korel to meet Franz—or what was said at their meeting. Surely, the two Nazi agents were brimming with questions for each other.

Yet the two spies don't have much time for discussion. Korel now needs Mayr's help to gather camels and supplies for a return trip through the desert to retrieve the other members of the mission. For over a week, they've been camping out in the Siah Kuh foothills.

Based on the time it took for Korel to reach the city, it'll take him another full week to get back to his colleagues, and then another week on top of that for the full caravan to return to Tehran. For Korel, that's three weeks of back-to-back treks through the Iranian desert. And that's just to get the mission started.

For now, though, Korel can at least take satisfaction that the first objective of Operation Franz has been completed. Despite a faulty parachute drop, their personnel and most of their supplies are still intact. More important, thanks to Korel's competence and a stroke of good fortune, the mission has achieved its initial goal of locating and establishing contact with SD agent Franz Mayr.

For Mayr, it must be even more gratifying. For almost two years, he's been operating mostly alone, in hiding, fearing for his life, with very little contact and no support from his home country. During that time, he never gave up his mission. Almost single-handedly, he built and cultivated a network of Nazi sympathizers and supporters in Tehran.

Now, for the first time, he's got the support he's craved. Soon, he'll supposedly have supplies, money, wireless radios, and new personnel to work with.

For Nazi spy Franz Mayr, it's a new day in Tehran.

For years, he has stuck it out here, never giving up, convinced that Iran would soon be vital to the Nazi war effort. Yet at this moment, Mayr and his companions are still unaware of just how important this city will soon be on the global stage. Indeed, the Nazi mission in Tehran is about to change into something none of them can imagine.

22

—— · ——

Tehran, Iran

May 1943

He looks like an ordinary teenager on a bike.

At nineteen years old, he's slender, with Eastern European features and smooth skin that's lightly tanned by the Persian sun. He spends most days traversing the streets and back alleys of the city on his bicycle, sometimes with companions but often alone, occasionally stopping to peer into doorways or to say a few words to shopkeepers or regulars at the city's outdoor markets.

Bicycles are a common mode of transportation in Tehran, so this teenager looks no different from many ordinary residents who get from place to place on two wheels.

But this young man is far from ordinary. Every day, his bike rides have a special purpose.

His name is Gevork Vartanian, and he's an undercover Soviet agent. He belongs to a team of young recruits called the "Light Calvary," named after their mode of transportation.

So how does a young man still in his teens end up as a Soviet spy?

In Vartanian's case, it's the family business.

Vartanian was born in 1924 to Armenian parents near Rostov, in southern Russia. His father, a recent immigrant to the Soviet Union, was eager to serve the family's new homeland. The elder Vartanian took a position with the NKVD—the primary Soviet intelligence service of the era, and precursor to the KGB—and quickly distinguished himself.

In 1930, before the war, the NKVD transferred the Vartanian family to Tehran, where Gevork's father worked undercover in the guise of an Armenian businessman.

Young Gevork therefore spent most of his childhood and adolescence in Tehran. He learned to speak fluent Farsi and got to know the ins and outs of Iran's complicated capital city. When it came time to contemplate a career, he knew exactly what he wanted to do. "As a child, I saw what my father was doing," Gevork later recalled. "He raised me in the spirit of patriotism and love for the Motherland."

It was time to follow in his father's footsteps. By the age of sixteen, young Vartanian was already working for the NKVD in Tehran.

At first, he served in an administrative position as a recruiter. But after the Soviets and British took over Iran in 1941—suddenly bringing the focus of Soviet intelligence to the region—Gevork's superior, an experienced Soviet spy named Ivan Ivanovich Agayants, gave him greater responsibility.

"My first task was to create a group of like-minded people," Gevork later explained, "and I quickly recruited seven guys."

These seven weren't typical recruits. They were young—mostly still teenagers—and they all worked on bikes. It was Agayants, Vartanian's superior, who jokingly called them the Light Cavalry, and as Vartanian would recall, "This name stuck to my group."

The Light Cavalry began acting as the eyes and ears of the NKVD. It was a clever idea. The cavalry could get around the city quickly and easily; they didn't need expensive vehicles or gasoline; and as bike-riding teenagers they would blend in and draw little attention to themselves.

This made them perfect spies.

Their job was to seek out enemy activity in Tehran. More specifically, "to monitor and identify fascist agents." There were still several thousand residents of German descent in the city, and while most were leading civilian lives, this population still needed to be monitored.

It was no secret that many Iranians resented the Allied occupation of their country. Some were still loyal to the previous Iranian government under Reza Shah, who was friendly to Hitler. The last thing the

Soviet, British, or American authorities in Iran wanted was an internal pro-Nazi resistance movement to develop and threaten Allied control of the region.

For the Soviets in particular, the stability of Tehran was a matter of supreme importance. Just over the border to the north, the Soviet Union was fighting for its very existence against the invading Nazi armies, sacrificing hundreds of thousands of lives every month. Sometimes the nation was barely hanging on by a thread. This extraordinary effort depended on the daily flow of American arms and supplies into the Soviet Union—a flow that went straight through Iran.

On a typical day in the spring of 1943, Vartanian and his fellow Light Cavalry members cruised the city, checking in on informants, passing messages from their superiors to intelligence sources, monitoring suspected pro-Nazi dissidents, and generally looking out for anything unusual.

Lately, though, there's been more to worry about. According to local reports, German planes have been spotted in the sky over the desert. There've been rumors of enemy paratroopers being dropped outside the city—and now, possibly, they're within it.

Soviet intelligence has known, of course, about a suspected Nazi spy operating in Tehran. They even know his name: Franz Mayr. Through their British intelligence counterparts, they've learned that this spy, working undercover and in hiding, has been building a powerful pro-Nazi network in the city.

Yet the one thing that young Gevork can't possibly know is that on the morning of May 5, 1943, over six thousand miles away on the other side of the globe, President of the United States Franklin Roosevelt is handing a top secret note to one of his most senior aides.

The aide has instructions to board a flight to Moscow and deliver the note, by hand, to Soviet Premier Joseph Stalin. Only the aide and Stalin himself have permission to view the contents.

This secret note, written by the President, will set in motion a series of events that will soon greatly impact young Gevork Vartanian and his city.

Soon enough, these events will link this teenager on a bike in the most unexpected way to Franklin Roosevelt, the U.S. President; to

Mike Reilly, the head of Roosevelt's Secret Service; to Winston Churchill, the Prime Minister of the United Kingdom; and even to Joseph Stalin, the leader of Vartanian's own adopted homeland.

It will happen, in a few months, right here, in Tehran.

The Light Calvary better be ready.

PART III

·

Uncle Joe

23

Berlin, Germany

Late April 1943

Walter Schellenberg carefully eyes the uniformed man who has just entered his office and taken a seat in front of Schellenberg's desk.

Schellenberg's spacious corner office is in a modern building in the Schmargendorf neighborhood of Berlin. A prolific Jewish architect named Alexander Beer originally designed the structure in 1930 as a retirement home for Berlin's then thriving Jewish community. In 1941, the Nazi Party seized the compound, deported the aging Jewish residents to prisons and labor camps where most of them were killed, and repurposed the structure for the Reich's use. Beer is himself arrested in early 1943 and sent to the Theresienstadt concentration camp, where he dies a year later.

Today, however, this building is where Walter Schellenberg oversees the day-to-day operations of Nazi foreign intelligence services, also known as the Sicherheitsdienst, or SD.

The uniformed man in Schellenberg's office does not know it, but the desk in front of him has some unusual hidden features.

Schellenberg, as a high-ranking intelligence officer in the Reich Security Main Office, has many potential enemies. Some could be secret foreign agents lurking in Berlin; others could be internal rivals within the cutthroat world of the Reich. "There were times when I felt more like a hunted beast than the head of a department," Schellenberg later recalled. Whether his enemies are from outside of the Reich or within it, he knows what happened to his mentor. He's always on high alert for plots against him.

Indeed, to protect himself, he's taken special precautions.

"Microphones were hidden everywhere, in the walls, under the desk, even in one of the lamps," Schellenberg later recalled, "so that every conversation and every sound was automatically recorded."

These recordings chronicle any threat made against him in his office. Still, that's no help if a visitor attacks him or uses violence. For that, he'd prepared something more elaborate. "My desk was like a small fortress," he later described. "Two automatic guns were built into it which could spray the whole room with bullets. These guns pointed at the visitor and followed his or her progress toward my desk. All I had to do in an emergency was to press a button and both guns would fire simultaneously."

If that didn't work and an attacker escaped, Schellenberg has a backup plan. "I could press another button and a siren would summon the guards to surround the building and block every exit."

The uniformed man currently seated before Schellenberg's desk likely has no idea that two automatic guns are at that moment pointed at him. But if he did he would probably not be intimidated, for he's someone used to facing danger without backing down.

His name is Otto Skorzeny. At thirty-four, he's a veteran officer with the equivalent of a Lieutenant's rank in the Waffen-SS, the military force run by the SS alongside the traditional German armed forces. He's a loyal Nazi, recently injured in a battle on the Eastern front, so he can no longer serve on the front line. Yet he's far from useless. Skorzeny has a unique skill set—engineering, explosives, flight training, advanced weaponry, as well as leadership in battle—that makes him potentially valuable.

Schellenberg summoned Skorzeny to his office, at least in part, because of Operation Franz. The Iran mission has thus far been a success—the group of paratroopers successfully met up with Nazi agent Franz Mayr in Tehran, the Berlin SD office has learned—and Schellenberg wants to build on that success.

The concept of Special Forces—small, mobile teams of specialized soldiers sent to fulfill discreet tasks—has recently gained currency in Nazi leadership circles. The vast German armies have encountered stiff resistance from the Soviet armies on the Eastern front, and the progress of the war has stalled. Utilizing small, elite, fast-moving teams to accomplish specialized and often secret missions is a way to take advantage of Germany's superior technology and training. Nazi leaders hope it'll tip the balance in the Axis's favor.

Schellenberg already has plans for another Iran mission, soon to be called Operation Anton, that would parachute a team of agents armed with weapons and explosives into the northern tribal regions of the country. There, they would link up with another German spy on the ground, an Abwehr agent named Berthold Shulze-Holthus, to sabotage rail lines and other targets, provide weapons and money to local collaborators, and complement the Operation Franz mission. This is just the beginning. For Iran and elsewhere, Schellenberg has other plans in the works.

To accomplish these objectives, Schellenberg knows he needs help. He needs someone to better strategize and equip these Special Forces missions. And he needs a leader with the skills to recruit and train agents, to prepare them for elite field operations.

That is where Otto Skorzeny comes in. Skorzeny is a physically powerful presence, six foot four and wide-shouldered. He has a fencing scar on his cheek from his teenage years—a source of pride among a certain set of German men. He speaks firmly and exudes confidence. Most importantly, he has the skills and knowledge for the job.

By the end of the interview, the two men have all but agreed on a plan. Skorzeny will take over and expand the training program for agents and soldiers in the SD's newly created Special Operations program. He'll be the commander of the Sonderlehrgang z.b.V. Ora-nienburg unit, translating roughly to "special course for special assign-ments." The term "Oranienburg" refers to the location of the training

In spring 1943, Nazi foreign intelligence leader Walter Schellenberg recruited veteran Waffen-SS officer Otto Skorzeny (above) to lead an expanded "Special Operations" training program for the SD. Skorzeny would recruit, train, and oversee elite commando teams for clandestine foreign missions. (Courtesy of Shawshots / Alamy Stock Photo)

grounds: in Oranienburg, roughly twenty miles north of Berlin and home to the site of one of the first Nazi concentration camps.

In these unglamorous surroundings, Skorzeny will recruit soldiers and intelligence agents, training them in explosives, sabotage, and paramilitary operations.

In this new position, Skorzeny will remain an officer of the Waffen-SS but will receive a new commission with a Captain's rank, and he will answer directly to Schellenberg.

In typical Reich fashion, the two Nazi operatives have been pretending to get along while they secretly judge each other. Skorzeny, who considers himself a soldier first, perceives the physically unimpressive Schellenberg to be a bureaucrat and "a man who neither had the determined character nor was as clever or clear-seeing as he thought he was."

Schellenberg, meanwhile, considers himself a person of refined taste and intellect; he prefers to do business with the social elite of the Nazi hierarchy. He doesn't have much patience for crude military men like Skorzeny.

Still, the arrangement is mutually beneficial—and they agree to work together.

What neither man realizes is that because of their short meeting today, soon-to-be-Captain Otto Skorzeny—previously a midlevel Waffen-SS officer little known outside his division—is on his way to being known all over the world as the "Most Dangerous Man in Europe."

24

Washington, D.C.

May 5, 1943

It's just a letter.

It's typewritten, single-spaced, only a few paragraphs. The President believes, though, that this short letter could alter the alliance for the better—and therefore help win the war.

In fact, Roosevelt thinks it's so important, he insists that a single person should carry this letter by hand across the world and personally deliver it.

The chosen messenger now sits in the Oval Office, across from the President's desk, trying to understand his mission.

Roosevelt's plan to send this letter was initiated back on April 29, the day FDR returned from his cross-country train journey. The *Ferdinand Magellan* had arrived at Union Station at 10 a.m.; Roosevelt did a press conference at 12:05 p.m.; and then, at 1 p.m., he had lunch in his office with a former member of his administration whom he asked to see immediately upon return.

That person was Joseph E. Davies, who from 1936 to 1938 served as Roosevelt's ambassador to the Soviet Union and was one of the few people in Washington the President trusted to do business with Moscow. While ambassador, Davies had developed a positive rapport with the Soviet government, and Roosevelt knew that both

Foreign Minister Molotov and Premier Stalin himself thought favorably of him.

During this lunch meeting, FDR finalized plans for Davies to serve as a "special envoy" to the Soviet Union, to carry out a single discreet mission. Roosevelt asked Davies to block out several weeks for the trip and to stand by.

Now, six days later, on May 5, 1943, Davies is back in the White House for another one-on-one meeting. Here, in the Oval Office, Roosevelt hands Davies a one-page typewritten letter.

The recipient? Joseph Stalin, the Premier of the Soviet Union. Davies is told to personally hand it to Stalin in Moscow. According to Roosevelt, the letter is so confidential that no other means of delivery is safe enough—and that the President trusts no one other than Davies to carry it out.

Davies then reads the letter, which Roosevelt composed himself. It begins:

My Dear Mr. Stalin:

I am sending this personal note to you by the hands of my old friend, Joseph E. Davies. It relates solely to one subject which I think it is easier for us to talk over through a mutual friend.

I want to get away from the difficulties of large Staff conferences or the red tape of diplomatic conversations. Therefore, the simplest and most practical method that I can think of would be an informal and completely simple visit for a few days between you and me.

As he has before, Roosevelt is communicating that he wants to meet Stalin in person. "It is my thought that neither of us would want to bring any staff," Roosevelt's letter continues, "and that you and I would talk very informally and get what we call 'a meeting of the minds.'"

Roosevelt goes on to suggest a timetable: "[Y]ou and I ought to meet this summer."

After showing Davies the letter, the President repeats that no one except Davies, Stalin, and Stalin's Foreign Minister is allowed to read it.

Now aware of its contents, Davies responds with two obvious questions: Why isn't Churchill invited—and does Churchill know that Roosevelt is planning this meeting without him? At this point, it's public knowledge that Roosevelt and Churchill have been pushing for a meeting of the Big Three.

"Three is a crowd and we can arrange for the Big Three to get together thereafter," Roosevelt says somewhat cryptically. "Churchill will understand, I will take care of that."

In other words, Churchill clearly does *not* currently know that Roosevelt is pursuing this meeting without him. Roosevelt's wording to Stalin also confirms this. "Africa is out of the question in Summer and Khartum is British territory," Roosevelt writes in the letter. "Iceland I do not like because for both you and me it involves rather difficult flights and, in addition, would make it, quite frankly, difficult not to invite Prime Minister Churchill at the same time." He concludes, "Therefore, I suggest that we could meet either on your side or my side of Bering Straits."

To put it more bluntly, Roosevelt is purposefully making sure Churchill won't come, and by doing it behind Churchill's back, FDR is secretly undermining their publicly stated desire to meet as a trio.

To make matters more complicated, at this very moment, Churchill is on a ship with his senior military staff, bound for the United States for his first conference at the White House since his landmark visit, now eighteen months ago, in the aftermath of Pearl Harbor. His arrival is scheduled for May 11, one week from today's meeting with Davies.

Much like his previous visit, Churchill will arrive in Washington to great fanfare. Once again, the British and American war planners will meet extensively over the course of many days, working to shape strategy based on the latest developments in the war. And once again, Churchill and Roosevelt will spend considerable time together, including personal time as friends, away from Washington, D.C., at Roosevelt's country retreat.

All the while, the President will be anxiously waiting for a response from the Soviet Premier regarding a secret plan that undermines the Prime Minister.

So why is Roosevelt deceiving his closest and most loyal partner?

The answer is related to the single biggest decision the Allies must make in the course of the war—one that could be the key to defeating Nazi Germany.

25

—·—

Washington, D.C.

May 19, 1943

The cross-Channel attack.

In the weeks and months since the Casablanca Conference, this is the most critical military question on the Allied side—when and how the United States and the British will finally attack Nazi Germany directly by sending forces across the English Channel into occupied France. Planning this cross-Channel attack has begun to dwarf every other military consideration and become a major source of debate, confusion, and division among the Allied nations.

The leader who was always consistent on the issue was Joseph Stalin. Since the very beginning of the alliance, he's been adamant in his conviction that his Western partners must open a "second front" against Germany by striking directly from the west, presumably across the English Channel onto the beaches of northern France. This and this alone, Stalin believed, would force Hitler to divert enough ground forces from the Eastern front that the Soviet army could gain a decisive advantage and push the Nazi armies back.

Some military leaders in the United States were initially optimistic that such an assault could be launched quickly after America's entry into the war. Shortly after Pearl Harbor, the U.S. Joint Planning Staff presented a strategy for a combined American and British cross-

Channel attack to take place July or August of 1942. Although the idea was still under debate internally, President Roosevelt told Soviet Foreign Minister Molotov during his spring visit to the White House to expect a "second front" in 1942. Molotov took this message home to Stalin.

Roosevelt, however, would regret making this prediction. The problem was the British weren't yet on board. Roosevelt's military leaders were making plans that would impact places three thousand miles from U.S. shores; but for the British, this would be an attack launched from their own soil, against an enemy just across the Channel. The idea of diverting hundreds of thousands of Nazi troops away from Russia to the beaches of northern France—only a few dozen miles from England's southern coast—meant something entirely different for the British.

On top of that, the British planners pointed out the many tactical and logistical difficulties of an amphibious landing in the face of the most powerful army in the world, arguing that U.S. troop and arms production were not yet sufficient for such an operation.

The issue would be debated strenuously both within and between the military leadership on both sides, but ultimately the U.S. and British Combined Chiefs of Staff fell back on the shared conclusion that "it does not seem likely that in 1942 any large-scale land offensive against Germany, except on the Russian front, will be possible." The Russian front, of course, would not involve American or British troops.

Instead, in 1942 the Americans and the British embarked upon Operation Torch, the mission to push Italian and German forces out of North Africa and thereby gain control of Mediterranean ports and sea lanes. This was the beginning of the "Southern front" that would become the main European theater of operations for American and British ground troops for the first two years of the war.

The United Kingdom and the United States would continue to support the Soviet army with an increasing flow of arms and supplies, but they would not directly challenge the brunt of Hitler's armies in Europe or the Soviet Union.

Needless to say, this decision deeply frustrated Stalin. His armies and his country were facing annihilation, suffering millions of losses, enduring famines and massacres, while the Americans and the British were, in his mind, tinkering with sea lanes in a faraway region that was of minor consequence. In his eyes, they were not really confronting Nazi Germany. The Mediterranean theater was not the "second front" he had hoped for from his new partners.

Stalin didn't have much choice but to go along with his Allies' strategy. He desperately needed the U.S. arms and supplies that Roosevelt was sending, so the Russians had to continue enduring the Nazi onslaught largely on their own.

If the United States and the United Kingdom couldn't or wouldn't attempt a cross-Channel attack in 1942, then, Stalin assumed, surely 1943 would be the year they would do so. The Soviet Union would keep weathering the Nazi storm throughout 1942, its soldiers and civilians would die by the millions month after month, but at least the U.S. and Britain would join the fight the following spring or summer.

Roosevelt believed this too. Throughout 1942 U.S. and British war planners did try to come up with strategies to strike Western Europe from England in 1943. A series of plans for a proposed cross-Channel attack took on many names and variations: Operation Sledgehammer, Operation Bolero, Operation Roundup, Operation Roundhammer. Yet the war leaders could never agree on the specifics or the timing. With every proposed operation, someone would decide it was too complex or too risky, with a cost of failure too high.

The back-and-forth had many phases, but in general the same pattern continued to emerge: The Americans were ready to move forward with a cross-Channel attack, but the British would come up with reasons to reject or delay every plan.

Churchill, especially, became more and more drawn to the Mediterranean theater of war, where the Allies could achieve small but decisive victories. The Mediterranean, Churchill believed, was the "soft underbelly" of Europe through which the Allies could safely advance. This would be the "Southern Strategy" or "Soft Underbelly Strategy" by which Allied forces could defeat Italy's weak army along with any German forces Hitler was willing to send to the region to defend his smaller ally.

Although this strategy led to Allied victories in North Africa throughout 1942, it wasn't doing much to stop the cataclysm in Eastern Europe or the Soviet Union. Nor was it directly threatening Hitler's domination of Western Europe, including France, Belgium, Norway, the Netherlands, and elsewhere.

At the conclusion of the Casablanca Conference in January 1943, Roosevelt and Churchill had still not resolved this critical issue of the second front. Together, they made many grand proclamations about the progress of the war in the Pacific and around the Mediterranean, but they couldn't affirm a plan for attacking the heart of Nazi Germany—which is to say, attacking across the channel into northern France.

In the months after the conference, Churchill's constant negativity and wavering on the cross-Channel attack was threatening to corrode the Allied relationship. Every time they seemingly put a plan in place, Churchill and his team would undermine it and cause more delay, pushing instead to devote more resources to the Mediterranean campaign.

As the early months of 1943 wore on, Roosevelt began to fear what was once unthinkable: that again the Americans and British would not be ready to execute a cross-Channel attack before the onset of winter, and would therefore once again have to postpone the mission until the following spring.

It's in this context that Roosevelt had gone behind Churchill's back and set up his one-on-one meeting with Stalin. Roosevelt's goal is to establish a personal connection with the Soviet leader and assure him that the United States is fully committed to supporting the Soviets in the war. They may have to delay the cross-Channel attack again, but in the end, the Americans would come through on the second front, and Roosevelt would make sure that Churchill complied.

Roosevelt also knows that Stalin has never fully trusted the British, and he fears that if the three of them met in person and Churchill were to display any hesitance about the idea of attacking Hitler in France, Stalin might lose faith in the alliance with disastrous results. FDR simply believes, as one Roosevelt aide put it, that "he would get along better with Stalin in Churchill's absence."

Will Churchill be offended? Of course he'll be offended. But while Roosevelt is well aware that his personal loyalty to Churchill is important, it's not as important as defeating Hitler. And to defeat Hitler, the alliance with the Soviets must be solid.

A few days after Davies leaves for Moscow, Churchill arrives in Washington, D.C. On May 19, 1943, in the middle of the two-week-long conference—and after considerable time spent between Roosevelt and Churchill personally, sometimes including their wives and families—Churchill walks into the Capitol building where both Houses of Congress are assembled.

Once again, Churchill gives a long address where he's received rapturously by his American audience. He speaks at length about the tight bond between the two nations, and of his unity with Roosevelt.

In the speech, he specifically brings up the possibility for a Big Three conference. Referring to Roosevelt and himself, he declares: "We, both of us, earnestly hope that at no distant date we may be able to achieve what we have so long sought—namely, a meeting with Marshal Stalin."

As he speaks those words, the Prime Minister has no idea the machinations currently underway to cut him out of any such meeting.

Indeed, roughly twenty-four hours after Churchill's speech, former Ambassador Joseph Davies, special envoy to President Roosevelt, enters a spacious, grandly appointed room in Moscow, over 4,800 miles from the U.S. Capitol.

After over ten days of travel across the world, Davies, with Roosevelt's secret letter in his hand, is ready to carry out his mission for the President.

26

Tehran, Iran

No one can say that Franz Mayr isn't ambitious.

Since being forced into hiding nearly two years ago, his goal has been nothing less than the overthrow of the Allied government in Iran—with himself in the leading role.

Almost single-handedly, he's built up a pro-Nazi underground resistance movement in Tehran, with outreach to elsewhere in the country. This organization—known as the Melliun movement—has a network of local support, including elements within the Iranian army, the police force, and many business interests.

Under Franz Mayr's leadership, they've developed detailed plans for what they believe would be the coming Nazi liberation of the country, in which the Melliun's internal resistance would be a key component.

In planning for this grand event, they've already determined that "Azerbaijan East should be the first area to be entered by German forces" and that their own task was to "open the way for advancing troops."

In addition to Mayr and his network's plans for the coming Nazi military takeover, they also have ideas for how to exact revenge on their enemies afterward. According to the Melliun's internal documents:

The Managing Committee should have a list of the traitors to Iran so that, in time of need, when the German Army arrives in Iran and starts governing it, these people should be caught by the new government and handed to the Court.

The Jews.
The Bahais.
The Refugees (all of them).
Pro-British and Pro-Russians.
Former traitorous ministers.

The Melliun's plans were entirely consistent with standard Nazi methods: Take over a region, punish the Jewish population, then punish all others perceived to be enemies of the Reich.

With the unexpected arrival of new personnel, weapons, wireless transmitters, and other supplies from Berlin via Operation Franz, Mayr must have felt that his grand vision was closer to being realized.

But that didn't mean things were easy.

From the moment Karl Korel returned to Tehran with the other member of his team—all of whom survived their time camping in the desert—Mayr has found himself at odds with his new companions.

For starters, he's annoyed to learn that they called their mission "Operation Franz." Sure, it was a tribute to him, but he's a man hiding in an enemy country. If any of the team were captured and interrogated by the Allies, or if documents were confiscated, the mission's name might be revealed—meaning *his* name would also be revealed. After all his subterfuge, the last thing he needs is to be undone by a childish error.

Even worse, Mayr learns that the goals of Operation Franz do not entirely match his own. For the past two years, Franz has developed an underground resistance movement, prepared to help overthrow Allied control when the Nazi armies make their move. The Operation Franz team, however, was sent on an unrelated mission: to sabotage the Trans-Iranian railroad, with the goal of halting or slowing the flow of U.S. arms to the Red Army in southern Russia.

In Mayr's mind, this latter mission—sabotaging the railroad—is foolish. The railroad is well protected by British and Soviet security forces. A handful of novice German saboteurs will most likely be caught and arrested—threatening Mayr's long-running operations in Tehran.

Mayr also doesn't approve of the fact that the Operation Franz team brought a cache of explosives and heavy weapons into the city. These supplies now need to be stored in safehouses or basements, and if the wrong eyes see them, the entire mission could fall apart, taking Mayr with them.

Finally, Mayr is disappointed with the team itself. Other than Karl Korel, they're young and inexperienced. None of them know anything about the region, much less about espionage. A few of them are trained in explosives and sabotage, but that's not helpful to what Mayr sees as the main operation. Otherwise, they barely know how

Franz Mayr (standing, right), photographed with five of the six members of the Operation Franz team that traveled from Berlin to join him undercover in Tehran. Karl Korel, the oldest member of the team, is not pictured. (Courtesy of the National Archives of the UK)

to operate the equipment they traveled with—and Mayr is now responsible for keeping them safe in a foreign enemy city.

At this point Mayr has no choice but to work with these fellow Germans, but he's disappointed in the caliber of person the Berlin SD spymasters chose to send.

The one exception is Karl Korel. Mayr, of course, had met Korel a few years earlier in Tehran. Korel is mature and experienced; he speaks Farsi and knows his way around the city. The fact that he found Mayr at all is impressive. In Korel, Mayr believes he has a real partner.

Unfortunately for them, however, Karl Korel is about to cause one of the team's biggest problems.

27

Moscow, Soviet Union

May 20, 1943

He's about to be face-to-face with "The Man of Steel."

At roughly 4 p.m. on May 20, President Roosevelt's envoy Joseph Davies enters a room at the heart of the Kremlin, the fortified building complex in central Moscow that houses and protects the Soviet government.

After uniformed aides usher him inside, Davies finds himself in a large, ornate office room facing three people: Vyacheslav Molotov, the Soviet Foreign Minister; an unnamed interpreter; and Joseph Stalin, the Premier of the Soviet Union.

Davies knows that the Soviets like to get right to the point. Talking through the interpreter, Davies makes a few rehearsed introductory remarks. The President and the American people, he says, are "unequivocally devoted to winning the war over Hitler and the Jap[anese] and preserving the peace of the world from the threat of either Hitler or the Axis."

Stalin is known as a man of few words who's difficult to read in person. He rarely engages in small talk or reveals what he is thinking. As Davies makes his opening remarks through the interpreter, he notices that Stalin starts doodling on a piece of blank paper, apparently listening but not looking at Davies or at the others in the room.

"I was directed to state," Davies continues, "that the President believed that there are no differences which cannot be worked out with mutual self-respect to preserve the physical securities of each of the allies, through discussion and mutual effort."

Roosevelt's primary reason for sending him, Davies then explains, is to urge a personal meeting between the two leaders.

With this, Davies hands Roosevelt's secret letter to the interpreter, so the interpreter can read it to Molotov and Stalin.

The interpreter opens and begins reading the letter. As the interpreter reads, Stalin maintains what Davies calls a "grim face"—and all the while, he keeps doodling.

Only once during the reading does Stalin stop and interrupt. It's the part where Roosevelt makes clear that Churchill isn't invited.

"Why?" asks Stalin, clearly surprised.

Following Roosevelt's instructions, Davies explains that the American and Soviet leaders will likely be able to reach agreement faster and understand each other better in a one-on-one setting. Roosevelt promises he will then fill in Churchill on every part of the discussion.

Stalin doesn't respond. The interpreter continues reading the letter and soon reaches the end, concluding with Roosevelt's colloquial send-off, "You are doing a grand job. Good luck!"

When the translator finishes, Stalin, still doodling, asks Davies a few quick foreign policy questions, which Davies does his best to answer.

Then, Stalin goes silent. He seems to be thinking. Finally the Soviet leader puts his pen down and looks up at Davies. "I think your President is right," he says. "I think he represents America, as I understand it . . . You may tell your President I agree with him and it is necessary that we meet, as he suggests."

Davies finally exhales.

Stalin asks for an aide to bring him a map and a ruler. With the map in front of him, the Premier begins measuring distances on it. After completing a few measurements, he says he agrees with Roosevelt's suggestion that Alaska is a fair midpoint between the two nation's capitals. He suggests Fairbanks or Nome as potential locations.

Finally, he promises that within a day or two he'll have a letter of his own for Davies to carry back to Washington, D.C., and deliver by hand to Roosevelt. Meanwhile, for now, they all agree to maintain silence about what was said in their meeting. Roosevelt's letter will remain top secret.

Davies leaves the meeting knowing he's done exactly as Roosevelt asked. The next day, he sends a cable to the President indicating that he met with Stalin and Molotov, and that the President's letter "seemed to be favorably and cordially received." He'll wait to convey everything else in person.

A few days later, as promised, Stalin and Molotov present Davies with a letter he's supposed to hand-deliver to Roosevelt in Washington, D.C. They also add some personal gifts from the Soviet Premier to the President. Some world leaders give works of art or national delicacies. Stalin gives a Soviet tommy gun and a captured German light hand machine gun. Automatic weapons.

Davies's trip home matches his trip there: he takes a circuitous

Former U.S. Ambassador to the Soviet Union Joseph Davies (left) meets with Soviet Premier Joseph Stalin (center) in the Kremlin during Davies's visit to Moscow in May 1943. President Roosevelt sent Davies as a special envoy to hand-deliver a secret letter from Roosevelt to Stalin requesting a one-on-one meeting between the two leaders. On Stalin's left is Soviet Foreign Minister Vyacheslav Molotov, who received Davies with Stalin. (Courtesy of Sovfoto / UIG / Bridgeman Images)

route since he can only fly through friendly airspace. It takes a full ten days.

Finally, on June 3, roughly a month after he departed, Davies arrives back to Washington, D.C., with Stalin's letter.

Within hours, Davies is at the White House. The President, who only a few days earlier concluded his weeks-long meetings with Churchill and his team, is eager to see his envoy as soon as possible.

Davies hands over the letter from Stalin. Molotov had given Davies both a Russian version and an English version, so the President can immediately begin reading. As usual, Stalin gets right to the point. "I agree with you that such a meeting is necessary and that it should not be postponed," the letter begins. "Therefore I would suggest that our meeting should be arranged in July or in August." Roosevelt is pleased to read this, because this timing works for him too.

"If you agree to this," the letter continues, "I undertake to inform you two weeks before the date of the meeting when this meeting could take place." In other words, based on developments on the Eastern front, Stalin will give Roosevelt two weeks' notice to arrange the trip.

When it comes to the location, Stalin apparently believes it should be so top secret he can't even put it in this hand-delivered letter. "As to the place of the meeting," he writes, "this will be communicated to you by Mr. Davies personally."

After reading this line, Roosevelt looks up. Davies explains that Stalin measured the distances on a map and agreed to Alaska as a potential meeting place.

Roosevelt's unusual strategy of sending an envoy to Moscow seems to have paid off. Stalin will meet with him one-on-one, in a reasonable time frame, at the location that Roosevelt had suggested.

"Joe, you have done a grand job," Roosevelt says to Davies. He asks him to file a follow-up written report, and the two men part.

On the surface, it sounds like the mission was a success. But there're still two problems. First, Roosevelt now has to inform Churchill that he's planned to meet with Stalin without him—and that he kept this planning a secret from Churchill even while the two of them spent the past few weeks in close quarters.

Indeed, Churchill will realize that at the very moment he was telling Congress and the world that he and Roosevelt were seeking a Big Three meeting with Stalin, Roosevelt was making different plans with Stalin behind Churchill's back.

On top of that, it'll signal to Churchill that Roosevelt doesn't entirely trust him—or worse, that the United States is attempting to make a geopolitical move with Stalin that is not in Britain's best interest.

It's a bad time for a potential rift. Although the President and Prime Minister got along well personally during Churchill's visit, the talks between the American and British war planners were sometimes heated, even acrimonious. Behind the scenes, the relationship between the two countries is troubled.

As usual, the issue was where to focus the U.S. and British military effort in Europe. Churchill was determined to double down on the Mediterranean strategy—the "soft underbelly" of Europe—and was negative about the prospects of a direct attack against Nazi Germany across the English Channel into northern France.

British war planners raised the many logistical difficulties of such an attack and claimed the American and British armies were not yet prepared with adequate troops or landing crafts.

Supporting their argument to double down on the Mediterranean, the British have a certain logic on their side. The Allies had just spent the past year clearing North Africa of Axis troops. Having done so, it'd be foolish to not seize the opportunity, cross the Mediterranean, and invade the Italian island of Sicily. Once Sicily was captured, they could proceed to the Italian mainland.

Basically, the Allies have a chance to knock Italy out of the war. But there's no way the Anglo-American armies can do that *and* simultaneously attack northern France across the Channel.

For that reason, the U.S. agrees with the British plan. For now they'll again prioritize the "Southern Strategy" at the expense of opening a second front in Western Europe. The cross-Channel attack will have to wait until the next calendar year.

This leads to Roosevelt's second major problem: how to communicate this disappointing news to Stalin. On June 2, the day before

Davies's arrival back in Washington, D.C., Roosevelt and Churchill drafted a message to the Soviet Premier with a summary of their plans. After a few revisions went back and forth, they sent it.

It clarifies what they're doing for the remainder of 1943. "In the Mediterranean the decision was made to eliminate Italy from the war as quickly as possible," the message states, explaining their plan to invade Sicily in early July and then move to the mainland in late summer. This will demand most of the British and American forces in the region and, as a result, "the concentration of forces and landing equipment in the British Isles should proceed at a rate to permit a full-scale invasion of the Continent to be launched . . . in the Spring of 1944."

For Stalin, it's the year that will jump out. The cross-Channel attack isn't happening until 1944.

At this point, Stalin has already waited impatiently for a year and a half for the Americans and British to strike at Hitler's armies in Western Europe and give the Soviets relief from the Nazi onslaught. Now, the President and Prime Minister are saying the Soviet Union will have to weather the storm alone for another full year.

So, on the same day that Davies has brought him good news from the trip, Roosevelt knows that Stalin is about to read a message that he won't like at all.

How will Stalin respond? Will this affect their proposed one-on-one meeting? And most important, what will it mean for their Alliance?

The President has no choice. All he can do is wait.

28

May 1943

For a while, things had been looking up for Franz Mayr.

His long-shot message to Berlin was received. His superiors at the foreign desk of the SD, led by Walter Schellenberg, had not only responded to his request but sent a team of six to support him.

While he is disappointed in the quality of some of the mission personnel, he's impressed by the team's interpreter and de facto leader Karl Korel, who managed to cross the desert by himself, locate Mayr in Tehran, then cross the desert again to successfully retrieve the rest of his team. Korel, it seems, is someone Mayr can work with.

But in no time, a new problem rears its head. And it's a terrible one.

Shortly after his return with the rest of the Operation Franz team, Karl Korel begins to look unwell. They all see it. He's feverish and exhausted, with terrible stomach pains. Soon, he can barely move. His living conditions—hiding in basements or attics of local safehouses—don't help matters.

So, how should the group handle a sick undercover agent in this hostile occupied city? Mayr and the Operation Franz team can't just take him to a hospital. Doing so could easily alert local authorities to the team's presence in the city.

And yet, Korel clearly needs medical care.

The group tries to provide the best care possible, and finally, through local connections, Mayr finds a doctor willing to visit Korel in secret. After assessing the patient, the doctor has bad news. Korel has typhoid fever, a deadly disease normally contracted by ingesting a deadly food-or water-borne bacteria. Proper treatment requires the use of antibiotics to which neither the doctor nor anyone else in the group has access.

It's a worst-case scenario for Korel. His condition slowly worsens. At some point in mid-May, he's dead.

It's a devastating loss for Mayr and the Franz team. But it also poses an immediate logistical problem. What do they do with Korel's body?

For the same reason they couldn't take Korel to the hospital when he was ill, now they can't bring his lifeless body to the city morgue. It would alert city officials to their group. Nor can they get caught transporting a mysterious corpse through the streets to throw in a dump or a river. Somehow, they need to get rid of the body quickly and discreetly.

The team realizes they have no choice. It's time to bring out the knives and handsaws.

Mayr enlists some local collaborators to do the dirty work. "We had to cut his body into pieces and take them out of the city in cases and rucksacks," one of these collaborators descibes it. Then, in a moonlit deserted field on the outskirts of Tehran, Mayr and the surviving members of Operation Franz give their teammate's chopped-up remains a proper German burial.

Korel's grisly demise casts a pall on the Operation Franz mission. They've lost one of their more experienced members, and the only one who could speak the local language.

For Mayr in particular, Korel's death is a tough blow. In his mind, the remaining young members of the group are mostly incompetent. They don't know how to conduct themselves as foreign agents, and they depend on Mayr for everything. Housing them, feeding them, and protecting them soon becomes an endless burden.

Still, not everything is a disaster.

As Mayr originally requested of Berlin, the parachutists brought with them wireless radio transmitters. After a few false starts, the team has been able to set up the transmitters and obtain a usable signal. To avoid detection, Mayr has set up a complicated system by which members of the group regularly rotate a transmitter between six different locations, each with a code name 101 to 106, and keep it set up for only a short time before switching to the next location.

None of the team members are accomplished signals operators, but through trial and error they figure out how to send and receive semiconsistent messages to and from the German embassy in Turkey, and sometimes directly with Berlin.

By early summer of 1943, the Nazi mission in Iran is in an uncertain place. On one hand, the Operation Franz mission has some money, supplies, and a working means of communication with the SD offices in Berlin. On the other, they've just buried the chopped-up remains of their most experienced member.

For this struggling team of undercover agents, more surprises are on their way.

29

Washington, D.C.

June 11, 1943

Roosevelt and Churchill had it wrong.

They thought Stalin would be disappointed that the cross-Channel attack into northern France would be delayed a full year. But Stalin isn't disappointed.

He's furious.

After receiving the news in Roosevelt's and Churchill's message, Stalin writes them back on June 11 with a long, detailed response. As might have been expected, he zeroes in on one thing: their delay in the timing of the cross-Channel attack. He starts by laying out the many times in the past they had promised the attack and then failed to come through. And as for this latest delay:

> Your decision creates exceptional difficulties for the Soviet Union, which, straining all its resources, for the past two years, has been engaged against the main forces of Germany and her satellites, and leaves the Soviet Army, which is fighting not only for its country, but also for its Allies, to do the job alone, almost single-handed, against an enemy that is still very strong and formidable.

Using the term "single-handed" is strong language, especially given that the U.S. has been steadily supplying the Soviets with planes, tanks, weapons, and raw materials while also fighting a war against Japan on the other side of the globe. Not to mention, the Americans and British have been engaged against the Axis powers in North Africa for a year and are now about to attack Sicily.

Still, in Stalin's mind the Mediterranean theater is a sideshow. To him, the heart of the war comes from the massive Nazi armies in Western and Eastern Europe. The Soviet Union has been doing the vast majority of the fighting against Hitler's armies—and Soviet soldiers and civilians alike have suffered many orders of magnitude more than the Americans or British.

In his message, Stalin describes the "disheartening negative impression" that "this fresh postponement of the second front" will have on the Red Army and the Soviet public.

"As for the Soviet Government," Stalin's message concludes, "it cannot align itself with this decision, which, moreover, was adopted without its participation and without any attempt at a joint discussion of this highly important matter and which may gravely affect the subsequent course of the war."

Churchill bristles at the message. He wants to push back and defend his position. In a long response to Stalin that Roosevelt agrees to cosign, the Prime Minister lists the risks and logistical difficulties of the cross-Channel attack, and argues it would be foolish to attempt it before the end of the year:

> I quite understand your disappointment but I am sure we are doing not only the right thing but the only thing that is physically possible in the circumstances. It would be no help to Russia if we threw away 100,000 men in a disastrous cross-Channel attack such as would, in my opinion, certainly occur if we tried under present conditions . . . I cannot see how a great British defeat and slaughter would aid the Soviet armies.

Churchill's fear of losing one hundred thousand men may ring hollow to the Soviet leader, whose country, by that point, had sacrificed *ten million* lives to the war, including over one million casualties in the recent battle at Stalingrad alone.

Needless to say, Churchill's message is not well-received in Moscow. The Premier writes another long response, even more strongly worded. Again, he recounts the many times the British and the Americans have rescinded on their promise. And then he goes further:

> You say that you "quite understand" my disappointment. I must tell you that the point here is not just the disappointment of the Soviet Government, but the preservation of its confidence in its Allies, a confidence which is being subjected to severe stress. One should not forget that it is a question of saving millions of lives in the occupied areas of Western Europe and Russia and of reducing the enormous sacrifices of the Soviet armies, compared with which the sacrifices of the Anglo-American armies are insignificant.

These are loaded words, and Stalin knows it. Since the start of the partnership, one of Roosevelt's and Churchill's great fears is that if Stalin were able to obtain a decisive military advantage over the Nazi armies now in the Soviet Union, he might use his leverage to negotiate a separate peace directly with Germany on terms favorable to him. The Soviet Union could demand its conquered territory back and gain other concessions but allow Germany to maintain control over Western Europe with no interference from the Soviets. This would create a strong Nazi Germany controlling Western Europe, and a weak and isolated Great Britain.

The result would also run directly counter to what Roosevelt articulated at the Casablanca Conference: namely, that the Axis powers must be defeated completely—they must surrender unconditionally—and their fascist regimes toppled and destroyed for good.

For the leaders, it's a precarious moment. Stalin knows that Roosevelt and Churchill don't want him to seek a separate peace, but by saying that the Soviet's "confidence in its Allies" is being "subjected to severe stress," he's making it clear he's prepared to leave the alliance if the United States and the United Kingdom fail to keep their promises. And as Stalin had stated in two consecutive messages, this is precisely what he believes his allies have done.

Churchill is offended by the accusatory tone, especially by an implication at a few points that they're being cowardly.

Responding with another angry message, Churchill reminds Stalin that at the start of the war "we British were left alone to face the worst that Nazi Germany could do to us," and yet they still gave aid to the Soviet Union after Hitler launched his surprise invasion. "I am satisfied that I have done everything in human power to help you," Churchill's message continues. "Therefore the reproaches which you now cast upon your Western Allies leave me unmoved."

Churchill, always temperamental, is now in his own full rage. He tells some aides that after this late message, his communication with Stalin might be over for good.

To make matters worse, around this time a Swedish newspaper publishes stories about mysterious meetings in Stockholm between unnamed high-level Soviet and German officials. Is this Stalin making good on his implied threat to abandon his allies and seek his own agreement with Germany? If so, it could leave Hitler in control of Western Europe with most of his massive armies still intact.

A few months ago, the Big Three alliance seemed stable and strong. Today, at this critical juncture, their unity is starting to crumble.

30

Washington, D.C.

June 23, 1943

The President needs to mediate.

The Churchill and Stalin relationship was troubled from the start, and now it's in flames. If ever there's a time for Roosevelt to step up and pull the Allies back together, it's right now.

The trick is, it won't be easy. At this point, Roosevelt doesn't have credibility with Stalin, who's still angry about the cross-Channel delay. With Churchill, he has a reservoir of trust, but all that may be gone when he reveals that for the past month, he's been trying to make plans with Stalin behind Churchill's back. Roosevelt knows that won't go well.

In fact, when it comes to telling Churchill about his clandestine plan with Stalin, the matter is so sensitive that Roosevelt can't bring himself to do it face-to-face, or even in writing. Instead, he sends his soon-to-be new ambassador to the Soviet Union, Averell Harriman, to London. In a meeting with Churchill, Harriman will break the news of the President's plan.

To carry out this "difficult assignment from Roosevelt," as Harriman would later describe it, the ambassador flies to London on June 23. The next night, Harriman relays the message to Churchill during a contentious three-hour dinner. As expected, Churchill isn't happy.

"I must emphasize his disappointment," Harriman reports to Roosevelt the next day. In addition to feeling betrayed, Churchill thinks that the British people will view a one-on-one meeting between Roosevelt and Stalin as publicly humiliating to Churchill, or worse yet as an insult to Britain's war effort.

No question, the three-way relationship is devolving fast. Stalin is furious at Roosevelt and Churchill for breaking their promise on the cross-Channel attack; angry messages are flying back and forth between Moscow and London; Roosevelt has offended Churchill by planning to meet with Stalin behind his back; and the U.S. and the United Kingdom are genuinely concerned that the Soviet Union could abandon its partners.

It is, as Harriman puts it, a "low point in the history of the alliance."

On June 25, the day after his dinner meeting, Churchill is still stewing as he writes a carefully worded message to Roosevelt.

"Averell told me last night of your wish for a meeting with U.J. in Alaska *a deux,*" the message begins.

Who's "U.J."? It's shorthand for "Uncle Joe"—a nickname that Churchill and Roosevelt sometimes use for Stalin when writing to one another. It's not clear exactly how the nickname started, but by early 1943, it was a running joke in the correspondence between the Prime Minister and the President.

Having opened with a reminder of the informality between them, Churchill proceeds to lay out a case for why he disagrees with Roosevelt's plan for a one-on-one meeting.

> The whole world is expecting and all our side are desiring a meeting of the three great Powers . . . It would seem a pity to draw U.J. 7,000 miles from Moscow for anything less than this.
>
> I consider that a tripartite meeting . . . not only of us three but also of the Staffs, who will come together for the first time, would be one of the milestones of history. If this is lost much is lost.

He goes on to explain, "I do not underrate the use that enemy propaganda would make of a meeting between the heads of Soviet

Russia and the United States at this juncture with the British Commonwealth and Empire excluded. It would be serious and vexatious and many would be bewildered and alarmed thereby."

To Roosevelt, it's clear that his war partner is upset. Three days later, on June 28, the President responds. His message begins with a striking sentence: "I did not suggest to U.J. that we meet alone, but he told Davies that he assumed . . . that we would meet alone."

It's a striking sentence—because it is simply not true. Roosevelt was the one who suggested to Stalin that they have a one-on-one, and as Davies witnessed, Stalin was surprised and taken aback that Churchill would not be invited.

"Of course, you and I are completely frank in matters of this kind," the President's message continues, compounding his dishonesty by specifically alluding to the history of trust between them.

Clearly, Roosevelt's fabrication is an attempt to save face with the Prime Minister, perhaps assuming there's no way Churchill will ever learn the truth.

Still, it begs the question, why would the President casually lie, potentially undermining the loyalty between them?

Roosevelt himself is never asked, but the likely answer is simple pragmatism. For the President, winning the war is the absolute priority. Roosevelt genuinely believed that a one-on-one meeting between himself and Stalin was in the best interests of the war effort, so he did what he could to set it up; he also knows that maintaining Churchill's goodwill is also critical to the alliance, so he said what he could to appease the Prime Minister. When a war is raging and millions of innocent people are being slaughtered, a question of personal honesty between two individuals may not seem so important.

The good news is, the President's little fabrication works. Churchill is appeased, at least for the moment. However, the two leaders now have a bigger problem in front of them.

Right now, Stalin is so furious, chances for a face-to-face meeting with the Soviet leader—whether one-on-one or all three together—have all but disappeared.

31

Berlin, Germany

Late July 1943

For the intelligence chief, spy craft is a passion.

Walter Schellenberg, the SD leader, delights especially in the more cerebral aspects of intelligence work. Not just the complicated intrigue of foreign policy and relations, but the technical details of espionage: wiretaps, surveillance, ciphers, and signals interception.

Every few weeks Schellenberg hosts at his home a dinner party with the technical heads of the various German intelligence departments to share techniques and ideas. "These meetings," Schellenberg later reported, "were perhaps more than any other single factor responsible for the high standard of the scientific and technical side of my service."

Within the constantly evolving labyrinth of the German intelligence agencies, one of the most secretive organizations—and one that Schellenberg and other leaders rely on the most—is the Forschungsamt, roughly translated as the "Research Agency" or "Research Bureau," and often abbreviated as the FA.

Unlike the other German intelligence services, which are often driven by political, military, and ideological agendas, the FA is a highly technical organization that focuses entirely on tapping telecommunications lines, intercepting enemy signals and radio transmissions, and breaking ciphers and codes.

Largely a brainchild of Nazi leader Hermann Goering, the FA doesn't normally interpret the information it receives—it simply gathers enemy intercepts, decrypts the codes, translates the material, and organizes the results to be distributed.

The FA's top secret daily reports are known in the Reich as "Brown Sheets" because of the light-brown paper they are printed on. At FA leader Goering's discretion, the daily Brown Sheets are shared with only a select few in the upper echelons of Nazi leadership.

The Brown Sheets are so sensitive, in fact, that they are transported exclusively in locked pouches. Each sheet is carefully accounted for by the agency, and the recipient must return each sheet in full to the agency within one month to be permanently destroyed. On the rare occasion in which the contents of these sheets are revealed beyond their audience of upper-level Nazi leaders, it is usually because one of the recipients has written about them.

For example, one regular recipient of the FA's Brown Sheets is Joseph Goebbels, the Reich Minister of Propaganda and one of Hitler's closest confidantes. Because Goebbels kept regular voluminous diaries, some details of the FA's work are contained in his diary entries and known to us today.

These entries reveal, among other things, that the agency was sometimes able to intercept Allied communications at the highest levels, up to and including communications involving Roosevelt, Churchill, and Stalin.

Specifically, we know that since the Casablanca Conference in early 1943, the FA had been intercepting clues related to the planning of an Allied conference later in the year, this time to include both the American President and the Soviet Premier.

To that end, on April 17, 1943, Goebbels recorded in his diary that "I have received from the *Forschungsamt* secret information supporting the belief that Roosevelt is planning to meet Stalin somewhere." The revelation is quite remarkable, given that FDR began considering the idea of a one-on-one meeting with Stalin in early April, when he first spoke to former Ambassador Davies about it. Somehow, the FA had discerned Roosevelt's top secret plan within a week or two of its inception.

A month later, on May 16, Goebbels recorded that "news has reached us that Roosevelt intends to meet Stalin soon," once again citing the Forschungsamt as his source. This report from the FA was similarly prescient, since Roosevelt had already dispatched Davies to Moscow at that point, and the former ambassador was only days away from meeting Stalin to give him Roosevelt's written request for a meeting.

In addition to Goebbels, Himmler, and Hitler himself, one of the few Nazi leaders who receives the FA's Brown Sheets is Walter Schellenberg, the head of foreign intelligence.

How exactly the codebreakers at the Forschungsamt had obtained the top secret decrypts regarding Roosevelt's intention to meet Stalin is unknown. But Schellenberg would later brag about the complicated systems by which the Nazi intelligence agencies monitored U.S. and British communications:

> Through collaboration with experts . . . we succeeded in tapping the main cable between England and America. The word "tapping" is used here in a figurative sense. In spite of the insulation of the cable we were able, by the use of short-wave instruments, to record the high-frequency impulses running through it, and by an incredibly complicated process to decipher them. The cable that we "tapped" was used for communication between England and the United States.

It's not clear whether Schellenberg is referring here specifically to the work of the FA to which he is privy, or whether he is referring to the experts within his own department in the SD. In either case, he clearly takes pride in the intelligence services for being able to monitor enemy communications at the highest levels; and he himself clearly takes pains to track such information.

One night in late July, Schellenberg has a late meeting over drinks at an exclusive private hotel with a fellow German spymaster. He is Admiral Wilhelm Canaris, the head of the Abwehr, Germany's long-running military intelligence agency. Unlike Schellenberg's SD, which was created by the SS and answers directly to Adolf Hitler, the Abwehr predates the Nazi Party and maintains at least some autonomy. Admiral

Canaris is an intelligence veteran, much older than Schellenberg, and although their two agencies are sometimes considered rivals, Canaris and Schellenberg maintain open communication.

Recently, the two organizations have been collaborating with some frequency, specifically on the Iran operations. Operation Anton, the latest mission into Iranian tribal regions outside Tehran, is premised upon paratroopers from Berlin linking up with an Abwehr agent on the ground—just as Operation Franz was based on paratroopers linking up with the SD agent Franz Mayr in Tehran. But while Operation Anton is technically an Abwehr mission, it is being overseen by the new Special Operations leader Captain Otto Skorzeny, whom Schellenberg recently hired on behalf of the SD. It's essentially a shared operation between the two agencies.

In any case, as the two spymasters sip their drinks, they have much to talk about . . . not just regarding Iran, but about the larger and increasingly troubled picture of the war.

Tonight, Canaris also has a specific message to impart to Schellenberg.

Hitler, Canaris tells him, has taken particular interest in stories about a supposed Big Three conference rumored to be in the planning stages. A summit, supposedly, to include the Allied leaders Roosevelt, Churchill, and Stalin.

As both men know, the FA intercepted communications earlier in the year regarding a possible Allied meeting with Stalin. But by this point in July, it doesn't take inside intelligence to know that a plan for such a meeting is being at least discussed. Speculation about a Big Three summit has been written about openly in the Allied press since the spring, and it has been something of an international parlor game to predict if, when, or where such an event might take place.

Six months ago, the German intelligence services got it wrong when it came to Casablanca. Not just wrong, but *very* wrong. Hitler, according to Canaris, does not want this to happen again. If there's to be a Big Three summit, the Führer wants to know in advance when it is and where it is.

Since the few shards of information about a proposed meeting, intercepted back in spring, the German agencies have learned no further details. If there is to be a Big Three summit in 1943, the Germans haven't the slightest idea when or where.

But these two men, Schellenberg and Canaris, have between them enormous resources at their disposal. They have the apparatus and staffs of their respective intelligence agencies. They have access to the daily reports from the Forschungsamt. And they have a directive that comes from Hitler himself.

For these Nazi intelligence leaders, the mission is clear: Find out where the Big Three will meet—and this time, don't get it wrong.

32

Washington, D.C.

July 1943

Roosevelt needs Stalin back.

Although FDR technically cosigned Churchill's messages during his angry exchanges with Stalin, Roosevelt himself had been careful not to enter the fray. He's always believed, and still believes, that maintaining goodwill with the Soviet Union—in other words, goodwill with Stalin—is essential to the war.

For that reason, back on June 16, while Churchill and Stalin were sending angry words to one another, Roosevelt quietly sent a separate message to Stalin regarding U.S. airpower shipments:

> In addition to our new protocol agreement I have directed that six hundred additional fighters be sent to you during the balance of 1943. They are P-40N type of fighter . . . This is the most maneuverable fighter we have. It provides our best protection against dive bombers and gives excellent protection to the ground strafing of the P-39s. I have also directed the shipment of seventy-eight additional B-25s during the same period.

Now he's speaking Stalin's language.

Several days later, on June 22, the President wrote another message to the Premier, paying tribute to the two-year anniversary of Hitler's invasion of the Soviet Union and commemorating the Soviet defense:

> Two years ago by an act of treachery in keeping with the long record of Nazi duplicity the Nazi leaders launched their brutal attack upon the Soviet Union . . . During the past two years the freedom loving peoples of the world have watched with increasing admiration the history-making exploits of the armed forces of the Soviet Union and the almost incredible sacrifices which the Russian people are so heroically making.

Roosevelt's words—especially the promise of all those American fighter planes—were designed to soften the Soviet Premier's anger. By continuing this mix of flattery and regular arms shipments, he's hoping to bring Stalin back from the brink.

Ultimately, though, it is a series of global military events that mend the bad feelings and disagreements within the Alliance, more than any letter from Roosevelt ever could.

In early July, German armies on the Eastern front launch Operation Citadel, a huge tank-based offensive designed to overwhelm and destroy a mass of Soviet armies near the city of Kursk. Since the German loss at Stalingrad earlier in the year, Hitler is hungry for major victories on the Eastern front. He's desperate for a win.

Unbeknownst to the Germans, a combination of Soviet and British intelligence efforts gave the Allies advanced knowledge of the German attack plan.

The Red Army, therefore, has prepared a meticulous defense—including a surprise counteroffensive to launch after the first wave of German attacks. Even worse for the Nazi armies, Hitler postponed the operation at a critical juncture to wait for a sophisticated new model of German tank to be ready; the new tank doesn't make much of a difference, but the delay gave the Red Army even more time to prepare and bolster their defense.

The attack launches on July 5, and what transpires over the next several days will become known as the largest tank battle in world history. "Everything was enveloped in smoke, dust, and fire," one

Red Army commander described. "It wasn't a battle, it was a slaughterhouse of tanks." The entire region is overwhelmed by the massive swell of mechanized infantry on both sides, swarming the countryside from all directions, swallowing nearby towns and villages.

Losses are tremendous on both sides—eventually the casualties will total over two hundred thousand Germans and around eight hundred thousand Soviets. Despite the immense Soviet losses, after two weeks of fighting, the Red Army holds firm and prevents the Wehrmacht from advancing. Operation Citadel has largely been a failure for the Germans, leaving Nazi forces in Russia more depleted, with little to show for it.

Seizing on the good news, Roosevelt uses it as another opportunity to make amends with Stalin. "Although I have no detailed news, I think I can safely congratulate you on the splendid showing your armies are making against the German offensive at Kursk," he writes in a short note on July 15. He adds, almost as an aside, that "I hope to hear from you very soon about the other matter which I still feel to be of great importance to you and me." Roosevelt is referring, of course, to the plan for a face-to-face meeting.

At this point, it's been nearly six weeks since any discussion of the in-person summit. Stalin's fury about the delayed cross-Channel attack had shut down the dialogue. But now, Roosevelt sees a chance to revive it.

What's also helpful to the cause is that, at nearly exactly the same time as the massive battles around Kursk, British, American, and Canadian forces in North Africa cross the Mediterranean and launch their planned invasion of the Italian island of Sicily. Code-named Operation Husky, it represents the first major American and British attack against Axis ground forces on European soil since the U.S. entered the war.

On July 10, the first Allied troops land on the island, meeting stiff resistance from the defending Italian and German troops. But the Allies' careful planning and superior naval and airpower prevails, and soon, the American and British forces hold key cities and ports. Within days, the remaining Axis troops are forced to evacuate.

Even Stalin, who has always held the Mediterranean campaign in contempt, can see that that the victory in Sicily represents a shift in momentum. The invasion makes headlines around the world, and Allied troops now occupy a fortified island only a few miles from the Italian mainland.

The number of casualties still do not compare to those of the massive battles on the Eastern front, but, as Churchill and Roosevelt make sure to remind the Soviet Premier, the attack on Sicily forced Hitler to divert some troops from the Eastern front that might otherwise have fought against the Red Army in Operation Citadel.

Even more remarkable is the larger impact that the capture of Sicily has on Italy's standing in the war.

For the past year, the Italian army has been generally performing poorly. The Italian people have begun to lose faith in their fascist government and the Axis alliance, leaving many Italians wondering why their nation is engaged in a dangerous war to support Germany's territorial ambitions. The invasion of Sicily suddenly makes clear how vulnerable the country is to Allied attack, and a feeling of panic overtakes the nation.

While the Allies are securing Sicily, the Italian government falls into chaos, splitting into factions that are torn between sticking with the German alliance or trying to make a deal with the Allies. The pro-Allies faction takes the lead, but they quickly realize they have no chance to negotiate with the British and Americans so long as Prime Minister Mussolini, Hitler's fascist ally, remains in power.

In an extraordinary series of events, the Italian monarch, King Vittorio Emanuele III, secretly conspires with the Grand Council to remove Mussolini from office in an attempt to save Italy from ruin. These machinations culminate on July 25 when King Emanuele summons Mussolini to the royal palace and promptly informs him that the council has already held a vote to remove him as Prime Minister and strip him of power. When the stunned dictator exits the building, he is quickly surrounded by armed carabinieri—royal soldiers—who arrest him and throw him into the back of a van.

Benito Mussolini, who has ruled Italy for nearly twenty years and once seemed invincible, is now being carted to prison as a criminal.

As the world learns of these dramatic events, fighting continues along the Eastern front. After Germany's failed Operation Citadel, the Soviet counteroffensive is a success. On August 4, Soviet troops achieve an enormous psychological victory by recapturing Orel, a city that the Germans had invaded back in October 1941 and occupied since.

By now, the city has been mostly destroyed—the original population of 114,000 is now only 30,000. These numbers are grim reminders of the devastating loss of life throughout the region. But now, at least, the city is back in Soviet hands.

It's a dizzying few weeks in the war, with most of it breaking in favor of the Allies. Determined to build on the good news, Roosevelt continues his charm offensive on Stalin. On August 4, he writes:

> Sincere congratulations to the Red Army, the People of the Soviet Union and to yourself upon the great victory of Orel.
>
> During a month of tremendous fighting your forces by their skill, their courage, their sacrifices and their ceaseless effort have not only stopped the long planned German attack but have launched a successful counter offensive of far-reaching import.
>
> The Soviet Union can be justly proud of its heroic accomplishments.

Roosevelt doesn't raise the issue of the head-to-head summit, which Stalin still hasn't responded to since the President's previous message.

Then, finally, on August 8, Stalin writes, "Thank you for your congratulation sent on the Red Army and the Soviet people on the occasion of successes at Orel."

The most vital part of the letter is how Stalin ends it, bringing up his previous promise to meet, and the reasons why it has been difficult for him to follow through:

> I have at the present time to put aside other questions and my other duties, except the primary duty—the direction of action at the front . . . I hope that under such circumstances you will fully understand that at the present time I cannot go on a long journey and shall not be able, unfortunately, during this summer and autumn to keep my promise given to you through Mr. Davies . . . I regret it very much, but, as you know, cir-

cumstances are sometimes more powerful than people who are compelled to submit to them.

This is not what Roosevelt was hoping to hear, but as he reads on, he sees that Stalin is only rejecting the previously agreed time and place, not the meeting itself. In fact, Stalin explains, "I consider that a meeting of the responsible representatives of our countries would positively be expedient." The message continues, "Under the present military situation, it could be arranged either in Astrakhan or in Ar[khangelsk]. Should this proposal be inconvenient for you personally, in that case, you may send to one of the above-mentioned points your responsible and fully trusted person."

Astrakhan and Arkhangelsk are both cities in the Soviet Union, making them highly impractical for the President. Also, Roosevelt believes the meeting should ideally not be held on any one leader's home turf, so the three can meet as equals. Still, Stalin's suggestions are much better than his previous silence.

The Premier's next comment is even more interesting. "I do not have any objections to the presence of Mr. Churchill at this meeting, in order that the meeting of the representatives of the two countries would become the meeting of the representatives of the three countries. I still follow this point of view on the condition that you will not have any objections to this."

In other words, despite his personal distrust of Churchill, Stalin has apparently decided that if any of them should meet, they should meet as a team of three. Perhaps Stalin is making an effort to put aside his past differences with Churchill. Or maybe it's more practical: He only wants to make one trip, so better to have all three of them there.

Either way, almost all the specifics that Roosevelt proposed during the Davies mission have been overturned. The date of a potential meeting is now later, the location has changed, and the possibility of a one-on-one meeting has apparently evaporated.

Still, Roosevelt knows good news when he sees it. At the end of the day, the most important thing is this: The plan for a face-to-face meeting between the Allied leaders seems to be back in play.

Assuming nothing gets in the way.

33

Berlin, Germany

July 26, 1943

Otto Skorzeny, Captain of the Waffen-SS, is bored.

Some of his complaints are with his new boss, Walter Schellenberg.

Skorzeny, the head trainer of Special Operations for the Nazi foreign intelligence services, doesn't particularly respect Schellenberg, and has grown tired of the long-winded meetings with him.

"Schellenberg was a talker," Skorzeny later explained. "He loved to tell stories and especially to talk about himself to a newcomer to the magical world of the secret service. We often ate together at noon and he recalled his former chief, Reinhard Heydrich, who had been murdered in Prague the year before."

Skorzeny finds these lunch meetings tedious. But it's not just Schellenberg and the rest of the foreign intelligence leadership that Skorzeny doesn't like. As a former Waffen-SS soldier used to fighting in the field, he's frustrated by the office politics and infighting of the SD and other agencies within the Reich Security Main Office.

"I must say that if I had suspected in advance all the intrigues, the narrow-mindedness and the clumsiness of the bureaucracy," he later wrote, "I would probably never have accepted this commando post."

A good portion of Skorzeny's time has been devoted to planning and executing missions to Iran and elsewhere in the Persian Gulf region.

He's quickly grown to appreciate the importance of Iran to the war effort on the Eastern front, particularly of the Trans-Iranian Railway. At this moment he is overseeing Operation Anton, the mission that will drop parachutists into the northern tribal regions of Iran to provide support to the German Abwehr agent Berthold Shulze-Holthus who, like Franz Mayr in Tehran, had been operating there mostly alone.

Now that Skorzeny's Iran missions are up and running, Schellenberg and the other leaders have upgraded his training grounds from Oranienburg to nearby Friedenthal. He's also received increasing resources and autonomy to hire his own personnel and direct the Special Operations as he sees fit. Skorzeny's goal is to train a full unit of skilled commandos who can be dispatched quickly in small teams for elite missions into enemy territories:

> I had drawn up an extensive program for my special unit. The men were to receive the most comprehensive training possible to enable them to be used at any point and for any purpose. Infantry and engineering training was a *sine qua non,* but each man must also be familiar with the handling of mortars, light field artillery and tank guns. It was elementary that he should be able to ride a motorcycle and drive a car and lorry as well as specialized vehicles. The syllabus even included the driving of railway engines and the handling of motorboats.

Skorzeny is proud of what he's accomplished. Still, the bureaucracy and pencil-pushing required of his new job is an endless source of frustration.

He's feeling particularly listless on the afternoon of July 26. He has just finished a long lunch with a former classmate in a hotel restaurant, drinking coffee and talking about old friends. He wears civilian clothes, not anticipating anything of importance from the day. Because several hours have passed since he left his office at the training grounds, he calls to check in.

Expecting little, he is surprised when his secretary answers the phone in a "state of wild excitement." She explains hurriedly that everyone on his staff had been frantically looking for him for the past two hours.

Why the commotion? "FHQ has sent for you, Chief. A plane will be waiting for you at five o'clock at the Tempelhofer airfield," she answers.

Skorzeny takes a moment to make sure he's heard correctly. FHQ stands for "Führer Headquarters."

That's Hitler's headquarters in the Wolf's Lair.

For anyone working in the Reich, it's an honor to be summoned there. And it's usually the sign of something important.

Trying to conceal his excitement, Skorzeny calmly asks the secretary, "Is there any hint as to what it's all about?"

"No," she replies, "we know nothing at all."

He tells her to instruct his assistant to go to his office and retrieve his uniform, then meet him directly at the airfield where the plane is waiting for him.

After hanging up the phone, Skorzeny quickly says goodbye to his friend. A moment later he's in a car, rushing to the airport. His plane leaves in a few hours.

As Skorzeny's driver races him across the city, he tries to figure why he's been summoned. "Could it be connected with 'Operation Franz'?" he wonders. "It was not probable," he decides. Nor can he think of anything else he's involved in that could rise to the level of being flown to Hitler's headquarters in East Prussia.

Arriving at the airport, he meets his aide and obtains his uniform. Among the airport officers, he hears some chatter about the surprise downfall of Mussolini—this dramatic news has just broken—but he doesn't pay it much mind.

After he changes into his uniform, he rushes to the tarmac. There, a massive Junkers Ju 52 aircraft is waiting.

Once inside the plane, he sees that he's the only passenger. This huge plane was sent to Berlin just to retrieve him.

As the plane takes off, the questions return to his mind. "What [is] in store for me at FHQ? Whom should I meet? Everything was shrouded in mystery, a mystery impenetrable at the moment."

He doesn't even really know where he's headed. "I had only a vague idea of the whereabouts of the Führer's headquarters, which was a secret carefully kept from ordinary mortals," he later wrote. "Beyond its code name . . . and the fact that it was somewhere in East Prussia, I knew nothing."

That's about to change. After a three-hour flight, the Junkers lands on a small airstrip deep in the Prussian woods near a remote lake.

Exiting the plane, Skorzeny discovers that a large Mercedes sedan is waiting for him at the base of the airfield. "Are you Captain Skorzeny?" a sergeant asks. "I'm here to take you to headquarters at once."

With Skorzeny in the back seat, the driver races on winding roads through forests and fields for several miles. The drive isn't long. Eventually, a checkpoint with guardhouses comes into view.

Here, they tell Skorzeny to exit the vehicle and sign his name into a book. A few miles later, they reach another checkpoint, where the guards ask him to do the same. One of them picks up a phone and calls inside for permission to let the vehicle in.

Soon after, the Mercedes heads through barbed wire fence gates, past barracks and more guard towers.

It's getting dark when Skorzeny finally arrives to a compound of buildings. The car stops at one of them, a building called the Tea House. Inside are dining quarters for some of the top generals, along with a large antechamber.

Inside the antechamber, Skorzeny discovers he is one of six military officers who has been summoned, and they now all wait together. The others are Colonels and Majors, all of them outranking Skorzeny, who is a Captain.

Two of the officers are from the Wehrmacht, two are from the Luftwaffe, and another is a fellow Waffen-SS officer. None appear to have any knowledge of why they're there.

Right then, a uniformed aide appears, announcing, "I'll take you to the Führer, gentlemen."

This isn't just a trip to the Wolf's Lair. He's been summoned to meet Adolf Hitler himself.

"I thought I could not be hearing right and trembled in every limb," Skorzeny later recalled.

He should be scared. He's about to be face-to-face with the Führer.

34

The Wolf's Lair, East Prussia

The six uniformed officers stand at attention. They form a straight line, side by side, in a dimly lit room with dark curtains and maps on the walls. They all stare directly ahead.

Captain Otto Skorzeny, the lowest in rank, is the farthest to the left.

They've been standing here for a few minutes, waiting. Can it possibly be true? Are they really about to meet the Führer?

Skorzeny hears a door open. He and the others click their heels and stand at attention. After so much anticipation, the tension is almost unbearable.

"Now I was to meet the man," as Skorzeny puts it, "who had played so great a part in German history."

Adolf Hitler enters.

Since Skorzeny must stare straight ahead and is on the opposite side of the room, he can barely see the Führer raise one hand in the familiar Nazi salute. Hitler then immediately starts asking questions of the highest-ranking officer, who's on the opposite end of the line.

At this point, Skorzeny still can't see the Führer clearly, but he can hear him. "All I heard was the Führer's deep voice as he put his curt questions," Skorzeny later described. "The sound of that voice was well known to me . . . there was no mistaking it."

One by one, Hitler asks each officer several quick questions about their military backgrounds. Skorzeny, at the far end of the line, will be last.

Finally, the Führer stands right in front of him. The Captain feels like his every gesture is being scrutinized. "I made a great effort not to bow too low and I think my bow was correct," he would recall. Then, the Führer asks him some basic questions about his past and his rank. Skorzeny tries to answer, but struggles to maintain composure with Hitler right there. "His word, his bearing, the entire man radiated an extraordinary power."

After the individual interrogations, Hitler addresses all of them at once, surprising the group with a question: "What do you think of Italy?"

The rest of the officers begin mumbling generic statements about Italy as an Axis partner. Skorzeny has a different thought.

"I am Austrian, my Führer!" he exclaims loudly, interrupting everyone else.

The room goes silent, with Skorzeny's words hanging in the air.

Why does Skorzeny make this loud statement?

As everyone in the Reich knows, Hitler is also from Austria. Although now joined with unified Germany, Austria has its own distinct history. At the end of the First World War, the Treaty of Versailles granted a favorite region of Austria to Italy, infuriating native Austrians. Italy may now be a close ally, but the matter remains a grievance to those from there. Skorzeny sees an opportunity to bond with Hitler over their shared background.

The question is, will the strategy work?

Immediately, Hitler walks back down the line and stands in front of Skorzeny, staring at him intently.

Finally the Führer declares, "The other gentlemen may go. I want you to stay, Captain Skorzeny."

Now Skorzeny is alone, facing the German leader.

Hitler no longer seems interested in interrogating Skorzeny. Instead, he begins to explain what this highly unusual meeting is about.

"Mussolini was betrayed yesterday," Hitler says. "His king had him arrested. But the *Duce* is not only my great ally, he is also my friend . . . and I cannot abandon this statesman."

What does this have to do with Skorzeny? Hitler quickly explains:

We must find out where the Duce is being held and free him. That is the mission I have for you Skorzeny. And I have chosen you because I am convinced that you will succeed with this operation. And you must risk everything to carry out this action, which is now most important to the conduct of the war. Naturally this mission is to be kept absolutely secret, otherwise it will fail . . . But you must act quickly, very quickly! You will understand that the life of the *Duce* depends on it!

This is why Skorzeny was originally summoned. He's a Special Operations expert, running a Special Operations training facility. Hitler needed someone to lead this secret mission, to discover where Mussolini is being held and free him.

As Hitler describes the assignment, Skorzeny falls under the Führer's sway. "The longer Hitler spoke the more I could feel his influence upon me," Skorzeny later described. "His words seemed to me so convincing that at that moment I had not the slightest doubt about the success of the project. There was such a warm, human inflection in his voice when he spoke of his loyalty to his Italian friend that I was deeply moved."

After describing the mission, Hitler goes silent, staring at Skorzeny for a long moment. "I have full confidence in you, Skorzeny. I hope I shall hear from you soon and wish you the best of luck."

Skorzeny can only mutter, "I fully understand, my Führer, and will do my best."

They shake hands, then Hitler's aide leads Skorzeny out of the room. As the Captain leaves, he still feels Hitler's eyes on him.

Moments later, Skorzeny is catching his breath in the large antechamber. He fumbles for a cigarette in his pocket and raises it to his lips.

His head is buzzing. The Führer just gave him a mission wilder than any fictional spy story. He must learn where Hitler's closest ally Benito Mussolini is held—and then lead the commando raid to rescue him.

For this dedicated Nazi soldier, it's the assignment of a lifetime.

35

---·---

Tehran, Iran

August 14, 1943

For months they've been hunting Nazis.

Tonight, just after dark, on an otherwise typical late summer evening in Tehran, a group of armed British officers are on the move. Since the start of the year, they've been closely monitoring enemy activity both within the city and in the surrounding regions, often sharing information with their Soviet counterparts.

Much of the work has been tedious, sorting through paperwork and filing detailed reports. But tonight, they're ready for action—and they're on to something big.

They're agents of the British Defense Security Office in Persia—or DSO Persia—the Tehran-based office of the Combined Intelligence Center in Iraq and Iran.

Accompanying the British officers are two Iranians. One is a member of the Persian Army Reserve; the other is a Lieutenant of the Persian Police. What they have in common is that the British have recently identified them as operatives of the Melliun, the underground pro-German movement in Tehran. Tonight, on the dark Tehran streets, these two Iranians now lead the British officers to what could be a secret safehouse of the Nazi underground.

Why are these pro-German Iranians leading the British to one of their hideouts? They don't have much choice. Two nights ago, the British agents apprehended one of these men—someone they strongly suspected was guilty of collaborating with Nazis in Tehran—and after some interrogation he admitted he was guilty in "actively participating in German activities." From there, he led them to the other man, giving the British two admitted Nazi collaborators.

In truth, the British DSO office doesn't really care about these two relatively low-level locals. They want the higher-ups at the very top of the chain. More specifically, they want notorious Nazi undercover agent Franz Mayr, who's known to be the ringleader.

These two Iranians are just pawns in the game. So the British agents cut a deal with them that "no action by D.S.O. would be taken against either of them" if they cooperated and shared useful intelligence.

Lucky for them, they did know something, or at least they claimed to. As the British interrogators wrote in their report, "After much bargaining, a plan was devised and the informers . . . promised to lead the D.S.O. to the hiding place of a German W/T [wireless transmitter] operator."

So right now, these two Iranians are leading the British officers to the Nazi safehouse.

Are the informants telling the truth? Do they really have solid info, or are they making empty promises in hopes of saving themselves? As the DSO agents approach the address, they're about to find out.

At exactly 9:30 p.m. local time, the agents burst through the door. Raiding the home doesn't take long. Within minutes they locate and secure a German-made wireless transmitter on the premises, and more importantly, they apprehend the young man in the house who is there to operate it.

Unlike the two informers, this young man is not a local. He has light-brown hair, blue eyes, and European features.

As the British soon learn, the young man is SS Corporal Werner Rockstroh—one of the five remaining parachutists of the Operation Franz mission from Berlin. He's in the middle of his shift in one of several rotating safehouses that serve as wireless transmission stations for the team.

It's a huge score for British intelligence. But even better, while they're on premises, the British learn that Rockstroh is expecting visitors later that night.

For the next few hours the officers wait, making sure that from the outside, the house bears no sign of unusual activity. Sure enough, in quick succession, not one but two visitors arrive at the house to meet with Rockstroh.

The first man is a Sergeant Major with the Iranian army. Clearly, the army remains a key recruiting ground for the local pro-Nazi movement. The British quickly apprehend him. But it's the second man who's more interesting. Unlike the first visitor, he puts up a physical fight against the DSO agents. It doesn't take long for them to restrain him.

His identity? A local dentist.

Which begs the question: Why's a dentist consorting with Nazis— and why would the Nazis care about him?

The British agents take the two men to the DSO headquarters for immediate interrogation. If the team works fast, maybe they can get some new leads while the trail is still hot.

The dentist's name, the interrogators learn, is Dr. Quidsi.

Quidsi, it turns out, is a liaison between the local Melliun movement and the German wireless operators in Rockstroh's group.

But when it comes to Dr. Quidsi, there's one other detail that's even more interesting. He's from a well-known family in Tehran: the Sanjari family. His niece, he reveals, is Lili Sanjari.

The British intelligence officers know that name.

And just like that, a local dentist becomes the most important discovery of the night.

36

---·---

Quebec City, Canada

August 21, 1943

The war is moving fast and there are critical decisions to make.

Only three months after Churchill's latest visit to Washington, D.C., the President, Prime Minister, and their staffs meet again in August, this time in Quebec City.

After the successful invasion of Sicily and the fall of Mussolini, the most pressing questions concern military strategy along the Mediterranean front. Germany has already rushed troops to the Italian mainland to defend against a possible Allied attack. The King and Grand Council are prepared to abandon the Axis powers and make a deal with the United Kingdom and the United States. The Italian army is divided, with some factions planning to fight with the Germans, and some ready to switch sides.

It's a chaotic situation that demands complex decision-making.

Churchill has always favored the Mediterranean campaign, so at the Quebec summit, he pushes hard—and wins Roosevelt's support for—a plan to follow up the Sicilian campaign with an invasion of the Italian mainland to capture or push out the Axis forces in the country.

During the conference, top British and U.S. military leaders are on hand to relay orders to the ground commanders as decisions are being made. Preparations begin for a multipronged attack on Italy, set to begin on September 3.

But the Mediterranean strategy isn't the only priority. Having agreed to follow through on the Italian campaign, Roosevelt insists that the combined Anglo-American powers remain focused on what is, in his mind, of greatest importance: clarifying the plan for a cross-Channel attack into northern France, now delayed until the spring of 1944.

Once again, debates between the Americans and British are heated. Churchill's constant wavering on this issue—the same issue that only a few months ago nearly pushed Stalin out of the alliance—continues to aggravate Roosevelt and the Americans. Every time an agreement seems close, the Prime Minister or one of his advisors presents some new idea to delay or downgrade the cross-Channel attack in favor of his Southern Strategy.

This time, though, Roosevelt holds firm. He demands that Churchill and the British remain true to what they mutually agreed upon in May and subsequently shared with Stalin: an invasion of northern France early the next year.

After much back and forth, the Combined Chiefs of Staff draft a confidential report outlining key elements of the plan, setting a target date of May 1, 1944, to launch the cross-Channel attack. Simply locking this date on paper gives military commanders a clear deadline to work toward and allows planning to commence according to a master schedule.

Still, Roosevelt and his staff push for one more important concession from the British, namely, that an American commander should be the one to lead the cross-Channel attack. FDR and the American war planners don't have faith that the British leadership is truly committed to the plan, so they want the U.S. military to take the lead.

Also, the leaders need to come up with a good name for the mission—and when it comes to names, well, that's Winston Churchill's specialty. The Prime Minister gives names to even minor events in the war, including the current meeting in Quebec, which he code-named the "Quadrant" Conference. He was trying to stay on a Roman theme that he'd established earlier in the summer when he named the "Trident" Conference in Washington.

Usually, for inspiration, he drew from literary or historical sources. For military affairs, he preferred epic and powerful words, often from ancient myths. He once sent a memo to his military assistant giving guidelines for how to name military operations, insisting that names carry appropriate dignity and "do not enable some widow or mother to say that her son was killed in an operation called 'Bunnyhug' or 'Ballyhoo.'"

So what should they call next year's much anticipated cross-Channel attack into northern France? The Prime Minister, despite all his reservations about the mission itself, comes up with a winner. Operation Overlord.

Everyone likes it. From that point on, no other name is considered.

In addition to pinning down Churchill on opening the second front in France, Roosevelt has another key priority for the conference: pushing aggressively for the meeting with Stalin. Since Casablanca, FDR's goal has always been to meet with the Soviet Premier in person before the end of the year; with September now approaching, that window is closing.

Remarkably, despite Stalin's most recent request that Churchill be present at any in-person meeting, the President was still holding out hope for a last-minute, one-on-one meeting with Stalin in the original agreed-upon location of Alaska. Even though the chances were remote, the President had arranged for a secret plane to be on standby near Quebec so that he could fly to Alaska on short notice.

Given Stalin's latest communications, this notion is beyond farfetched, and Roosevelt soon accepts that he needs to give up the one-on-one idea and instead join forces with Churchill and hold Stalin to this three-way meeting. It's been several weeks since Roosevelt's last communication with Stalin on the matter, and the Soviet Premier has once again gone silent. To Roosevelt, it feels like he might be once again trying to slip out of it.

But Churchill, who seems to have gotten over the earlier insult of Roosevelt wishing to exclude him, is once again eager to make the Big Three summit happen. He also supports Roosevelt's wish that the proposed location is not in the Soviet Union.

On August 18, in the middle of the Quadrant Conference in Quebec, the two leaders write a combined message to Stalin. They quickly update him on the latest plans for Italy, then move on to the question of the summit:

> We wish to emphasize once more the importance of a meeting between all three of us. We do not feel that either Ar[khangelsk] or Astrakhan are suitable but we are prepared ourselves, accompanied by suitable officers, to proceed to Fairbanks in order to survey the whole scene in common with you. The present seems to be a unique opportunity for a rendezvous and also a crucial point in the war. We earnestly hope that you will give this matter once more your consideration.

A few days later, Stalin writes back but his message doesn't mention the summit. Instead, he complains about them not sharing enough information about Italy. Then, on August 24, as the Quadrant Conference is wrapping up, Stalin cables them again.

This time he finally responds to their request for a meeting. By the time they receive the message, the Prime Minister and President are both leaving Quebec, so each reads it separately.

"I entirely share your opinion and that of Roosevelt about the importance of a meeting between the three of us," Stalin writes. He proceeds to describe how busy he is with matters of war, when "our armies are carrying on the struggle against the main forces of Hitler with the utmost strain." Given these circumstances, "I cannot without detriment to our military operations leave the front for so distant a point as Fairbanks."

Interestingly, Stalin doesn't offer up any alternative locations, or possible dates. Basically, it's no different than what Stalin last communicated to Roosevelt several weeks ago: no specifics, no commitments. This could be just a version of the same evasion Stalin has been giving Roosevelt and Churchill in one way or another since the previous December, when the President first invited the Soviet leader to join them in Casablanca and Stalin declined.

Still, Roosevelt remains optimistic. After reading Stalin's message, he sends a quick note to Churchill. "I hope you have seen Uncle Joe's new message which is greatly improved in its tone . . . my first feeling is that he has come around to our meeting and that it should be held very soon."

Roosevelt and Churchill decide not to press the issue right away, and instead send Stalin another message filling in the rest of the details from their conference. This includes an update on the subject closest to Stalin's heart: the cross-Channel attack into northern France, now officially planned for the following spring.

"A large scale buildup of American forces in the United Kingdom is now under way," Churchill and Roosevelt write. "It will provide an initial assault force of British and American divisions for cross channel operations."

They don't share the exact target date with Stalin—they probably don't want to be held to it—but they state emphatically that "this operation will be the primary British and American ground and air effort against the Axis."

On August 31, a week after the conference, Churchill takes to the radio airwaves to give a lengthy public address about the state of the war effort. Within the address he specifically raises the subject of a proposed Big Three meeting, and applies strong public pressure on Stalin to engage:

Nothing is nearer to the wishes of President Roosevelt and myself than to have a threefold meeting with Marshal Stalin. If that has not yet taken place it is certainly not because we have not tried our best or have not been willing to lay aside impediment and undertake further immense journeys for that purpose . . . the President and I will persevere in our efforts to meet Marshal Stalin.

Lest anyone not get the point, the Prime Minister continues, "It would be a very great advantage to everyone and indeed to the whole free world if our unity of thought and decision . . . upon strategic problems could be reached between the three great opponents of the Hitlerite tyranny."

He's not hiding his intentions, but it still doesn't get a response from Stalin.

A few days later, on September 4, Roosevelt decides to press the issue, sending the Soviet leader a message and bringing up the summit one more time. "I still hope that you and Mr. Churchill and I can meet as soon as possible. I personally could arrange to meet in a place as far as North Africa between November fifteenth and December fifteenth."

Between the two, Roosevelt and Churchill have now asked Stalin a half-dozen times in just a few weeks. That's in addition to their many requests during the summer, *and* Roosevelt's elaborate ploy of sending a special envoy to Moscow, *and* their pleading with the Premier to join them for the Casablanca Conference, and then for another proposed meeting in spring.

It seems like the one question Stalin is determined to avoid.

But on September 8, Stalin finally writes back to Roosevelt. "As to our personal meeting with participation of Mr. Churchill I am also interested to have it arranged as soon as possible. Your proposal regarding the time of the meeting seems to me acceptable."

That all sounds promising. But the key question is the location, which has continued to be the biggest sticking point.

Thankfully, Stalin has a new idea. "I consider that it would be expedient to choose as the place of the meeting the country where there are the representations of all three countries," he writes, adding, "for instance, Iran."

Iran? This is a genuine surprise.

At this point, the trio had considered and rejected proposed meeting locations in Morocco, Egypt, Scotland, Norway, Russia, and Alaska. No one has ever suggested Iran. For that matter, no one has ever suggested a location in the Near East or Persian Gulf regions.

For Roosevelt, it's a complicated suggestion.

On one hand, Iran is farther from the United States than any other location proposed by Roosevelt or Churchill. If traveling as far away as Casablanca had been a major effort—and it certainly was—a journey to Iran would be over 50 percent longer. What's more, the United States has no infrastructure for high-level visits to the region and so would have to plan logistics and security from scratch.

On the other hand, Stalin is correct that Iran is a nation where all three major powers have representation. Because of the critical importance of the Trans-Iranian Railway, the country is relatively well secured by British and Soviet troops. Both the United Kingdom and the Soviet Union have existing embassies in the capital city of Tehran, and the United States has a legation,[2] or diplomatic office. Furthermore, the relatively remote desert location could allow for greater secrecy than most places in Europe or near the Mediterranean.

Iran.

It just might work.

---

2 "Legation" refers to a diplomatic office of lower rank than an embassy, headed by a minister rather than an ambassador. The distinction between the two ceased to be used after the Second World War.

PART IV

Eureka

37

---·---

Italy

Late Summer 1943

For Captain Otto Skorzeny, the rest of the summer is a whirlwind.

After his meeting with Hitler in the Wolf's Lair, when the Führer ordered him to rescue Benito Mussolini, Skorzeny immediately starts preparing for his mission.

He's instructed to leave the Wolf's Lair at 8 a.m. the following morning and take a plane directly to Rome, Italy, so he can begin his search for Mussolini. But before he leaves, he must make sure that his own people, who are back in Berlin, get sent at the same early hour to a location in southern France where they'll be on standby.

Right after the meeting, Skorzeny calls his assistant, Karl Radl, and tells him that no one in the Berlin office will be sleeping that night. He explains that although he can't reveal the reason, he needs a commando unit that'll be ready to go the next morning. "Pick fifty men—only the best," he orders.

In addition to men, Skorzeny needs supplies—and since no one has the slightest idea where Mussolini is being held, they have to be ready for any sort of mission. Skorzeny decides that every soldier who gets on the plane the next morning must be outfitted with machine guns, pistols, hand grenades, plastic explosives, fuses, helmets, rations, and both warm- and cold-weather uniforms. If any of this equipment isn't currently available at the training grounds, they need to find it—overnight—somewhere in Berlin.

The following morning, Skorzeny, who didn't even bring a bag with him to the Wolf's Lair, is on a scheduled flight from East Prussia to Rome. In the air, he learns that fifty soldiers from Berlin, led by his second-in-command Karl Radl, somehow made it to their morning flight and are now bound for France, where they'll eventually board another flight that will take them to a secure barracks in Italy.

Arriving in Rome, Skorzeny immediately begins trying to figure out where Mussolini is being held. German officers in the city introduce him to friendly assets within the Italian state police and to other city officials who may be able to help him track down clues.

The search, however, soon becomes maddening. "We learned that all sorts of rumors were flying round as to where Mussolini could be found," Skorzeny later recalled. "Many professed to know that he had committed suicide, while some said he was very ill and had been sent to a sanatorium. Such speculations turned out to be rubbish and we found no real clue."

The quest to find the former dictator is all the more confusing because every few days, the royal authorities are moving their high-value prisoner to a different secure location. Every time Skorzeny's team receives intelligence that Mussolini is in one place, they soon learn that he's already been moved elsewhere.

Still, for each credible lead, they make elaborate preparations. At one point, Skorzeny believes that Mussolini is being held in a police barracks in Rome, so he and his team devise a plan to storm the barracks from the city streets—only to learn at the last minute that he's no longer there. When they hear that *Il Duce* might be on a sea cruiser bound for the Port of La Spezia, they corral dozens of boats and map out a seabound mission to storm the cruiser in transit, take over the captain's chair, and steer the ship to a German-controlled port. Later, when they hear Mussolini is being held captive in a fortress on one of the La Maddalena islands, they devise a complex amphibious landing to storm the island and rescue him.

Transfer after transfer, as the chase continues, the country is falling apart. British and American forces begin bombing raids over Rome and other northern cities; at one point, the barracks where Skorzeny's team is staying gets badly damaged and they have to relocate. An Allied ground invasion of the country seems imminent, with German forces also flowing in to prevent it.

Soon enough, Skorzeny's mission appears to be in peril when rumors spread that the King is planning to offer Mussolini to the Allies as part of a peace deal. The rumor proves to be false, but in these unprecedented circumstances, anything seems possible.

Amid this chaos, on September 2, Skorzeny and his team receive compelling intelligence that the royal authorities have just moved *Il Duce* to a remote mountaintop hotel on the Gran Sasso range within the Apennine Mountains northeast of Rome. The national police have apparently converted the hotel—a former elite ski resort left abandoned during the war—into a prison to house their high-value prisoner.

At an elevation of 7,200 feet, the only way to reach the hotel is via a single cable car that traverses the side of the mountain. A unit of armed carabinieri supposedly guard Mussolini in this alpine fortress.

Although Skorzeny isn't sure that the intelligence is reliable, he knows that an Allied invasion can come any day. This might be their last chance to launch a rescue mission, so he has no choice but to roll the dice and hope his sources are correct.

So, how do you possibly conduct a successful rescue mission in the heart of the Italian Alps? First, he needs to study the location.

On September 8, he and Radl arrange a reconnaissance flight to circle above the range so they can take photographs of the peak, identify the precise location of the hotel, and try to figure out how their relatively small team can reach this extremely remote target.

To avoid detection, their reconnaissance plane flies at an altitude of 16,000 feet, at which height Skorzeny is able to see and photograph the hotel. But he also notices something else: a triangle-shaped clearing that's adjacent to the building. It appears to be an empty field or meadow.

This unexpected discovery becomes the key to an unusual plan. Instead of storming the mountain from below and relying upon the single cable car to ascend to the hotel, Skorzeny's commando team can use the triangular meadow near the hotel as a makeshift landing strip. While no conventional aircraft could ever land on such a small and uneven space, perhaps lightweight motorless gliders could. If so, any passengers aboard would be within striking distance of the hotel prison. Once Mussolini is liberated, a small two-passenger plane could then swoop down to pick him up and transport him to safety.

In addition to providing the only practical approach to the mountaintop, the glider plan also maintains the element of surprise. "It was certain that no one expected an attack from the air," Skorzeny concludes, "and this was our one and only chance" to attempt a rescue.

When he shares the idea with his commanding officers, they say it's too risky. One aviation expert estimates that given the thin air at such an altitude, the team would have an 80 percent casualty rate just from the glider landings—and that's *before* the raid on the hotel even begins. Still, no one has a better plan, and the window of opportunity is closing.

Obtaining approval from Berlin, Skorzeny secures a dozen lightweight DFS 230 gliders from the Luftwaffe, each of which can carry nine passengers and a pilot.

After a few frantic days of preparation, the takeoff is set for September 12, first at 6 a.m. and then, after a delay, at 1 p.m. In another unforeseen obstacle, a recent Allied bombing raid left craters on the airfield, causing two of the gliders to run aground during takeoff. The remaining ten make it into the air, with Skorzeny himself in the lead glider.

Now, roughly an hour after taking off, his glider is finally approaching the Gran Sasso peak. Through the small windows, he and his team of commandos spot the snowy mountaintop as it comes into view.

"Helmets on!" Skorzeny yells to everyone on board. Within moments the hotel itself is visible.

Yet as the aircraft get closer, something doesn't look right.

"The pilot turned in a wide circle, searching the ground . . . for the flat meadow appointed as our landing-ground," Skorzeny recalled. "But a further, and ghastly, surprise was in store for us. It was triangular all right, but so far from being flat it was a steep, a very steep hillside!"

The so-called landing strip—this supposed meadow—is actually a smooth, sloping rock face on the mountain peak and, as Skorzeny clearly sees, "landing in this 'meadow' was out of the question."

As a result, with no landing strip in sight, ten gliders carrying a hundred men and still flying at top speed are about to ram into the side of a mountain.

Skorzeny only has a few seconds to think. According to the direct orders of his General, he's forbidden to land without an airstrip, meaning he should order the pilot to swerve away from the mountaintop, glide down to the valley below, and hope to land safely. The rest of the gliders can then follow suit. In other words, he should abandon the mission.

Or . . . he could do something else.

"Crash landing!" Skorzeny bellows at the top of his lungs. "As near as the hotel as you can get!" He's in charge of the aircraft—this is a direct order.

The pilot tilts the starboard wing toward the mountaintop. As the wind shrieks around them, the glider hurtles straight toward the rocky face of the rugged mountain peak.

38

Washington, D.C.

September 1943

There's new hope for the summit.

After Stalin's message to Roosevelt and Churchill on September 8, signs point to the long-sought-after Big Three meeting finally occurring, most likely in late November.

If anything, after the summer, President Roosevelt feels an even greater urgency for this meeting to take place.

The Allies just had a run of successes on the battlefield. It's now critical to seize that momentum and press every advantage. Roosevelt believes that a grand show of unity on the world stage—the unity of the Big Three—is now essential to the war effort.

The Casablanca Conference taught Roosevelt that in this new age of global media, meetings of world leaders can carry enormous symbolic weight. Simply the photograph of Roosevelt and Churchill together in Morocco—accompanied at the time by the leaders of the French resistance—had been instantly transmitted around the globe. The story of the conference was covered by newspapers everywhere. The event had created a powerful perception of organization and strength.

In a war where nations around the world are forced to pick a side, or to offer assistance in one direction or the other, this perception of strength is crucial. Most governments will choose, sometimes for their very survival, to be on the side that's winning. The Allies need neutral or wavering countries to move in their direction.

Even within nations under total Axis control, the resistance movements—also important to the war effort—need momentum; they rely on the perception of Allied success as much as the reality of it.

If Roosevelt and Churchill's event in Casablanca created this perception, then a three-way meeting with Stalin would do even more. The world has long known that Roosevelt and Churchill are closely aligned, but Stalin is another matter. One of the great questions surrounding the Allies has always been whether the Soviets could work with their Western partners.

In fact, Nazi leaders have long thought that a key to their victory would be the unraveling of the relationship between the Soviet Union and the other two countries. The Soviets are simply too different, Germans believed, and the alliance is doomed to fail.

A Big Three summit would help put this issue to rest. So not only would the event bolster the Allies—it would demoralize the enemy at a key juncture in the war.

Apart from the theatrics, a Big Three summit would also allow the three leaders, face-to-face, to discuss many difficult and pressing issues. At this moment, there are several complex questions to answer. How to best lure Turkey into the war on the Allied side? Will the Soviets ever agree to join the fight against Japan? What's the status of the fractured Baltic states that Soviet armies are now liberating from Nazi occupation?

Roosevelt hopes to forge an understanding with Stalin to answer these questions. With the three leaders together in person, these tough issues and others can be confronted directly, with decisions made in the room.

Finally, there's the matter of the cross-Channel attack. In this new phase of the conflict, with momentum on their side, Roosevelt is adamant that they must agree on a definite plan of attack. With Stalin there in person to apply double pressure on Churchill, Roosevelt hopes to finally corner the Prime Minister and get him to agree on an irrevocable schedule for striking northern France.

The stage is now set for all of this to happen.

With every passing day, however, there's one detail that keeps gnawing at the President: the proposed location.

Iran, Roosevelt realizes, is simply too far away. It'll take too long for him to get there. Any other world leader should surely understand how valuable time is, but FDR must be careful about broaching the subject to Stalin, especially considering how hard it's been to bring the Soviet leader on board. The last thing Roosevelt needs is to let the opportunity slip away.

On September 9, the day after receiving Stalin's message, he writes back, "I am delighted with your willingness to go along" with the summit. Trying to show enthusiasm, he adds, "And the time about the end of November is all right."

Here's the trickier part. "My only hesitation is the place," he continues, "because it is a little bit farther from Washington than I had counted on." He decides to provide the concrete reasons why it's such a problem. "My Congress will be in session at that time and, under our Constitution, I must act on legislation within ten days. In other words, I must receive documents and return them to the Congress within ten days and Tehran makes this rather a grave risk if the flying weather is bad."

As an alternative, he writes, "I hope that you will consider some part of Egypt, which is also a neutral state and where every arrangement can be made for our convenience."

Following Roosevelt's lead, American diplomats start pushing for Egypt. The next day, the U.S. ambassador to Egypt sends Roosevelt a message from Cairo to report that the Egyptian leader, Mostafa El-Nahas Pasha, just confirmed publicly that "he would welcome holding a conference between Great Britain, the United States and Russia in Cairo and would be pleased to provide facilities."

The Egyptians have open arms, and it's a perfect location. Hopefully, this puts the matter to rest.

Unfortunately, Churchill sends a mixed message to Stalin, writing on the same day as Roosevelt and accepting Tehran as the site. Brimming with excitement that the summit is back on—and that he himself is now definitely included—the Prime Minister gushes to the Premier, "I am pleased and relieved to feel that there is a good prospect of this taking place . . . I have for some time informed you that I will come anywhere at any time for such a meeting." The message continues, "I am therefore prepared to come to Tehran unless you can think of a better place in Iran . . . I defer to your wishes."

Stalin, in response to these two simultaneous messages, simply latches on to Churchill's positive response. In a September 12 message to both leaders, Stalin writes, "As regards the meeting of the three heads of the Governments, I have no objection to Tehran, which, I think, is a more suitable place than Egypt where the Soviet Union is not yet represented."

Churchill takes this as a green light. Still apparently bursting with enthusiasm, he sends Stalin another note on September 27, further affirming the choice of location.

Churchill also raises a subject of enormous importance for all three of them: security.

Given the intense international scrutiny and heightened excitement surrounding the proposed conference, keeping the date, location, and other details secret will be extremely difficult. Each of the three leaders know that they have targets on their backs.

"I have been pondering about our meeting of heads of Governments at Tehran," Churchill writes. "Good arrangements must be made for security in this somewhat loosely-controlled area." As a sort of decoy, Churchill suggests that he make elaborate preparations in the city of Cairo, Egypt, to throw off the world press. While the spotlight shines on Cairo, they can secretly prepare and lock down the real location:

> Then perhaps only two or three days before our meeting we should throw a British and a Russian brigade round a suitable area in Tehran, including the air field, and keep an absolute cordon till we have finished our talks. We would not tell the Iranian Government nor make any arrangements for our accommodation until this moment comes. We should of course have to control absolutely all outgoing messages. Thus we shall have an effective blind for the world press and also for any unpleasant people who might not be as fond of us as they ought.

Churchill seems to revel in all this—the heightened security planning, the secret code words, the feeling of high drama on the world stage.

Yet, there's one final detail that captures the Prime Minister's attention: The conference, in his mind, needs a good name. Naturally, he's already given it some thought.

"The code name for the operation should be 'Eureka,'" Churchill suggests to Stalin, "which I believe is ancient Greek." He adds, "If you have other ideas let me know and we can put them to the President."

A week later, Stalin writes back regarding Churchill's idea of sending British and Russian military brigades to surround Tehran during the proposed conference. "I do not think the measure advisable—it could lead to undue commotion and exposure," Stalin argues. Instead, each country should simply "take a strong police force with them" to the summit.

Otherwise, he says, "I have no objection to the other proposals for the coming meeting, and I agree to the code names suggested for the correspondence on the meeting."

The best strategy for security will be an ongoing question for the three leaders, but for now at least, Stalin agrees with the Prime Minister's word choice.

Eureka.

The new code word for the proposed first-ever in-person meeting of the three Allied leaders during the Second World War.

They have a name. Now they just need to make this conference happen.

39

Gran Sasso, Italy

September 12, 1943

The mountain face is coming at them fast.

The glider pilot desperately scans the uneven, sloping field of rocks, looking for something, anything, that will provide a flat enough surface for a crash landing.

"I closed my eyes and stopped thinking," Captain Otto Skorzeny later described, as he and his team of eight SS commandos prepared for the coming crash.

During several seconds of pure commotion there is a "frightful din" and "the noise of shattering wood" as the bottom of the glider smashes hard along the ground then "bounced several times" along the uneven rock face. Yet somehow, after a "last mighty heave," the badly battered aircraft comes to rest.

Skorzeny thankfully realizes he's still intact. He and a few others tumble out the broken hull of the aircraft and spill onto the jagged rocks. Miraculously, after skidding about twenty yards, the "completely destroyed" glider is now within fifteen yards of the mountaintop hotel.

Barely looking to see the status of the pilot or the rest of the team, Skorzeny grasps his machine gun in both hands and begins running toward the hotel. Behind him, he can hear the panting of some of his armed commandos following. They're under strict orders not to fire any shots until their leader fires first, and to "stick to him like glue."

Of course, Skorzeny and his men still have no idea if Mussolini is even inside the building. But to maintain the element of surprise, they push forward with maximum speed.

As they race toward the side of the building, they spot a single stunned carabiniere—a guard—standing near a door, staring at them wide-eyed. "*Mani in alto!*"—"Put your hands up!"—one of the Nazi commandos shouts.

The Italian guard drops his weapon.

With the guard subdued, they smash through the door, which leads to a small utility room where another Italian soldier is frantically trying to operate a wireless radio transmitter set up on a chair. The soldier probably ran to the radio as soon as he saw a glider heading toward the mountain.

Before the soldier can get off a message, Skorzeny lunges at him. "A hasty kick sent his chair flying from under him," Skorzeny later described, "and a few hearty blows from my machine-pistol wrecked his apparatus."

The room has no other doors, so Skorzeny and his men race back outside and circle around the building, searching for another entry. He jumps up on a stone terrace and, in a stroke of good fortune, this vantage provides him a perfect view of the main face of the building.

"My eyes swept the façade and lit on a well-known face at one of the windows of the first story. It was the Duce! Now I knew that our effort had not been in vain!"

Sure enough, Mussolini is inside. From his position at the window, the prisoner can undoubtedly see them coming.

Skorzeny knows that there is probably a full unit of armed carabinieri inside standing guard. So how should Skorzeny proceed?

"Duce, get away from the window!" Skorzeny shouts.

Mussolini instantly recedes into the room.

By remembering the location of the window, Skorzeny should now be able to go straight to Mussolini's room once he enters the building. He continues circling the building until he sees a larger front entrance. Making sure some of his men are behind him, he storms straight in.

A handful of carabinieri are in the front foyer, but before they know what's happening, Skorzeny rushes straight through them, knowing his men behind him have the element of surprise and will quickly overpower the Italian soldiers.

He sees a staircase and immediately bounds up, three stairs at a time. Based on his memory of the room's location from outside, he makes a guess and charges into the second door in a long hallway.

Sure enough, there's *Il Duce.*

Next to him are two stunned guards. Knowing they don't have a chance against the team of armed Nazis facing them with guns raised, they drop their weapons.

Up to this point everything had happened so fast that the carabinieri were simply too surprised and unprepared to put up any resistance at all. After a total of about four minutes since the first glider landed, Skorzeny and his men have found and secured their target without firing a single shot.

As his teammates secure the hotel hall, keeping their guns aimed at the Italian soldiers, Skorzeny formally addresses the prisoner they've come to liberate.

"Duce, the Führer has sent me! You are free!" he exclaims.

Stunned, Mussolini reaches out to shake Skorzeny's hand, then embraces him. "I knew my friend Adolf Hitler would not leave me in the lurch," he says.

Mussolini was "extremely moved and his black eyes glistened," Skorzeny recalls. "I must confess this was one of the greatest moments in my life."

By this time, more of the gliders have crash-landed around the mountaintop. One glider had careened straight into a rock face during the attempted landing, smashing it to bits and badly injuring several on board. But most of the teams survived and have surrounded the hotel.

To finalize the victory, the German commandos ask for and receive an official surrender from the carabinieri's commanding officer. The Italian soldiers use a hotel bedsheet as a makeshift white flag.

With the hotel secured, Skorzeny and a few teammates walk Mussolini out of the room, into the hall, and down the hotel stairs. When they emerge from the front entrance out to the mountaintop, the assembled commandos stand at attention, raising their arms in salute.

A light snow has started falling, and as the German soldiers surround Skorzeny and Mussolini to celebrate, someone takes out a camera and captures the moment.

While Skorzeny and *Il Duce* enjoy themselves a team of soldiers get to work clearing boulders and brush to create a more flat and usable airstrip near the hotel. Once the job is done, one of them waves a green light; this is the signal for a small two-engine Fieseler Storch plane that has been circling overhead to descend and land on the strip.

Once the plane is on the mountaintop, Skorzeny and Mussolini board the tiny aircraft and brace for a rocky takeoff.

A few moments later, the plane accelerates along the makeshift runway and shoots off the edge of the steep mountain peak. At first,

SS Special Operations leader Captain Otto Skorzeny (with binoculars) celebrates alongside former Prime Minister Benito Mussolini (in black) just after Skorzeny's commando raid freed Mussolini from a remote mountaintop hotel where pro-Allied Italian forces had been holding him prisoner. (German Federal Archives)

it appears that the Storch is carrying too much weight for the thin alpine air, and the plane's nose dips down toward the valley for what appears to be a precipitous nosedive. But the pilot slowly rights the plane and soon is headed away from the Gran Sasso mountains.

In a few hours, the Storch will land safely on an airfield outside Rome. There, the two passengers will board another plane, this time bound for the Austrian city of Vienna, where German authorities will receive them and *Il Duce*'s safety will be guaranteed.

Skorzeny did it. He rescued and freed Mussolini.

He also proved something that Nazi leaders will soon take to heart: With the right person in charge, anything is possible.

40

Vienna, Austria

September 13, 1943

"You have performed a military feat which will become part of history. You have given me back my friend Mussolini."

It's close to midnight when Adolf Hitler speaks these words by phone to Otto Skorzeny, shortly after the Waffen-SS officer was shown to his suite in a grand hotel in Vienna.

The energy at the hotel has been electric since Skorzeny and Mussolini arrived there an hour earlier, surrounded by the military escorts who met them at the airfield outside the city. Entering the hotel, they were received like conquering heroes.

Since the moment Skorzeny arrived in his suite, people have been coming in to congratulate him. Shortly before midnight, a Colonel from the Viennese garrison entered to formally bestow upon him, on behalf of the Führer, the Knight's Cross of the Iron Cross, the highest military honor in the Reich. Shortly after that, he received the personal call from Hitler.

It will continue like this for days. Skorzeny travels with Mussolini from Vienna to Munich, where the Germans have set up a headquarters for the deposed Italian Prime Minister. Here, with Nazi help, he'll plan his next moves. And here, too, Skorzeny is wined and dined, feted like a hero.

The news of Skorzeny's spectacular rescue of Mussolini quickly spreads throughout Germany. After a difficult stretch in the war, Nazi officials have been so starved for good news, the story of *Il Duce's* rescue comes at just the right time.

Perhaps no one is more thrilled than Nazi Propaganda Minister Joseph Goebbels, who has just been handed a gift. "Let us rejoice with all our hearts that the Duce has been restored to liberty," he writes. "The news of his liberation will create the greatest sensation throughout the world . . . I now have a feeling that our lucky streak has set in."

Goebbels is on hand in East Prussia, along with dozens of other top Nazi leaders, when Mussolini and Skorzeny make their grand arrival at the Wolf's Lair so that fellow fascists Mussolini and Hitler can be reunited.

"Hitler and Mussolini embraced after their long separation," Goebbels records in his diary. "A deeply moving example of fidelity among men and comrades was here shown. I suppose there is nobody in the world who can fail to be impressed strongly by so touching a ceremony."

The world press, of course, picks up the story about Skorzeny's stunning rescue of Mussolini from the mountaintop prison. At first, most of the Allied press assumes that the account of the rescue, initially broadcast by the Reich's news services, is Nazi propaganda. It seems simply too far-fetched to be true. Some American newspapers instead print false rumors that Mussolini was actually killed or committed suicide.

But journalists all over the world soon learn that this story is one of the very few cases where the Nazis are telling the truth.

Once the details are confirmed, both the Axis and Allied press include Skorzeny in almost every account of the rescue. Sometimes his photo appears, and soon—it's not clear exactly when or how it begins—he starts being referred to as the "Most Dangerous Man in Europe."

For now, Otto Skorzeny is happy just to be the most popular man in Germany. Upon his return to Berlin in late September, every Nazi leader wants to personally meet with him. He is the guest of honor at elaborate ceremonies. In private and in public, he is asked to recount the story of the rescue over and over again.

But finally, after all the fanfare, it's time for Skorzeny to get back to work.

He's a Major now, rather than a Captain—that's two promotions just this year—but otherwise he will still operate from his position as the head of Special Operations for the SD, running his training facility in Friedenthal.

He quickly goes back to what he was doing before he left for Italy. Among other things, that means training and overseeing missions to Iran.

At some point after his return to the SD, Skorzeny learns Iran has, since he was away, suddenly taken on a new, unexpected potential importance on the world stage. In fact, it could become the site of one of the most important events of the entire war. And if Iran has become more important, that means the missions there are more important too.

On top of that, after the hype and sensation surrounding the Mussolini rescue, one of the key takeaways—for Nazi leadership and for Skorzeny himself—is a simple one: Special Operations work. Small teams working in secret can often accomplish things that big armies can't.

Skorzeny proved it. And with the right elite team, he can prove it again.

41

·

Berlin, Germany

Late September 1943

When and how do the Germans first learn that Tehran is a possible location for the Big Three summit?

There's no precise answer—no definitive record of when the Reich first obtained this information. There are only a few clues to invite speculation.

Of course, the Forschungsamt, or FA—the Nazi signals intelligence organization, sometimes called the "Research Bureau"—had all the way back in April and May intercepted multiple Allied communications regarding Roosevelt's efforts to set up an in-person meeting with Stalin.

Given those interceptions, it's certainly plausible that the FA, through the same or similar high-level intercepts, also gained knowledge of the proposed summit locations discussed between Roosevelt, Churchill, and Stalin, up to and including Stalin's first reference to Iran in his September 8 message to Roosevelt and Churchill.

After September 8, references to Tehran pepper the correspondence of the Big Three, as well as the correspondence of their high-level military and diplomatic staffs. Because Nazi foreign intelligence leader Walter Schellenberg later bragged of his decrypts of direct correspondence between Roosevelt and Churchill—even the ability to intercept and decrypt a complete phone call between them at one point—it could be that Schellenberg's SD soon learned that Tehran was the likely place for the summit.

After Schellenberg's meeting with Canaris in late July, where the two intelligence chiefs discussed Hitler's desire for information about any pending Big Three summit, Schellenberg would certainly have been making an effort to learn what he could by any means necessary.

One Russian intelligence source would later assert that the Germans learned about Tehran as a location for the conference by "decipher[ing] the American Naval codes." This assertion may be true, but it's vague and there's no documentation to verify or further explain it.

One sign that the SD or other entities within the Reich Security Main Office become aware of Tehran as a potential location is the continued expansion of Nazi Special Operations missions into the Iran region. In the wake of the original Operation Franz mission back in April, the SD has embarked or is planning several follow-up missions, including Operation Anton, Operation Dora, Operation Berta, and several unnamed excursions involving German planes dropping parachutists into Iran.

Finally, in roughly late September—the period immediately following the Allied leaders' first mention of Tehran in correspondence about the coming Big Three summit—the SD's Near East division begins preparing a new mission into the Tehran region called Operation Norma. Few formal records exist regarding this mission, and its goals are confidential.

There are two details about the staffing of Operation Norma, however, that are known and noteworthy.

The first is that at the SD level, the mission will be overseen by Roman Gamotha, Franz Mayr's former partner in Tehran who fled the city after the Allied invasion—and who made a dramatic reappearance in Berlin earlier in the summer. Given his extensive experience in Iran and his former partnership with Mayr, Gamotha probably has more firsthand knowledge of Tehran than anyone else in the organization.

Secondly, the mission's tactical training will be overseen by none other than Otto Skorzeny—now a Major—who after his spectacular mission to rescue Mussolini has returned to his position as the head of the SD's Special Operations recruitment and training program in Friedenthal. Although Skorzeny's role within the SD is technically the same as it was before he left for Italy, he's now a national hero whose name has appeared in newspapers all over the world. He's rubbed shoulders with the Reich's elite and has received some of the highest accolades possible within the Nazi Party, including direct praise from Hitler. Any mission with Skorzeny's name on it suggests heightened importance.

So when did Nazi intelligence services first learn of Tehran as a possible summit location? One of the most fascinating clues goes back to early August. On the third day of that month, SD offices in Berlin sent a wireless transmission to Franz Mayr and his Tehran team with a very specific directive.

"According to our information it is claimed that a meeting between Roosevelt, Stalin, and Churchill is imminent," the message from Berlin states. "Please send any confirmation as soon as possible."

The request is quite remarkable, considering that Stalin's first mention of Tehran as a possible location is on September 8, more than one month later. So how would the SD in Berlin possibly have advance notice that Tehran could be the site of a Big Three meeting?

To this day, any answer is speculation, though there are at least two plausible explanations. One is that the SD at this time still has no special knowledge that Tehran may be the site of the conference, and the SD's leader, Walter Schellenberg, is also sending similar messages to agents in other locations, hoping to find leads.

August 3 falls very shortly after Schellenberg's meeting with Admiral Canaris, during which Canaris impressed upon Schellenberg that Hitler was demanding intelligence on the Big Three conference. It stands to reason, then, that Schellenberg would, on or near this date, be sending inquiries to trusted agents in all foreign countries, hoping to learn clues about the rumored conference.

Or, perhaps the transmission indicates that the SD had already identified Tehran as a likely location. Although Stalin's first direct mention of Iran to Roosevelt or Churchill doesn't occur until September 8, the Soviet Premier would not likely urge Iran as the meeting place to the other Allied leaders without having discussed the idea internally at some length first. Perhaps in early August, the SD some-how received interceptions of internal Soviet communications that were pointing to Iran as a preferred location for a Big Three summit—and SD agents therefore immediately sent the message of inquiry to their agents on the ground there.

Franz Mayr and the other German agents in Iran never respond to the inquiry. Or at least, no response is ever recorded. Presumably, at this point, they have no knowledge or intelligence to offer on the matter.

In either case, when Schellenberg and the SD staff in Berlin do first learn that Tehran is a possible location for the summit—and based on the clues, it seems they learn it at some point in mid- or late September—it must come as a striking revelation.

Maybe it's just a coincidence that the Allied leaders happen to choose a country and a city where the Nazi spy agencies have recently spent considerable time and resources building up an intelligence in-frastructure, but if so, it's a detail they plan to use to every advantage.

In the end, it must seem like a remarkable stroke of luck—or even an act of fate—that SD agent Franz Mayr, long forgotten or left for dead, was able to miraculously reconnect to Berlin as he did early in the year. And it's almost too good to be true that Mayr had spent the last year and a half building up an underground pro-Nazi resistance movement in Tehran. Because now, out of nowhere, one of the biggest events of the war—the first in-person meeting between Hitler's great enemies—is potentially taking place in that very city.

For the Nazis, the timing couldn't be better. Walter Schellenberg, the Nazi leader of foreign intelligence, knows as well or better than anyone that the Axis position in the war has diminished greatly in recent months. Unlike others, he doesn't believe the rescue of Mus-solini, however spectacular, has much of an impact on the big picture.

The daily Nazi propaganda in Germany won't say it, but the fact is that with Italy on the verge of falling after the Allied invasion, and more importantly, with the mighty Wehrmacht suffering a series of defeats against the Red Army on the Eastern front, Hitler desperately needs a change of momentum.

Maybe Iran and this proposed Allied summit will offer the Reich just such an opportunity—a chance at something extraordinary.

If so, it would be thanks in large part to Franz Mayr, the Nazi's unlikely hero in Tehran.

But there's something Schellenberg doesn't know about Franz Mayr. In the past month, Mayr's circumstances have changed dramatically.

For the SD's newest plans for Iran, it's a change that could make all the difference.

42

ONE MONTH EARLIER . . .

Tehran, Iran

August 15, 1943

Dr. Quidsi is a dentist. But more important, he's related to Lili Sanjari, the known lover of undercover Nazi ringleader Franz Mayr.

It's this second detail that matters most to the agents of the DSO—the British intelligence services monitoring Tehran. They're the ones who captured Dr. Quidsi, along with his local collaborator, a Sergeant Major in the Iranian military. During their interrogations, both admit to being members of the underground pro-Nazi Melliun movement, and to interacting with the German agents of Operation Franz.

For months now, the British have been monitoring Lili Sanjari, getting regular reports from the young American GI, Private Robert Merrick, with whom Sanjari was having an affair behind Mayr's back.

The DSO weren't interested in apprehending or arresting Sanjari—there was no benefit in that. The person they were interested in was Franz Mayr. So the DSO strategy with Lili Sanjari was, in the words of British intelligence reports, that she "had been left at large as a decoy in the hope of capturing Franz Mayr through her."

Now, they've got Lili's uncle—Dr. Quidsi—in custody, and lucky for them, he's actively involved in Mayr's organization. Under interrogation, Quidsi admits that he's often the "go-between between Mayr and the German W/T operators." In other words the go-between between Mayr and the members of Operation Franz.

The more Quidsi talks, the more the circle around Mayr seems to shrink. Under interrogation, Quidsi eventually insists that he can lead the British to Mayr—in fact, Mayr will soon be staying at Quidsi's home.

For the British, it's a perfect break at a perfect time.

At 1:15 a.m. on August 15, a handful of DSO agents descend upon Quidsi's address. Given the late hour, the ground floor of the home is pitch black. After sneaking around, the agents find a staircase that leads up to the second floor.

"The DSO . . . entered a room at the top of the stairs and saw a man in the darkness," according to agency files. "He was challenged, and made no attempt to resist."

One of the British agents flicks on the light. The man before them resembles descriptions they'd been given over the course of two years. "Are you Franz Mayr?" the lead agent asks.

"Yes," the man says as guns are pointed at him.

Finally, here he is. The longtime Nazi ringleader in Tehran.

The agents spin Franz Mayr, pressing his face to the wall. But before they can arrest him, he suddenly crumples to the floor.

Franz Mayr, the undercover Nazi agent and leader of the Melliun underground resistance movement, has just fainted.

He's not out for long. Soon, the British have him back in DSO headquarters. Aside from cursing out the local Tehranis whom he believes sold him out, he doesn't have much fight left in him. Perhaps after leading a difficult life in hiding for so long—while also shouldering the burden of protecting the other German agents who arrived with Operation Franz—he's simply exhausted.

Within a few days, Mayr agrees to cooperate. He sits for interrogation. He stops fighting. He knows this will be a long, grueling process, covering weeks and months, but it's not like he has a choice. His physical safety is now in the hands of his enemies. No doubt, there's little hope for a happy ending.

For months, this loyal Nazi lived a double life, ran an underground network of operatives, and served as the de facto leader of the pro-Nazi movement in Iran.

Now, Franz Mayr is in custody and ready to answer any question.

43

---·---

SIX WEEKS LATER . . .

Washington, D.C.

October 1, 1943

For months, there's been a flurry of correspondence between the three Allied leaders.

Now, in the wake of Stalin's agreement to the Big Three meeting before the end of the year—and his unexpected suggestion of Tehran as his favored location—the flurry becomes a blizzard.

In addition to the summit itself, there are important ancillary events connected to it. Stalin had insisted earlier that any three-way meeting should be preceded by a cabinet-level conference, so the three nation's war planners and diplomats can iron out complicated issues in advance, allowing the leaders to focus on the big picture. The conference will also serve as a hedge in case the Big Three conference should never materialize.

After some back and forth, this cabinet-level conference is finalized for October 18, to be held in Moscow. The American Secretary of State, Cordell Hull, and the British Foreign Secretary, Anthony Eden, will attend, as will their Soviet counterpart, Foreign Minister Vyacheslav Molotov. Also present will be top war planners from all three countries.

At the same time, Roosevelt is determined to combine his own global travel with another important goal: a face-to-face meeting with

Chinese leader Chiang Kai-shek. As the country that has suffered more than any other in the face of Japanese aggression and imperialism, China has been a U.S. ally from the beginning, and Roosevelt wants to shore up China's logistical and strategic support for the next phase of the Pacific war.

The trick is, the geopolitics of a meeting with Chiang are complicated. When the U.S. first forged its alliance with the United Kingdom and the Soviet Union against the Axis powers, Stalin insisted that the USSR maintain its own separate peace agreement with Japan. Japanese imperial interests in Asia did not currently affect the Soviet Union—Japan had no desire for conflict with the Soviets—and Stalin, who needed every possible soldier and weapon for his epic defense against the invading Nazi armies, had no interest in fighting the Japanese. As a result, the two nations had agreed to a truce even while fighting on opposite sides of the larger war.

What this means now is that Stalin can't be present at any event also attended by Chiang, because that would signify that Stalin was taking sides in the conflict between China and Japan, which Stalin had assured the Japanese he wouldn't do. Roosevelt, however, doesn't want to travel halfway around the world without meeting the Chinese leader in person.

To get around this issue, Roosevelt organizes a conference with Chiang in Cairo, Egypt, for early November, after the conclusion of the Moscow Conference but before the proposed Big Three meeting. Churchill will also join for some part of it. From centrally located Cairo, Roosevelt and Churchill can then travel to meet Stalin or convince him to travel toward them in North Africa.

Otherwise, for Roosevelt, there's only one remaining obstacle: the proposed location of Tehran.

Congress will be in session in November, and the U.S. Constitution demands that the President must act upon and return any legislation passed by Congress within a ten-day period. Should legislation be passed while Roosevelt was abroad, the documents would have to be flown to him, signed or vetoed by him, and then returned within that window. The President's planners predict that if there is any inclement weather, delays on cargo flights over the mountains to and from Tehran would push him outside the ten-day limit.

Although Churchill had previously accepted Tehran as the location, he agrees to help Roosevelt try to convince Stalin to agree to another place.

From there, Roosevelt and Churchill offer other options. If Stalin won't come to Cairo because of Chiang Kai-shek, Roosevelt suggests instead the city of Asmara, the former Italian capital of Eritrea, which he says has "excellent buildings and a landing field." Or they could meet in Baghdad, Iraq, where, the President says, "we could have three comfortable camps with adequate Russian, British, and American guards." If those two cities aren't suitable to Stalin, perhaps the three leaders could each converge by ship to the Mediterranean Sea.

Churchill even throws out the suggestion that they meet in the middle of a desert in eastern Iraq, where "we could put up three encampments and live comfortably in perfect seclusion and security." As his excitement grows about this idea, he sends to Roosevelt some New Testament verses about the three tabernacles meeting in the desert.

The answer from Stalin is always the same: no.

"Unfortunately, not one of the places proposed by you for the meeting instead of Tehran is acceptable for me," he writes. He gives no other alternatives. Keep Tehran.

Roosevelt keeps pushing. In a long follow-up message to Stalin he suggests yet more locations: Ankara, Turkey, and Basra, Iraq. He expresses frustration that "I would have to travel six thousand miles and you would only have to travel six hundred miles from Russian territory." He presses upon Stalin the enormous stakes: "I regard the meeting of the three of us as of the greatest possible importance, not only to our peoples as of today, but also to our peoples in relation to a peaceful world for generations to come."

Stalin simply won't budge. It's Tehran or nowhere.

With November fast approaching, Churchill is frustrated. "It is very awkward waiting about for an answer from Uncle Joe," he complains to FDR. "It is urgent to get dates settled and preparations made."

Roosevelt shifts to a new tactic. When the Moscow Conference begins on October 18, he tasks his Secretary of State, Cordell Hull, who is attending the conference, to implore Molotov and Stalin in person to change their minds. Hull is prepared to suggest another location—Beirut, Lebanon—that the Americans believe will be convenient for the Soviets.

On October 20, Hull speaks to Molotov. It doesn't go well. As he reports back to Roosevelt, "He proceeded to repeat Stalin's attitude which seemed nearly adamant with respect to every other place except Tehran," and "unless there are further new developments, I fear that Stalin will continue immovable on the question."

Why is Stalin being so stubborn? His stated reason, repeated multiple times, is that the Soviets have an offensive against the Germans planned for later November, and Stalin will need to be in constant personal contact with his military leaders during that time. Only in Tehran, he says, do the Soviets have secure and reliable communication lines directly to Moscow. Any other place is too risky.

Stalin may be sincere in his focus on military affairs, but it's impossible for Roosevelt not to suspect that Stalin is also trying to flex some power. After his resentment for their long delay opening a second front in Western Europe, Stalin may be showing them that he gets to call the shots, too.

At Roosevelt's insistence, Hull secures a meeting with Stalin so that he can make the case to the Premier personally. Roosevelt quickly sends a letter to Hull to give to Stalin, in which the President once again lays out the reasons Tehran won't work for him.

But the meeting, held on the afternoon of October 26, hits the same brick wall. Stalin insists that "any other place but Tehran" is impossible because of the communication risks.

As for Roosevelt's constitutional issues, Stalin finds them trivial compared to the importance of his coming military operations. He tells Hull that "he did not see why a delay of two days in the transmission of any state papers could be so vitally important, whereas a false step in military matters . . . might cost thousands of lives."

If Roosevelt won't travel to Tehran, Stalin finally says, the Soviets will send a high-level representative to meet Roosevelt and Churchill anywhere they like, while he himself stays in Moscow. Or, he offers, they can wait and do the Big Three summit in the spring, when Soviet armies will not be as active.

For Roosevelt, this isn't a solution. After the recent string of Allied military successes, the President believes they must seize the initiative. The time for the Big Three summit is now, not next spring. As for Molotov or another lower-level Soviet emissary coming in Stalin's place, it simply won't have the same global impact. As Hull puts it, it would lack "the important factor" of "the broad psychological effect throughout the world of the presence at such a meeting of the Marshal himself."

And so . . . another stalemate. Stalin seems to be one of the most stubborn men on the planet, and Roosevelt needs a new solution for his problem with Congress. He doesn't want to cave to Stalin, but there's not much choice. The Big Three meeting is simply too important, and right now, all signs point to Tehran.

Meanwhile, the Americans, British, and Chinese have to get their parties to Cairo—not just the leaders and their staffs, but also their diplomatic corps and security teams.

As these complicated arrangements are made, the planned meetings in Egypt begin to take on greater significance, both because Chiang Kai-shek has officially confirmed his willingness to meet and discuss all aspects of the war, and because in the wake of the Moscow Conference, the British and Americans leaders now have a new array of issues to work through. Their hope to meet Stalin immediately following Cairo adds a heightened sense of importance to everything.

In the middle of all this, on October 29—now less than three weeks before Roosevelt is scheduled to be in Egypt, and less than a month before the monumental Big Three summit will occur—Churchill sends a message to the President, marked "Personal and most secret."

The message contains one word in all capital letters: SEXTANT.

Churchill was thinking about the Cairo Conference—and, finally, he came up with a name.

44

Washington, D.C.

November 2, 1943

Whenever Mike Reilly, the head of the White House Secret Service, is summoned to speak to the President in person, it's usually bad news. Today is no exception.

As Reilly takes a seat, Roosevelt gets right to the point. In three weeks, he has to get to Cairo. In Egypt. That's three thousand miles farther than their enormous trip to Casablanca earlier in the year.

All those records they broke for the longest trip ever taken by a sitting American President, they're about to break them again.

Reilly's nerves still haven't recovered from the two other major trips Roosevelt has taken this year—his cross-country train journey in April, and his visit to Quebec in September—and now he has to add what will clearly be the most stressful journey of all.

On top of that, the President tells Reilly he "hopes to talk to Stalin" during this trip. But since Stalin can't come to Cairo, Roosevelt may have to go somewhere else even farther.

For Reilly, it's a logistical and security nightmare. But his job isn't to challenge the President's travel choices—it's to keep everyone safe.

"Cordell Hull is in Moscow now," Roosevelt explains to Reilly, referring to the Secretary of State who is still at the Moscow Conference.

"He is trying to make the arrangements for a meeting between Stalin and me."

The President explains that Hull will be returning through Africa on his way back, so Reilly should go to Africa right now to meet him during that window, learn from him what the latest itinerary will be, and immediately start making preparations. "Whatever he has been able to arrange will be alright with me," the President says.

Any personal plans Reilly may have had in the next six weeks, they're now canceled.

Still, despite Roosevelt's request, Reilly can't just hop on the next flight to North Africa. As the person in charge of the President's safety, first he must help plan and authorize the President's travel itinerary to Cairo, which will inevitably involve stops and stayovers. Once a few key decisions are made, he can then fly to North Africa to meet Hull.

Thankfully, Reilly and his staff learned a lot from the Casablanca journey earlier in the year, and one takeaway was the inherent dangers of foreign air travel with the President. "Because the Boss couldn't use normal steps, it was necessary to build ramps wherever his plane was to land," Reilly later wrote, "and they were an absolute giveaway to any enemy agents or in German aerial reconnaissance pictures of our airfields."

So if possible, they should try to minimize the President's total number of flights.

There's no way to avoid air travel once Roosevelt reaches Africa, but for the first part of the journey, there is another option: Instead of a plane, the President can board a ship.

With the help of his military liaisons, Reilly secures the battleship USS *Iowa* for the Commander in Chief's voyage across the Atlantic. Travel by sea is not without its own dangers—German U-boats patrol shipping lanes on the ocean—but the team feels confident that with an escort fleet, the mighty *Iowa* can fend off any Nazi subs.

Once the ship makes it to the port of Oran in Algeria, Roosevelt will transfer to a plane that'll fly him to Tunis, and from there, the President will board another plane to Cairo.

Once those initial plans are in place, Reilly packs his bag. Having quickly arranged with the State Department to meet Secretary Hull in Morocco, he embarks on a travel route using the soonest available military aircraft and pilots. The journey takes him from Washington, D.C., to New York City, then to Cuba, then to Trinidad, then to Belem, Brazil, then Dakar in French West Africa, then to Morocco.

At the end of it, Reilly is at the Marrakesh airport. There, a sedan is waiting for him. When Reilly enters the vehicle, he's alone with Secretary of State Cordell Hull.

Reilly quickly explains that the President asked him to confer with Hull to determine where, after Cairo, Roosevelt will travel to supposedly meet Stalin.

"Well, it's Tehran then," the Secretary tells him. By this point, Stalin still hasn't budged, and Roosevelt has finally agreed to it. Reilly is one of the very first people outside of Hull and the President himself to hear this final location.

"Good luck, Mike," Hull tells him as they shake hands. "I'll tell the President I saw you."

Reilly's work in Marrakesh is done. But his work in North Africa is just beginning. He'll now personally scout every step of Roosevelt's planned journey to establish security for both travel and lodging adequate for a U.S. President during wartime.

These preparations will take him to Oran, to Tunis, and to Cairo to set up for the President's arrival there.

Then, it's on to Tehran.

45

Lublin, Poland

November 3, 1943

It starts with music.

Yesterday, SS officials at the Majdanek concentration camp in Lublin, Poland, had parked a car outfitted with a loudspeaker near the front entrance to the camp, then parked another on the opposite side.

Today, before dawn, both of the car's loudspeakers start blaring, the sound of traditional German songs filling the air. As the music rises, it drowns out another sound, the thudding of boots hitting the ground as SS guards march through the camp quarters. An extra five hundred guards had been sent to the camp the night before, and now, starting at 5 a.m., these guards march from building to building, corralling prisoners.

Following instructions, they methodically separate Jewish prisoners from the rest and force them into lines behind them.

The guards systematically march the lines of prisoners toward the outskirts of the camp. The prisoners, many of them sick and emaciated, are men, women, teenagers, small children, and the elderly.

It's still dark out when the prisoners get a glimpse of where they're going. A terrified wail rises above the music that floods the camp.

For the past several days, teams of prisoners had been ordered to dig a series of large, deep, zigzagging trenches around the camp perimeter.

The purpose of the trenches, according to SS officials, was to house antiaircraft weapons. But prisoners sensed something else was planned, something terrible, and now they realize they were right.

As the prisoners approach the trenches, guards organize them into groups of ten or fifteen. Any prisoner who tries to run or resist is beaten and pulled back in line, or simply shot.

The armed guards order each prisoner to strip naked. Then they push them, one by one, to the bottom of the trench. They tell each of them to lie face down. As the other prisoners watch and cry out, a line of SS soldiers standing along the trench raise their weapons and shoot each prisoner in the back of the neck.

The blaring music can't hide the gunshots and the screams. It goes on like this all day, group after group, the perimeter trenches gradually filling with corpses.

This massacre was held today because it is Erntefest, or "Harvest Festival," a traditional German holiday. Similar mass killings are taking place simultaneously at two nearby smaller camps, Trawniki and Poniatowa, also in the Lublin district. This premeditated combined massacre is named Operation Erntefest in honor of the holiday.

By the end of the day, an estimated forty-two thousand Jewish prisoners have been shot to death in the three camps. Some eighteen thousand are killed here in Majdanek, their corpses gradually filling the trenches that the Jewish prisoners themselves were forced to dig.

Back in Germany, Reich leaders have encouraged citizens around the country to celebrate the patriotic holiday with food, drink, and dancing.

Yet there's something else behind the day's unspeakable carnage.

Nazi leaders have grown alarmed because in the past few months, there have been multiple attempted insurgencies on the part of the surviving Jews in the camps and ghettos of Nazi-occupied Poland. These attempts were unsuccessful and resulted primarily in the slaughter of the prisoners involved. A few German guards were injured, however, and a small number of Jewish prisoners escaped.

Heinrich Himmler, the SS leader, decided that in the wake of these insurgencies, a swift, strong response was necessary. He personally gave the order to SS commanders at Majdanek, Trawniki, and Ponia-towa to plan and coordinate the holiday slaughter at the three camps.

Operation Erntefest will eventually be counted as one of the largest single-day massacres of civilians during the war. But although the number of total victims stands out, there's nothing particularly uncommon about it. Massacres in one form or another are ongoing daily at the death camps, by starvation, by bullet, or by gas chamber. The now empty prisoner's quarters at Majdanek will soon be filled with new prisoners. And the non-Jewish prisoners there who were spared during Operation Erntefest—a few thousand Soviet POWs and assorted Polish nationals—will also soon perish in the camp.

There's a terrible irony in the trajectory of the Nazi atrocities during the war. As the German military has begun to falter against the Soviet Union and its Western Allies, SS leaders have pushed even harder to enact the genocidal program of the Final Solution. The Nazi regime has learned that it may not be able to defeat the Soviet army or the U.S. Armed Forces on the battlefield—but they can achieve "victory" by slaughtering defenseless Jewish populations.

"The Jews have richly deserved the catastrophe they are suffering today," Nazi Propaganda Minister Joseph Goebbels wrote in his diary as the genocidal program expanded during the previous year. "We have to accelerate this process with a studied ruthlessness and we are thereby doing an invaluable services to a long-suffering mankind tormented for millennia by the Jews."

By the end of 1943, Majdanek is just one of thousands of camps throughout Nazi-occupied territories that were established for the purpose of working prisoners to death or killing them with guns or in gas chambers. Since the first formulation of the Final Solution at the Wannsee Conference twenty months earlier, the SS have created a vast apparatus to transport Jewish populations from all over the continent to these camps, most of them in Eastern Europe, where the explicit goal is death.

For a time, SS officials debated how Jewish children should be handled. Some officers and soldiers found it particularly difficult to shoot young children, or beat them to death, or watch them starve.

In a meeting with Nazi leaders in October 1943, a month before Operation Erntefest, Himmler addressed these qualms.

"We faced the question: what should we do with the women and children? I decided here too to find a completely clear solution," he explained. "I did not regard myself as justified in exterminating the men—that is to say, to kill them or have them killed—and to allow the avengers in the shape of the children to grow up for our sons and grandchildren. The difficult decision had to be taken to have this people disappear from the earth."

Children, then, are not to be spared. In the trenches of Majdanek and elsewhere, the corpses of children accompany those of adults.

By chance, Operation Erntefest occurs during the three-week-long Moscow Conference, where Allied diplomats and military leaders are meeting to plan war strategy in advance of the proposed Big Three summit later in the month.

The participants at the Moscow Conference aren't aware of these particular massacres in the Polish death camps that are taking place during their meetings, but they've already been drafting a joint declaration to address specifically the crimes against humanity carried out by the Nazi regime and its collaborators.

"The United Kingdom, the United States and the Soviet Union have received from many quarters evidence of atrocities, massacres and cold-blooded mass executions which are being perpetrated by Hitlerite forces in many of the countries they have overrun and from which they are now being steadily expelled," the statement begins.

The declaration proceeds to outline a judicial framework for how these crimes can be punished. "Those German officers and men and members of the Nazi party who have been responsible for or have taken a consenting part in the above atrocities, massacres and executions," the declaration states, "will be sent back to the countries in which their abominable deeds were done in order that they may be judged and punished according to the laws of these liberated countries."

This is not the first declaration by Allied leaders condemning wartime atrocities perpetrated by the Axis powers. But this new declaration from Moscow, soon to be signed by Roosevelt, Churchill, and Stalin, will provide the framework for the later prosecution of former Nazi officials accused of war crimes.

For now, though, they're just words on a sheet of paper. Words on paper do nothing to stop the ongoing horrors on the ground. While Allied diplomats and politicians meet around conference tables, children are being slaughtered all over Eastern Europe in an ongoing campaign of mass murder and genocide.

In this war, every passing day brings unimaginable tragedy.

It's not enough, then, for the Allies to achieve victory—they must achieve it with the greatest possible urgency and speed. To do so, Allied leaders must combine their resources and formulate a plan to strike back at the Nazi Regime, crippling them in the only place that currently matters: on the battlefield.

46

Berlin, Germany

November 4, 1943

The information sometimes comes so fast, it's hard to know what to do with it.

That's certainly true for the SD foreign intelligence in the fall of 1943, and as usual, Walter Schellenberg is at the center of it.

Like many intelligence agencies around the world, his team is focused on trying to answer some simple questions. Will the Big Three ever have their long-rumored conference, and if so, when and where will it take place?

While it's not entirely clear what the SD knew about Tehran—or when they knew it—the most likely scenario is that they had something close to the truth: The Big Three summit was most likely a go and Tehran was the probable location. In any case, it was enough for the SD to keep planning secret missions to Iran, and to keep Skorzeny in charge of them.

It's in this generally murky period that the Nazi spymasters in Berlin get some unwelcome news.

Throughout September and even before, Franz Mayr and the rest of the Operation Franz team in Iran were no longer responding to SD radio messages. Suddenly, they were unreachable. Even contacts on the ground couldn't find them.

This was troubling, of course, but there were plenty of possible explanations.

Perhaps, due to changing weather or other factors, the Franz team could no longer get a signal. Perhaps their radios were malfunctioning, stolen, or confiscated. Perhaps Mayr and the others had to leave Tehran for a short period to escape detection. Or maybe they simply feared that their radio signals were being somehow intercepted.

On October 20, the SD find out the truth. A courier named Firouz recently left Iran and crossed into Turkey, bringing news to the German intelligence stationed there. Here's the official report:

"FIROUZ, after crossing the frontier illegally, arrived here today. He reports that MAYR was arrested on 15th August at 2:00 a.m. at the house of the dentist QUIDSI."

Now the word is out. Franz Mayr, the SD's longtime agent in Tehran, was arrested. If Mayr himself was arrested, that probably means his network was compromised, and that others have been arrested too, including the members of Operation Franz.

Even worse, it happened over two months ago. That means for eight weeks now, the SD has been planning missions without realizing that they can no longer rely on Mayr and his network's ground support.

This is bad news.

Yet as they contemplate the grim consequences, they have no idea that a sudden stroke of good fortune is just around the corner—one that no one could've seen coming.

47

———— · ————

The Atlantic Ocean

November 14, 1943

Franklin Roosevelt loves the ocean.

He learned to sail as a child and practically grew up on boats. His lifelong fascination with seafaring would lead, in part, to his appointment as a young Assistant Secretary of the Navy under Woodrow Wilson. When he was stricken with polio at age thirty-nine—and his doctors predicted he would be incapacitated for life and could never work again—his only way to exercise was in water, and it was the countless hours of physical therapy submerged in ponds, lakes, and oceans that enabled him to slowly regain movement in his upper body.

After his return to politics and public life, he still turned to the sea for almost every break and vacation, bringing family and friends with him on endless sailboats and schooners for fishing trips and other excursions.

Now, today, in his wheelchair, he's gazing out at the vast expanse of the Atlantic Ocean on the deck of the battleship USS *Iowa*, northeast of Bermuda and several hundred miles away from the nearest shore.

Finally, after so much planning, he's on his way to Cairo.

Standing behind him, as usual, is a Secret Service agent—one of Reilly's men—who is there to protect Roosevelt but also doubles as a wheelchair-pusher. Also nearby is Admiral Ernest Joseph King, Commander in Chief of the U.S. Fleet and Chief of Naval Operations. Almost two years ago, Admiral King was one of the first people to inform Roosevelt of the Japanese attack on Pearl Harbor.

Roosevelt often does his best thinking from the decks of boats, and right now there's a lot to contemplate.

He had capitulated to Stalin on Tehran—there's no other way to put it. He would have to find peace with this.

After Stalin refused to compromise, Roosevelt had no choice. To deal with any potential Constitutional issues, the President's team devised a complicated plan. If Congress passes legislation during the trip, the documents would be flown only as far as Tunis in North Africa, rather than all the way East to Tehran. Roosevelt, if necessary, could fly from Tehran to Tunis to sign or veto the legislation, then immediately return to the conference. From Tunis, the legislation would safely make it back within the constitutionally mandated window.

Those are a lot of hoops to jump through, but for Roosevelt, the most important thing is this: The Big Three meeting is on. Given the overwhelming priority of winning the war—and the importance that Roosevelt has placed on the three of them achieving this objective—all other considerations are secondary. Whether Stalin was sincere in insisting on Tehran or engaging in a power play, it no longer matters.

On November 8, Roosevelt wrote to Stalin and formally accepted Tehran as the location. He tried to imbue the message with an elevated tone. "The whole world is watching for this meeting of the three of us," he wrote. "The fact that you and Churchill and I have got to know each other personally will have far reaching effect on the good opinion within our three nations and will assist in the further disturbance of Nazi morale." Finally, "I am greatly looking forward to a good talk with you."

Stalin's response, sent on November 10, was brief. "I thank you for your answer. Your plan concerning the organization of our meeting in Iran, I accept." No high-minded words or expression of shared principles.

Stalin is not the only partner in the Big Three who's been causing anxiety for the President. Churchill, unlike Stalin, shares the
President's wholehearted enthusiasm for the conference. Yet, when
it comes to the cross-Channel attack, Churchill is once again losing
his nerve.

"I now feel that the year 1944 is loaded with danger," he wrote to
Roosevelt on October 27. And then in the same letter, "I must add
that I am more anxious about the campaign of 1944 than about any
other with which I have been involved."

There's no question what he's referring to. Opening the second
front in northern France is the centerpiece of their plans for 1944.

Even more ominous, Churchill suggested directly that he and his
advisors are rethinking the entire strategy. "In view of the changes that
have taken place since Quadrant"—that's the Quebec Conference—
"we have had prolonged discussions here about our existing plans for
the campaign of 1944. On these the British Chiefs of Staff and War
Cabinet are deeply concerned."

The prospect of the cross-Channel attack—sending British and
American troops straight into the teeth of the Nazi juggernaut waiting on the other side of the English Channel—still fills Churchill
with terror. Despite the Allied victories in recent months, the Prime
Minister knows that invading the beaches of northern France carries
enormous risk. He could end up presiding over a disaster, only a few
miles from England's shores.

By this point, the Allied attack in mainland Italy is well underway, and its success has reignited Churchill's enthusiasm for the less
risky Mediterranean theater. Once the long and difficult but ultimately
winnable campaign in Italy is over, Churchill has been talking to his
ministers about moving the troops in Italy east to invade the Axis-
controlled Balkan territories.

These plans would presumably take place in the spring of 1944,
thereby directly conflicting with the plan for Operation Overlord. It's
a new version of the "soft underbelly" strategy.

Among U.S. military leaders, worries have spread that Churchill
and the British will once again delay, downgrade, or otherwise compromise Operation Overlord.

"Postponement to midsummer would be so serious that it ought to be avoided if that is possible," Secretary of War Henry Stimson wrote to Roosevelt's close advisor Harry Hopkins just before Hopkins and the President left Washington, D.C., to board the *Iowa*. "In added difficulties and delays in closing the war, such a postponement would cost many thousands of lives."

Stimson, by appealing to Hopkins, is trying to pass a frank message to the President. "The task for our Commander-in-Chief is to hold the situation firmly to the straight road which has been agreed to . . . He should tolerate no departures from the program," Stimson continues, clearly referring to the British vacillations. "So the one prayer I make for the Commander-in-Chief is steadfastness—a very difficult virtue but one more needed than any other in this particular problem."

There's much for Roosevelt to contemplate as he gazes out at the Atlantic on his way to Cairo and Tehran. On top of everything else, he must convince Stalin to commit to a truly shared, global vision for winning the war and dictating the peace—and simultaneously use Stalin's presence to exert maximum pressure on Churchill to commit fully to Operation Overlord.

As the bright afternoon sun shines down, Roosevelt's thoughts are interrupted.

Admiral King had specifically arranged for Roosevelt's wheelchair to be positioned with a wide view of the surrounding sky and ocean. For the President's benefit, the ship's officers have planned and are now about to execute a demonstration of the *Iowa*'s awesome defensive firepower.

For the demonstration, the *Iowa* launches a series of weather balloons in the air to serve as targets. Soon, the battleship's antiaircraft guns are blazing, the President, Admiral, and several dozen others watching from the deck as the ship's roughly one hundred turrets shoot down balloon after balloon. A few that drift out of range are taken down by a nearby destroyer serving as escort.

It's an altogether impressive display, and the assembled spectators are in awe as they watch the firepower of the vaunted U.S. Navy's finest ships. Running this exercise is without risk—as long as there are no nearby German U-boats who see it.

At that moment, the radio signal blares on the bridge, "Torpedo is coming your way!"

Must be part of the demonstration—but the ship's senior officers look utterly worried.

"This is not a drill!" blares a voice over the loudspeakers. "Torpedo on the starboard beam!"

Alarm bells ring, the air filling with the sound of crew members' feet pounding as they race to their battle stations.

This is most definitely *not* a drill.

A live torpedo is heading straight for the USS *Iowa*.

And the President of the United States is still on the starboard side of the bridge, in his wheelchair, unable to move or run.

48

Berlin, Germany

Early November 1943

At first, it seems too good to be true.

In late October, only days after learning of Mayr's arrest, Schellenberg receives an urgent message from the office of Hitler's Foreign Minister, Joachim von Ribbentrop. The Foreign Minister's office has just come into possession of an extraordinary set of documents that Ribbentrop would like Schellenberg's agency to investigate.

More specifically, they're photographs of documents—one photo per page. They came from Turkey. According to the source that delivered them, they're the confidential documents of the British ambassador to Turkey, Sir Hughe Knatchbull-Hugessen.

At the time, Turkey was a neutral country in the war. Recently, however, the Allies have been aggressively pressuring Turkey to join their side. The Axis powers have been strongly urging Turkey to resist this Allied pressure.

With its location adjacent to Iran, Turkey would be an obvious subject of conversation during any Allied conference in the region. This means the British ambassador would be privy to high-level discussions about the proposed Big Three summit—and would also be in possession of highly sensitive diplomatic documents.

At first, Schellenberg approaches the cache of photos with skepticism. Surely, this must be a hoax or some sort of Allied trap.

Yet as his team reviews the cache, he is stunned by the contents. "I could see that we had here highly secret correspondence between the British Embassy in Ankara and the Foreign Office in London," he later recalled. "There were also private notes in the Ambassador's own hand, dealing with developments between Britain and Turkey, and Britain and Russia."

For the Germans, it's an extraordinary intelligence coup.

What's even more extraordinary is how the photographs arrived in Ribbentrop's office. Apparently, the British ambassador's personal valet—his lead servant, essentially, stationed at the ambassador's personal quarters in the embassy—has been secretly taking photographs of his boss's documents when the ambassador is not at home.

Once the valet had a batch of photographs, he secretly approached German government contacts in Ankara and offered to sell them to Berlin for a large sum. The valet is a Turkish man whom the ambassador hired locally. His only motive, apparently, is money.

Yet, there's something even *more* extraordinary. This valet is willing to continue taking photographs of the ambassador's papers, so long as the Germans keep paying him. In other words, he's ready to be an ongoing source for the foreseeable future.

The valet is smart enough not to give his real name. At first, the Germans call him "Pierre" as a pseudonym, but they soon come up with a better nickname. Cicero, they call him, after the Roman philosopher, because "his documents speak so eloquently."

It takes a few days to set up the operation, but by early November, Schellenberg is receiving Cicero's photographs on a regular basis. It gives him access to the most sensitive Allied intelligence—especially from the Persian Gulf region encompassing Turkey, Iran, Iraq, and Russia—often within a few days.

The Cicero Affair, as it's soon called, will become one of the most sensational spy stories of the war. For right now, however—in the early weeks of November 1943—it has a very specific implication. Since Turkey is a critical subject of the coming Cairo Conference and the Big Three summit to follow, Schellenberg is about to have unprecedented access to the conference planning in almost real time.

At first, he learns that Stalin is insisting on Tehran as the location for the Big Three conference. He also learns that Roosevelt is saying no. Bit by bit, letter by letter, he's quickly got a front-row seat. Where there was only murky intelligence, pieced together from confusing Allied intercepts, now there is immediacy and clarity.

For months, various secret missions to Iran have been underway. Now, those missions have a whole new importance. And yes, Franz Mayr's capture was a setback, to be sure. But the operation must go forward.

Good fortune has just smiled on the SD. And Schellenberg knows they must take advantage of it.

As the SD leader considers his next moves, the Cicero documents cause quite a stir among the Nazi leadership. So how can they use this remarkable information?

The answer comes soon enough. In early November, Adolf Hitler invites Schellenberg to a private meeting at the Wolf's Lair. To join them, he summons none other than Major Otto Skorzeny—the Nazi star and Special Operations mastermind.

The topic of their meeting?

The Big Three summit in Tehran.

49

———•———

The Atlantic Ocean

November 14, 1943

There's a live torpedo headed toward the ship.

The obvious question is, *Where'd it come from?* A Nazi U-boat, or some other enemy nearby?

The truth is almost worse. It's a terrible mistake.

One of the nearby escort ships, the destroyer USS *William D. Porter*, was participating in the demonstration for the President. According to the program, the *Porter* was meant to discharge several harmless blank torpedoes for the *Iowa* to detect and intercept. Accidentally, the torpedomen on the destroyer erroneously failed to remove the explosive primer from one of the torpedo tubes before the missile fired. By the time the mistake was realized, the live torpedo was already shooting through the water at over fifty miles per hour, heading straight toward President Roosevelt and the *Iowa*.

Naturally, the *Porter*'s captain is horrified—and knows he must alert the battleship immediately.

The thing is, that's not so simple. All ships in the *Iowa*'s fleet are under strict orders not to send any radio signals, since they can be picked up by the enemy and reveal the presence of the fleet.

Instead, the *Porter* tries to warn the *Iowa* using a light signal, but the battleship doesn't receive it.

Now, the *Porter*'s commanding officer has a choice: disobey orders and send a radio signal, or let a live torpedo shoot straight toward a U.S. battleship carrying the Admiral of the U.S. Fleet, the Secretary of War, and the President of the United States.

There's no choice at all.

The captain sends the radio signal.

On USS *Iowa*, Captain John McCrea, the commanding officer, has one overwhelming reaction: turn the ship.

With his staff and crew moving as fast as they can, McCrea swings the massive ship's nose to starboard. By turning *toward* the coming torpedo at a chosen angle, the battleship—so much longer than it is wide—makes for a much narrower target.

The good news is, the officers got the warning signal early. This gives them a much-needed head start when it comes to rotating the ship.

As the battleship turns, it creates a swell of waves that fans out. The waves collide with the torpedo on the starboard side, detonating it less than 1,000 yards away. From on board the *Iowa*, the nearby underwater explosion makes it feel like a depth charge hit the ship.

As for Roosevelt, the President was initially confused by the commotion, as was everyone else assembled on the bridge. But once he grasped what had happened—and that he and his staff were out of harm's way—he asked to be wheeled to a rail on the bridge so he could try and catch a glimpse of the detonation.

The Secret Service agent with him followed the order and then, not sure what to do, took out his handgun as if to shoot the torpedo if it got too close.

The whole episode—an American destroyer shooting a live torpedo directly at a battleship carrying the President—would go down as one of the most embarrassing mistakes in the history of the U.S. Navy. Immediately following the incident, the Navy orders the arrest of every officer and crew member aboard the *Porter* and sends the ship straight to nearby Bermuda for a full investigation.

When the dust settles on the *Iowa*, Presidential advisor Harry Hopkins tries to lighten the mood by declaring that whoever shot the missile from the destroyer "must have been some damn Republican!"

Roosevelt also takes it in stride. It's not his nature to focus on negatives.

Still, for those whose job it is to keep the President safe, it's an unwelcome reminder of the perils of wartime travel with the Commander in Chief. Even here in safe waters, surrounded by a massive U.S. fleet, the President's life was put in danger.

In a matter of days, it'll be even worse: He'll be in an unfamiliar city, surrounded by agents of the enemy.

50

Late Fall, 1943

The Germans got a lucky break. Thanks to the disloyalty of the British ambassador's personal valet in Ankara, Turkey, they now have an unexpected new cache of intelligence, giving them regular updates on the Allies' upcoming conference.

Yet when it comes to intelligence gathering, good luck can flow both ways.

The Soviets are about to get an intelligence breakthrough of their own.

In western Ukraine, just over the border from Poland, the war and the ongoing Nazi occupation has left the area completely devastated. It's now home to some of the worst atrocities against civilians, turning it into a war-torn region that's overseen by a mix of German soldiers, military officials, and SS administrators.

Among these Nazi functionaries is a square-jawed young Lieutenant named Paul Siebert. Handsome and outgoing, Siebert is popular and well respected.

Unbeknownst to his fellow officers and soldiers, though, his name is not actually Paul Siebert. His real name is Nikolai Kuznetsov—and if this name doesn't sound German, that's because it isn't.

Kuznetsov is an undercover Soviet spy, working for the NKVD.

Every day, he risks his life gathering information about Nazi operations in the region, then sends it back to his superiors in Moscow. In fact, Kuznetsov has already had a remarkable career as a Soviet agent. With his Nordic appearance and flawless German, it's near impossible to tell that he's undercover. He's also personally brave. Operating under different aliases, he's had a hand in multiple assassination plots against high-ranking Nazi officials in the Ukrainian cities of Lviv and Rivne. By some accounts, he personally pulled the trigger on a few of them.

Tonight, though, he isn't interested in killing.

On this cold night in late fall—the exact date isn't known, but probably in early November—Kuznetsov, aka Lt. Paul Siebert, is having drinks with a German Special Operations officer named Hans Ulrich von Ortel. Kuznetsov has recently befriended von Ortel, just as he's befriended many other German officers and soldiers. Now, the two are relaxing and telling stories.

Kuznetsov notices that the more von Ortel drinks, the more he speaks. For a spy, this makes for a promising evening.

Sure enough, as Kuznetsov pours more cognac, von Ortel starts bragging. He says he's part of a team planning a top secret special mission. He's been training for it in the Carpathian Mountains. Best of all, he hasn't been training with just anyone. His mission's leader is none other than Otto Skorzeny, the Special Operations mastermind who led the famous mission to rescue Mussolini.

Now, Kuznetsov's really paying attention.

Officer von Ortel won't reveal anything else about the mission—but Kuznetsov remembers something useful. Von Ortel had previously mentioned that he needed a loan of money, and this gives Kuznetsov a small opening.

The Soviet spy tells his drinking partner that he has access to some funds, that a patriotic German will grant him a loan. This gesture generates trust—but more importantly, it causes von Ortel to slip up.

I'll repay you, the German officer says, "in Persian rugs."

It's a tiny detail—these Persian rugs—but this throwaway comment contains a major hint about the mission's destination. It must be Iran.

Kuznetsov, whose work is specific to Ukraine, doesn't have much knowledge about the Middle East, and probably has no idea that the Big Three are planning to meet in Iran. He simply files the comment away.

Refilling von Ortel's glass, he spends the rest of the evening trying to learn more, but von Ortel reveals nothing else regarding his top secret mission.

Thankfully, as he always does, Kuznetsov makes sure the details of his meeting are "promptly reported to Moscow." The spy on the ground may not know what to make of von Ortel's disclosure, but NKVD experts back in the main office are very interested in it.

It's a remarkable find: a Nazi Special Operations mission. In Iran. Led by Otto Skorzeny. And the training for it is taking place in the weeks just before the Big Three conference there.

Coincidence?

Doesn't seem likely.

Time for the Soviets to get to work.

51

———— • ————

Cairo, Egypt

November 23, 1943

Mike Reilly is on another plane.

He's been on a lot of them in the past two weeks, almost too many to count. He's also been on quite a few boats, trains, trucks, and jeeps. Since his arrival in North Africa to meet Cordell Hull in that empty sedan at the Marrakesh airport, it's been a whirlwind.

From there, he traveled to Oran, Algeria, then to Tunis, then Cairo, then Basra, then Tehran, then back to Oran, to Algiers, then back to Oran.

They were all scouting trips for the President's arrival, to make advanced security arrangements. Once Roosevelt and the USS *Iowa* pulled into the port of Oran in Algeria, Reilly joined the President's party and traveled by air with him from Oran to Es Sénia, then to Tunis, then, finally, to Cairo.

Once in Cairo, the President was joined by Prime Minister Churchill, Generalissimo Chiang Kai-shek, and Madame Chiang Kai-shek, who often serves as her husband's interpreter and advisor at important international meetings.

This was the beginning of the Cairo Conference—or the Sextant Conference, according to Churchill.

For Reilly, the advance security planning for Cairo had been fast and furious. During his earlier scouting trip, he had discovered a city "seething with unrest," including violent demonstrations occurring in front of the British and French embassies. According to Reilly's sources, the city was also "filled with Axis spies." Every possible precaution had to be taken to secure the conference.

Surveying the scene, Reilly ordered that a barbed wire entanglement be built to surround the entirety of the Mena district, where the meetings were to be held. American and British troops were quickly posted around the ambassador's compound where Roosevelt and much of the U.S. delegation would be staying. Every member of the local waitstaff and groundskeeping teams had to be replaced by Americans for the duration of the event; otherwise, an enemy agent or informant could end up being the one serving water at lunchtime.

The U.S. military was also involved. "The air raid defense system was reinforced with anti-aircraft batteries and Reconnaissance fighter planes," Reilly later recalled. Because intelligence photos of the nearby island of Crete showed the presence of German aircraft, U.S. military planes commenced heavy bombings of the island "before and during the time the President was in Cairo."

Once these and other precautions are taken, the event gets underway. Naturally, an armed team of Reilly's agents remains on hand for every moment of it, tasked to protect the President and the U.S. delegation, coordinating their efforts with the British and Chinese security teams who are also trying to keep their people safe.

With his team on duty and the location finally secure, Reilly heads for his next plane.

This one is bound for Tehran. If all goes according to plan, the President will be traveling there in four days, as soon as the Cairo Conference concludes.

Reilly has to get there first to get things ready.

It's not his first trip there. Reilly had already flown once to Tehran briefly a week earlier—but it was just to check the airfields and the roads to the city. For that earlier trip he wanted to keep the lowest possible profile and did not alert the British or Soviet security services to his presence.

Now he wants to see more than the airports and investigate the city itself, plus the President's lodging and the conference site. This time, he'll be in full coordination mode with his Soviet and British counterparts who are also setting up their own security in advance of the Big Three conference.

At 11:30 a.m., Reilly's plane takes off. After a nearly 1,600-mile journey, it arrives late that afternoon at the Gale Morghe airport a few miles outside Tehran. Gale Morghe embodies some of the complexities of wartime reality in the region: an Iranian airport used mostly by Soviet forces flying American planes.

Here at the airport, Reilly meets his Russian security counterparts— "my opposite number," as he puts it—in General Dmitri Arkadiev, a ranking officer of the NKVD, the Soviet intelligence service. Together, Reilly and Arkadiev will be sharing responsibility for the safety of the Allied leaders for the duration of the conference.

As for Reilly, his first priority is to inspect the American legation— that's a smaller version of an embassy—on the southern outskirts of the city, where Roosevelt is scheduled to stay. The most notable feature is its distant location, roughly a mile and a half across the city from the British and Soviet embassies where Churchill and Stalin will be staying and where most of the meetings will take place.

Roosevelt had made clear to Reilly that he wanted to stay on American turf to maintain his independence, but Reilly doesn't like the fact that the President will have to travel back and forth such a long way.

From there, Reilly begins his security check of the American legation. In addition to his standard checklist of precautions, Reilly reaches out to the local U.S. Command Center and requests a heavy guard of military police to patrol in and around the compound.

His next step is to inspect the British and Soviet embassies. Unlike the isolated American legation, the two embassies are side by side in the center of the city, both surrounded by high walls. Only a narrow street separates the two compounds, a street that could easily be walled off to keep people away. For all three leaders, he realizes, this setup would be a far safer and easier meeting place.

Yet as he continues to tour the Soviet embassy, his opposite number and security counterpart—General Dimitri Arkadiev—pulls Reilly aside.

The General has a grave look on his face.

Reilly reads it instantly. Bad news is coming.

52

Mike Reilly braces for the worst. He's not wrong.

According to General Arkadiev, Russian security forces have determined that "the Germans ha[ve] dropped parachutists in the Russian-occupied area near Tehran."

Even worse, at least some of them were dropped yesterday.

"This was bad news," Reilly thinks to himself. German parachutists. Near Tehran. Right before the three Allied leaders are supposed to be in the city.

Arkadiev goes on to say that the Soviet forces have "not caught any of the Germans," who, they suspect, are now "hiding in the mountains."

Reilly knows it can't get much worse. "The German parachutists could have been dropped for only one of two reasons," he later recalls. It's either "to sabotage the railroad between Basra and Tehran," which is "the life-line for Russian Lend-Lease supplies shipped to the Persian Gulf from the United States," or, he concludes, it's "to assassinate the Allied leaders."

If it's the former—to sabotage railroads—then why are the German parachutists suddenly arriving now, within a day or two of the Big Three's arrival? That seems a very unlikely coincidence.

The more realistic—and terrifying—possibility is that the Germans know about the conference and now are painting bull's-eyes on the Allied leaders.

For now, they need to assume the worst.

The two security experts spring into action. "We extended the protected area around the legations and doubled the guards," Reilly recalled. From that moment forward, "Russian, British and American Secret Service agents and intelligence officers combed Tehran, looking for the parachutists."

The problem is, in a city of three-quarters of a million people, plus the added chaos of a major international summit, how can they possibly locate and identify a few enemy agents?

It's not like the German parachutists are going to waltz through the city gates wearing Nazi uniforms. They'll find a way to blend in. To infiltrate.

And if they do that, they might already be here in Tehran, closer than anyone realizes.

53

———— • ————

Berlin, Germany

Iťs a one-of-a-kind opportunity.

For at least a few days, the three Allied leaders will be in the same city, in the same room—sometimes eating at the same table. When they're photographed together, it might even be in a public location.

For Nazi Special Forces, there'll never be a better chance to hurt them all at once.

The only question is, how do you get close enough to do it?

Given the nature of the event, iťs easy to predict where the three leaders are staying: at their countries' respective embassies or legations. Thaťs a starting point.

Of course, the Allies are aware that the enemy knows this, so they'll guard them like military fortresses. Any frontal assault on the individual compounds would be foolish. Better to find a subtle way in.

A simple map of the city reveals something important about the three countries' buildings. While the Soviet and British embassies are in the center of the city and next door to one another, the American legation is on the outskirts, isolated.

That might not change the level of protection, but it does mean that once the meetings start, either the American President is going to have to travel through the city to meet the other two, or the other two will be traveling to the American President. Sure, there's the possibility that all three would meet at some neutral location, but even so, then all three would be forced to travel through the streets.

In the compounds, they're safe. When they're traveling, they're exposed.

That's opportunity number one.

With a deeper knowledge of the city, which the Nazi intelligence services certainly have, there's a second opportunity. For each of the country's buildings, in addition to the ground-level doors and entrances, there's a network of underground tunnels.

It's designed that way for the water.

As most visitors to Tehran know, the city's supply of drinking water is unsafe for outsiders. In fact, it's not safe for locals either. Residents usually draw their water from a source connected to the city's uneven sewer system, and that water is notoriously contaminated by bacteria from human and animal waste. It's even worse for Westerners, who are particularly vulnerable. Typhoid fever—the disease that claimed Karl Korel—is just one of many maladies that you can contract.

Back when the Allies invaded and took over Tehran, they needed a solution to this problem. Instead of relying on imported bottled water or risking the local stuff, they set up a system to draw clean mountain water from outside the city, to those places where Russian, British, and American officials need it.

Hence the tunnels.

In those tunnels, the water flows directly to the three countries' diplomatic headquarters—the Russian embassy, the British embassy, and the American legation—as well as to the local U.S. Army Command compound.

So yes, a direct assault on one of the compounds might be doomed to fail. But a surprise attack through one of the underground water tunnels? That's a different story.

To this day, it's unclear whether the German intelligence agencies had their agents scout the tunnels—or whether they had maps or schematics to them. But the Germans most definitely knew that the tunnels existed and that humans traversed them.

Which leaves the big question: *When* would Roosevelt, Churchill, and Stalin all be together? Unless you know when to strike, there's no way to take down all three at once.

The tricky part is, in the days before the summit, the Allies' itinerary of meetings still hasn't been set—and once it's finalized, it'll be top secret. Making things even harder, each meeting has a different configuration of people—only a few have all three leaders, and most of them only include diplomats or generals, with no leaders at all.

For any potential assassin, trying to determine the exact right day and time is confounding. Yet even a novice enemy intelligence officer would notice that a particular date of note happens to fall during the conference.

November 30, 1943. Winston Churchill's birthday. His sixty-ninth, to be exact.

Whenever there's an international summit, there's the inevitable long, elaborate dinner where the leaders and attendees gather to socialize after their long day of meetings. These dinners don't necessarily take place every night, but the fact that Winston Churchill's birthday happens to fall in the middle of the conference?

It's a pretty good bet that all three will be in the same room at the same time.

If so, Winston Churchill could be in for a real birthday surprise.

54

Tehran, Iran

November 27, 1943

Churchill doesn't like what he sees.

After the Cairo Conference, the British plane departed a few hours before the American plane, so when the Prime Minister and his entourage arrive at Tehran's Gale Morghe airfield at 11 a.m., the American plane is still nowhere in sight.

No reason to wait. The Prime Minister and his entourage head straight for the city.

They put Churchill in the back of a car, in a long line of vehicles in the British convoy, all of them driving on the desert road toward downtown Tehran.

It's here, on this hot road, that Churchill starts to feel uneasy. He doesn't like the security arrangements that the British and their local contacts have made for him.

"As we approached the city the road was lined with Persian cavalrymen every fifty yards for at least three miles," he later wrote of his arrival. "It was clearly shown to any evil people that somebody of consequence was coming, and which way."

He goes on about the Iranian cavalry, "The men on horseback advertised the route, but could provide no protection at all." To further signify that someone important was coming, "a police car driving a hundred yards in advance gave warning of our approach."

As Churchill's vehicle approaches the city, this unfortunate mix of elements—lots of signifiers that a high-level person was arriving, but little in the way of security—soon leads to predictable results. "Presently large crowds filled the spaces between the Persian cavalry," Churchill notes, "and as far as I could see there were few, if any, foot police."

Any member of this crowd could pose a danger to the Prime Minister, with no apparent means to prevent it.

As the vehicle slowly makes its way into and through the city, the problem gets worse. Soon the crowds are "four or five deep," and when the car stops at intersections, the onlookers "pressed to within a few feet of the car."

The Prime Minister is appalled. "There was no kind of defence at all against two or three determined men with pistols or a bomb."

At the time, no one seemed unfriendly—"I grinned at the crowd, and on the whole they grinned at me," as Churchill puts it—but a hostile enemy agent could easily be hidden among them.

By the time the Prime Minister arrives at the British embassy in the center of the city, he is deeply unnerved. "If it had been planned out beforehand to run the greatest risks and have neither the security of quiet arrival nor an effective escort the problem could not have been solved more perfectly," he'd write.

Sure, some of his reactions come from the lack of security—but there's something else gnawing at him.

Both the British and Americans are entering a faraway city that they didn't choose to be in. It's in a country they don't readily understand, with different customs from their own. On top of that, it's common knowledge that the Iranian people once had German sympathies in the war, and that many do not like the Allied occupation. As a result, there's an active underground pro-German movement in the city, and a history of local Nazi agents.

To make matters worse, the local government has provided little in the way of security, leaving the Allied leaders to fend for themselves.

Winston Churchill is not a stupid man. He's been in Tehran for barely an hour, but what he's feeling more than anything else is that he's in danger.

55

Tehran, Iran

November 27, 1943

A few flights later, Mike Reilly returns to Tehran. This time, he's got the President with him.

They arrive at the Gale Morghe airport at 3 p.m., the President's plane carrying the U.S. delegation and other top U.S. officials. If all goes according to plan, the Big Three meeting will take place tomorrow afternoon.

With a large military escort, the Presidential entourage drives from the airport to the American legation on the southern outskirts of the city. Once the President is settled—and safe—Reilly knows it's time to work. There's a lot to do before tomorrow.

Thus far, he hasn't told anyone in the President's circle about the German parachutists. It's too uncertain—better not to alarm everyone. Yet now that Reilly is back in the city, he needs an update right away from the NKVD, the Soviet intelligence service.

Racing across the city to the Soviet embassy, he finally gets some good news. The NKVD chief explains that Soviet agents have "captured some of the parachutists."

They've also learned some more details, namely that "thirty-eight Nazis had been dropped around Teheran."

"Are you sure it was thirty-eight?" Reilly asks, trying to make a slight joke about the precision of the number.

"Very sure," the Soviet spy chief replies calmly. "We examined the men we caught most thoroughly."

The chief is dead serious. "The way he said it made me happy I had not been present when the Nazis were questioned," Reilly later wrote.

He doesn't want to know what interrogation techniques the Russians used on the captured Nazis, but he certainly wants their info.

The examinations "disclosed that there were at least six German paratroopers loose in the vicinity with a radio transmitter," the official explains.

That gives Reilly the current overall picture: thirty-two Germans captured, six still on the loose armed with a radio, which means they could be communicating with their handlers back in Berlin.

Needless to say, there are still so many questions: Did all the Germans recently arrive by parachute, or have some of them been in the region longer? Who or what entity in Germany sent them? Are there more agents still to come?

The NKVD chief isn't forthcoming with any more information, at least for now.

Soviet security forces seem to be handling the situation well, but even so, clear danger remains.

Six Nazi agents on the loose are a real threat. A group that small may not be able to directly assault the Big Three compounds, given the huge security details that the American, British, and Soviets have posted. But that's not how they would operate, even with a larger number. More likely, a potential Nazi assassin would sneak in and infiltrate.

No matter how tight the security, there will be moments where Roosevelt, Churchill, and Stalin are exposed. All three need to travel by car through Tehran. And all three have to be in contact with local workers or staff.

All it takes is one gunman blending into a crowded street, a sniper finding the right rooftop, or a disguised German agent somehow infiltrating one of the facilities. Capture all the parachutists you want—if one gets through, none of it matters.

So what should the Americans do? The NKVD chief tells Reilly directly.

With all these dangers, Stalin would like to officially ask "for the President to move from the isolated American Legation to either the British or the Russian Embassy, which were side by side in the heart of town and were both heavily walled."

Reilly likes the idea. It's the smart choice.

The trouble is, the President has already told Reilly that he wants to stay at the American legation. Reilly obviously doesn't have the authority to make a decision that overrules the President's wishes. After this conversation with the Soviets, he needs to decide who he should tell, and how to handle the confidential information he has just received.

As it turns out, someone else is about to make the decision for him.

56

Mike Reilly isn't the only American making arrangements for tomorrow's summit.

Like Reilly, W. Averell Harriman, U.S. Ambassador to the Soviet Union, arrived with the President's party. Also like Reilly, he's been racing around all afternoon.

As the President and other members of the U.S. delegation get settled, Harriman starts making the rounds, facilitating plans between the American legation, the Russian embassy, the British embassy, and the military compound of General Donald Connolly, the head of the U.S. Command in Iran, where Harriman himself is staying.

The bustle continues through the evening, until finally, just before midnight, Harriman lands back at General Connolly's compound. Harriman's day had originally started at 3:30 a.m. that morning in Cairo—then they flew to Tehran—and since then, Harriman has been in a pressure cooker almost every minute. He needs a few hours' sleep before another long and difficult day ahead.

Yet, just as the Ambassador hopes to settle in for the night, he receives an urgent message from the Soviet Foreign Minister, Vyacheslav

Molotov. Harriman had already met at length with Molotov earlier that afternoon to plan the conference itinerary. He's got no idea why Molotov would need to contact him again.

Molotov, the message says, needs to see him in person now—as in *right now*—at the Soviet embassy. Molotov requests that British Ambassador Archibald Clark Kerr also join.

So much for Harriman's sleep. He quickly tracks down an Army officer, Major John Bates, and asks him to accompany Harriman across town.

It's after midnight when the two ambassadors, Harriman and Kerr, arrive with their officer escorts at the Soviet embassy. At this point, they still have no idea why Molotov has called them so late.

In the darkness, they enter the walled Soviet compound, not sure what to expect.

Molotov meets them in person. He has "received bad news," Molotov tells the two ambassadors. "German agents in Tehran ha[ve] learned of Roosevelt's presence in the city," and they are planning a "demonstration."

What does that mean? Harriman asks him to explain.

Molotov looks at them both. "There might be an assassination attempt," he says.

An assassination attempt. At the hands of German agents. They're learning this the very morning before the conference is set to begin. Unbeknownst to Harriman and Kerr, this is exactly what Mike Reilly separately learned from General Arkadiev and the NKVD.

"Even if it failed," Molotov continues, this assassination attempt "would certainly lead to shooting and might result in the killing of innocent bystanders." Furthermore, such an incident would create "a most unfortunate scandal for the Allies, which was bound to be exploited by the Nazi propaganda machine."

Naturally, the Americans want every piece of information they can get from the Soviets. As Harriman later recalled, "I pressed him within the limits of civility for details." But Molotov, a Foreign Minister and not an intelligence officer, doesn't have much more to offer.

Apparently, it was Stalin who asked him to personally share this information.

So does Stalin have a plan?

He certainly has a suggestion. To avoid danger, Roosevelt should move to the Soviet embassy rather than stay at the American legation.

The Soviet compound is large, with plenty of room. The British will be right next door. If Roosevelt moves, none of the Big Three will have to drive through the Tehran streets in broad daylight to meet with one another. Basically, they'll all be under one roof.

To back up Stalin's offer, Molotov gives Harriman a quick midnight tour through the compound to show him a villa where Roosevelt and his top staff could stay and remain independent.

The Soviets have already started working on the plumbing and making other arrangements in the event the President accepts.

Harriman looks around the villa. "Although the furnishings were overelaborate and ugly," he later recalled, "the quarters looked comfortable enough."

So what should Harriman do?

His long day still isn't over. Thanking Molotov for the information, he says goodbye to Kerr, and then travels back to General Connolly's, where he arranges to speak to both Connolly and to Mike Reilly, the head of Roosevelt's security detail.

Harriman and Reilly share with General Connolly the conversations they had with the Soviets. Both stories match up. The General, they all know, has plenty of U.S. troops on hand, should they ever need them. From there, the three men discuss options and come up with a plan.

It starts with this: Tomorrow morning, they meet with Roosevelt . . . and tell the President his life is in danger.

57

Tehran, Iran

November 28, 1943

Franklin Delano Roosevelt, the President of the United States, arrived with the rest of his team at Tehran's airport at approximately 3 p.m. on November 27.

Now, the following morning, at 9:30 a.m., he's seated in his quarters, facing top members of his military staff and security team who arranged an emergency meeting.

There are other advisors in the adjacent room, talking hurriedly to one another and walking from room to room.

They're all trying to digest what they've just heard from the Soviets: The Big Three are in danger.

During the meeting, Averell Harriman, Ambassador to the Soviet Union, does a lot of the talking. But after being briefed, others pipe in too.

Stalin and Molotov, Harriman says, want to convey that "Teheran was filled with Axis sympathizers, and that an unhappy incident might occur to any of the Heads of State driving through the city to each other."

More specifically, Russian intelligence has discovered that the Germans have dropped paratroopers in the region around the city. Some are still at large. This echoes exactly what Mike Reilly has heard directly from the NKVD officials in charge of Soviet security.

Later this afternoon, Stalin is scheduled to visit the American legation for an initial greeting, with Churchill arriving soon after. As Harriman puts it, that means that today, in several hours, "the risk of assassination of Mr. Churchill and Marshal Stalin while coming to visit the President [is] very real."

He tells Roosevelt their solution, for the President to move his quarters to the Russian embassy. This "would bring the three Heads of State so close together that there would be no need for any of them to drive about town."

Harriman adds that he personally inspected the quarters offered by the Russians and found them acceptable.

Harriman's final point is that whatever decision they make doesn't just pertain to the safety of Roosevelt—it has larger implications. As he puts it, "If we persisted in our refusal to accept quarters in the Russian compound we would be responsible for any injury that Marshal Stalin might suffer in driving through the town to consult with President Roosevelt."

After hearing from Harriman, Roosevelt wants to know what others think.

Admiral Wilson Brown offers a dissenting opinion, saying he doesn't like deferring so quickly to Stalin's demands. He points out that "it was Stalin who suggested Tehran and why was he objecting now to security?"

It's a fair point. But there's one other person Roosevelt wants to hear from: Mike Reilly, head of Presidential security. Over time, Reilly has learned that when the President calls on him to speak, he has only a brief chance to state his case. He needs to get this right.

Talking as clearly as he can, Reilly says that he "is in full agreement" that Roosevelt should move from the American legation. With Nazi agents lurking in the city, "Stalin and Churchill would be subjected to unnecessary danger when they came to visit him and also that Russian NKVD men felt FDR was risking not only his life but theirs by living outside of town."

Reilly feels the need to explain this last point further. Having spent some time with the NKVD agents, he's learned how Soviet agencies work. He explains to Roosevelt, "If anything happened to the President of the United States, we in the Secret Service would be deeply embarrassed, but the Russian Secret Service men would be dead before nightfall."

It's a hell of a detail. In the end, it's Roosevelt's call.

"Do you care which embassy I move to?" he asks.

"Not much difference, Sir," Reilly answers.

The President takes a moment to think. Despite the alarming news he just heard, he's not really focused on his personal safety—that's the job of his security staff and of U.S. military personnel. He's thinking mostly about his master strategy at the conference. The fact is, this unexpected turn of events—a Nazi assassination plot—has given him a nice opportunity.

"All right. It's the Russian then," the President says. "When do we move?"

It's a fair question. But Roosevelt isn't just asking *when* to move. He's asking *how*.

Half a dozen Nazi assassins are supposedly in Tehran. As Harriman explained, the threat of an assassination attempt on Churchill or Stalin is "very real" if they drive to the American legation—so the same holds true for Roosevelt driving the other way.

Somehow, they need to get Roosevelt—and his entire entourage—to the other side of town. And they need to pull it off without anyone knowing.

The good thing is, Mike Reilly has a plan.

58

How do you guarantee the safety of a President in a large, loud, conspicuous motorcade as it rolls through the center of a densely packed city?

The simple answer is, you can't.

That's the conclusion that Mike Reilly and his team reach while contemplating how to transport President Roosevelt from the outskirts of Tehran to the walled Soviet embassy compound over a mile away in the city's center.

"I had no stomach for sending him through the crowded streets of Tehran," Reilly later recalled. "It would have been a tough enough job normally, but with six Nazi paratroopers around somewhere it was a real headache."

It's not that the Americans can't provide security for their President. After all, there's an active U.S. Army base nearby. But simply bringing in armed troops solves only part of the problem. "We could line his entire route with soldiers," Reilly puts it, "but half a dozen fanatics with the courage to jump from airplanes could probably figure out some way to get in a shot. And it was logical to assume that, with Nazi 'chutists shooting, one shot would be plenty."

A motorcade is too big to keep secret—and they can't guarantee the President's safety if he's part of it. So where does that leave them?

With one of the best weapons in the Secret Service arsenal.

Deception.

Even today, the Secret Service still use variations of the same trick. The single best way to keep the President safe is to make people look for him in a place where he isn't.

"We lined the entire route with soldiers, shoulder to shoulder. We set up the standard cavalcade with the gun-laden jeeps fore and aft, and it traveled slowly along the streets guarded by soldiers," Reilly later described.

As the entourage proceeds slowly into the city, the Presidential sedan is at the center of it all, right in the middle. In no time, the crowds come running. Everyone's excited to see the President.

The catch is, Roosevelt isn't anywhere near the procession.

"As soon as the cavalcade left the American Legation," Reilly later explained, "we bundled the President into another car" and "put a jeep in front of him."

The two nondescript vehicles head out in a different direction from the motorcade and then go "tearing through the ancient side streets of Teheran." Meanwhile, "the dummy cavalcade wended its way slowly through the main streets."

At the city center, spectators, onlookers, and soldiers are all craning their necks at the motorcade, trying to get a good look inside the sedan that supposedly contains one of the most powerful individuals in the world.

In reality, they're catching little glimpses of Bob Holmes, the nondescript Secret Service agent who gamely accepted the role as dummy President. He's literally prepared to take a bullet for the Commander in Chief should an assassin get off a good shot.

It's Holmes, not the President, who draws "the cheers of the local citizens and I hope the curses of a few bewildered parachute jumpers from Germany."

At the same time, in the little sedan transporting the real President, a small group of three men accompany him: Admiral Leahy of the Navy, Major Boettiger of the Army, and Roosevelt's trusted friend and advisor Harry Hopkins. They'll do their best to protect the President should they run into any trouble.

Roosevelt, true to his nature, isn't worried for his own safety. In fact, he enjoys the high drama as he ducks down to avoid being seen while the two vehicles race through the winding, picturesque back-streets of the city.

"The Boss, as always, was vastly amused by the dummy cavalcade trick and the other cops-and-robbers stuff," Reilly later put it. "I was glad it amused him, because it did not amuse me much."

Indeed, the entire episode is highly stressful for Reilly and the Secret Service. Playing this elaborate trick may have been the safest option, but that doesn't mean they're out of danger. If the Nazis figure out the truth, or stumble on this little two-car transport, the President is beyond vulnerable. And if they fall for the trap and take aim at the dummy cavalcade, there are potential victims there as well, including Reilly's agent Bob Holmes. Holmes may be wearing a bulletproof vest, but a well-aimed bullet could still take his life.

It's not until the armed guards in front of the Soviet embassy wave Roosevelt's sedan through the walled entrance of the heavily guarded compound that Reilly finally breathes a sigh of relief.

On day one of the conference at least, they've kept the President safe.

Now the real adventure begins.

59

Roosevelt made careful arrangements to meet Stalin informally, one-on-one, before Churchill arrived.

After the Soviet aides show Roosevelt and his staff to the villa where they're staying, he doesn't have much time to prepare.

A few minutes later, Mike Reilly receives word that Stalin is already on his way.

"I'll talk to him in the sitting room, Mike," the President says. "Stall him a second while I get ready."

Roosevelt is seated when the Americans waiting outside first see the Soviet leader.

Emerging from the main embassy building, Stalin is flanked by a security detail, all of them now heading across the tree-lined walkway within the compound. After a full year of buildup and preparation, this is what everyone has been waiting for.

"Seeing him for the first time was indeed a shock," Reilly later wrote. The iconic image of Stalin's face was so well known all over the world, it was strange for everyone to see a somewhat diminutive and ordinary-looking person walking toward them.

"His hair was white, and his yellowish face was pockmarked," Major John Bates, one of Roosevelt's military escorts, notices. Stalin's left arm was slightly deformed, and his gait was slightly awkward. At five foot four, he was shorter than everyone else present, especially the towering Russian guards who flanked him.

Yet there was a mysterious aura around him that commanded a mix of fear and respect. "He was a small man, indeed," Reilly put it, "but there was something about him that made him look awfully big."

The American aides open the door to the villa, letting Stalin enter. Roosevelt, waiting in his wheelchair, watches as Stalin "sort of amble[s] across the room" and, with a big grin under his trademark mustache, reaches down to shake the President's hand.

"At last!" Roosevelt says, also grinning. "I am glad to see you. I have tried for a long time to bring this about."

Stalin returns the greeting, offering Roosevelt a Russian cigarette. Stalin has done his homework—he knows the President likes to smoke.

Whenever he meets someone new, Roosevelt often likes to open with something lighthearted. Pointing to a photograph on the wall of Stalin smoking a pipe, FDR suggests that, during the conference, they should get a photograph of the three Allied leaders: Stalin with his pipe, Churchill with his trademark cigar, and Roosevelt with his cigarette and filter holder.

Stalin lets out a chuckle.

Soon, everyone exits the room except for the two leaders and their respective interpreters. Roosevelt asks about progress on the Eastern front, which begins a brief conversation about a few aspects of the war. They talk about shipping delays, the role of France, the latest developments in China. It's all informal, none of it touching on the topics they both know will be covered during the formal sessions.

For Roosevelt, his real plan here is to establish some rapport and get a sense of Stalin's personality. That way, during the real meetings, he can anticipate the Soviet leader's rhythms and manner of speaking. He also wants to establish that he's an independent entity—that he and Stalin can collaborate independently of Churchill.

With this goal largely accomplished, the Big Three summit can officially begin.

In the afternoon sun, the two leaders exit the American villa and head toward the central building embassy.

The first session is scheduled for 4 p.m.

The large American and Soviet contingents arrive from one direction—as always, flanked by their armed security teams—and the British arrive from the other. Soon, all three groups are mingling in the entryway to the main conference hall.

For Churchill, it's already been a rough day. He caught a bad cold back in Cairo, and now he's got a sore throat that makes it difficult to speak. In a bad mood, he's even more agitated when Roosevelt declines his invitation for a preliminary lunch meeting. Since arriving, the President's entire focus has been on Stalin.

Once the small talk is done and the participants are seated around the conference table, each leader makes introductory remarks. The personality of each can't be hidden.

Roosevelt, who agreed to preside over this session, goes first. "As the youngest of the three present," he says with a smile, "I would like to welcome my elders."

He then adds that "he wished to welcome the new members to the family circle," and that "meetings of this character were conducted as between friends with frankness on all sides." If so, the "three great nations" could "work in close cooperation."

Up next, Churchill aims for a more lofty approach. Between these three nations, he says, "was the greatest concentration of power that the world has ever seen." They should proceed with the "absolute certainty that we held the happy future of mankind," and that he "prayed that we might be worthy of this God-given opportunity."

As for Stalin, he speaks in a matter-of-fact tone. "I take pleasure in welcoming those present. Now let us get down to business."

60

———.———

Roosevelt begins the session with a survey of America's position in the war. He describes the recent advances of U.S. forces in the Pacific theater and gives an update on American arms production and shipping. But very quickly, he gets to the subject that everyone at the table knows is most important.

Operation Overlord.

The cross-Channel attack is the one subject that almost tore apart this alliance. It's also the one that everyone knows will determine the course of the war.

As a result, Roosevelt has a clear preplanned strategy: gain Stalin's trust; put pressure on Churchill.

The President starts by making it clear that a cross-Channel attack from England to northern France has been the centerpiece of their war planning, and that "the plan adopted at Quebec involved an immense expedition and had been set at that time for May 1, 1944."

He adds, however, that there are questions about what to do with the Anglo-American forces after the fall of Rome, which they expect to occur in January. He's heard some ideas from the Prime Minister for how these forces might be utilized for future missions in the Mediterranean, but that would draw resources from and delay the schedule for the cross-Channel attack:

> We cannot do everything we would like to do in the Mediterranean and also from the United Kingdom . . . If we were to conduct any large expedition in the Mediterranean, it would be necessary to give up this important cross-Channel operation, and certain contemplated operations in the Mediterranean might result in a delay in Overlord for one month or two or three.

The goal, Roosevelt says, is that "he and the Prime Minister had desired to ascertain the views of Marshal Stalin on this point."

It's a massive softball that Roosevelt's just lobbed to Stalin, and the Soviet leader is ready to swing.

"The best method in the Soviet opinion was getting at the heart of Germany with an attack through northern or northwestern France," he says, repeating what he always says.

Stalin acknowledges that the Mediterranean operations had been "of great importance in order to produce freedom of navigation," but that "now they are of no further great importance as regards the defeat of Germany."

Just like that, Stalin, with help from Roosevelt, has put Churchill on the defensive.

It's the Prime Minister's turn to speak. He begins by saying that he wants to make clear that he "had long agreed with the United States that an invasion of North and Northwestern France across the Channel should be undertaken."

He also says, however, that the British and American troops in Italy will soon be finished with operations around Rome, and he's been contemplating "what could be done with forces in the Mediterranean area during this period to bring the greatest pressure to bear on the enemy."

He's interested in various operations east of the Mediterranean, in Greece and the Balkans, and admits that "some of the operations which had been discussed might involve a delay of some two months in Overlord."

What Churchill wants, essentially, is to keep the start date for the cross-Channel attack flexible—which means to delay it.

To Stalin, this sounds like another repeat of everything he's heard for the past two years: They say they're in for the mission, then they delay repeatedly.

Stalin demands unequivocally that "Overlord be accepted as a basis for operations in 1944 and other operations should be considered as diversionary." If they're worried about Anglo-American forces in Italy with nothing to do, they could organize a supplementary attack on southern France just before the cross-Channel attack, so they are supporting Overlord rather than delaying it.

From that point on, Stalin is relentless on the issue. As Charles Bohlen, Roosevelt's interpreter, put it, "Stalin's aim at Tehran seemed to be single-minded-confirmation that the two Western Allies would go through with their decision, made in Quebec the previous summer, to invade France in the spring of 1944."

As the session continues, the issue remains unresolved. Even when they move on to other subjects, the question of Overlord looms over everything. Until they're in sync on this key matter, there can be no unity.

The meeting ends at 7:20 p.m., but the Big Three quickly reconvene at 8 p.m. for the first ceremonial dinner of the summit.

It's hosted by the Americans, with a menu of steak and potatoes. Roosevelt personally mixes the pre-dinner cocktails so he can show off his martini recipe.

Stalin dutifully tastes one, and decides that it is "all right, but a little cold on the stomach."

During dinner, the leaders discuss several other issues. Roosevelt would like to join, but he starts to feel queasy and excuses himself. His physician determines that it's just a bout of indigestion, but advises Roosevelt to go to his quarters and rest for the night.

Once he's settled back at the villa, the President feels better. Most nights on these trips, he likes to relax, usually accompanied by his son Elliott, his close advisor and friend Harry Hopkins, and a few others on the American team.

It's been a momentous day. He learned of a Nazi assassination plot, raced through the streets of Tehran, met Soviet leader Joseph Stalin for the first time, and had a lively first meeting during the summit he's been anticipating for over a year.

As far as the conference itself, Roosevelt feels good about his strategy. He formed the rapport with Stalin that he was looking for, and his plan to team up on Churchill regarding Operation Overlord seems to be working.

Now, at the end of the day, he can finally relax, talking through it with his most trusted advisors and friends.

The trouble is, those advisors and friends are not the only ones listening.

Hidden in the room's carpets, walls, and furniture are tiny microphones too small to see. As the President and his team talk about it all, a very different set of ears is hearing every word.

61

———•———

There are six of them still out there. They've got one wireless radio.

That's how Gevork Vartanian, the nineteen-year-old NKVD agent and member of the Light Cavalry, later described the challenge they faced during the conference.

The weeks leading up to the summit had been a busy time for Vartanian and his bicycle-riding comrades in Tehran. In fact, it was a busy time for the entire NKVD working in the region.

First, they needed to crack down on the Nazis in the city. So Soviet intelligence and security forces made a sweep of arrests. No German sympathizers were spared.

The urgency increased even more when rumors started to spread—based on intelligence from a Ukrainian source—that the Germans were planning some sort of action at the conference.

Vartanian, riding his trusted bicycle, raced around the city "fourteen or sixteen hours per day," he later recalled, following suspects, tracking down leads, and sharing information.

The British did the same. The two sides don't always cooperate, but in the lead-up to the conference, Vartanian and the others were given some big news: British intelligence captured Franz Mayr, the German spy and leader of the pro-Nazi Melliun movement in Tehran.

Like others on the Soviet side, Vartanian felt a pang of jealousy when he heard that the British captured Mayr. "We wanted to get him first!"

Regardless, they had plenty else to do. The rumors of mysterious German parachute drops in and around the city kept coming. Plus, the Soviet crackdown was producing results. Exact numbers vary, but the Russians had arrested approximately two to three hundred Nazi sympathizers since the dragnet started.

Now, though, the search has narrowed to the most important group of all.

There are six of them with a radio. Six Nazi agents.

Some of the intelligence is confusing, but according to Vartanian, they parachuted in "near the town of Qom," roughly fifty miles from Tehran. The group consists of "six radio operators" though they were also "loaded with weapons."

Fortunately, the NKVD tracked the landing and "followed them to Tehran," where pro-German associates "had readied a villa for their stay."

Once the Nazis reached the villa, the NKVD made a key decision. Instead of apprehending them, they chose to simply observe. It's the right call. The Light Cavalry will follow their every move.

"While we were watching the group, we established that they had contacted Berlin by radio," Vartanian described. Even better, "we recorded their communication."

"When we decrypted these radio messages, we learnt that the Germans were preparing to land a second group of subversives for a terrorist act."

It's a key detail. According to the Soviet decryptions, these six radio operators were just the *advance* group—a scout group—with another team to follow.

Their theory on what's to come? "The assassination or abduction of the Big Three."

Of course, it's the Allies' worst fears come true—and the radio decrypts give the NKVD a key new detail.

"The second group was supposed to be led by Skorzeny himself," Vartanian recalls, referring to the SS Special Forces leader and Mussolini rescuer.

Now the NKVD must decide what to do. They can continue to surveil these agents, purposely allowing the mission to proceed so they can capture or kill the action team when they arrive in the city. Or they can try to disrupt the mission right now by storming the house and shutting down this advance team's operation.

Either way, time is short. The Allied conference has already begun.

In as few as twelve hours, another group of Nazi commandos are coming—and according to the Soviets, they'll be led by the "Most Dangerous Man in Europe."

62

November 29, 1943

Churchill still has a cold.

Plus, on the second morning of the conference, he's frustrated. Day one didn't go as well as he'd hoped. The other leaders are disregarding his arguments.

He wants to talk to Roosevelt, frankly and confidentially, as they always have. For two years, they've confronted every challenge together. Now, at this critical moment, there's distance between them.

That morning, Churchill again invites Roosevelt to lunch so they can get aligned before joining Stalin in the afternoon.

As he did the day before, Roosevelt refuses, worried that Stalin would learn about it. The last thing he needs is Stalin thinking that Roosevelt and Churchill are colluding against him.

Churchill is savvy enough to understand Roosevelt's motives, but that doesn't ease the sting.

When Averell Harriman, Roosevelt's ambassador to the Soviet Union, delivers the news, he relays that Churchill growled that he could "accept rebuffs as well as the next one." But the Prime Minister also has another message: "I shall insist on one thing: that I be host at dinner tomorrow evening. I think I have one or two claims to precedence. To begin with, I come first both in seniority and alphabetically.

In the second place, I represent the longest established of the three governments. And, in the third place, it's my birthday."

The date is set. Tomorrow. November 30. The last night the Big Three will all be together.

A birthday party.

It'll be the perfect send-off.

63

It's a sword.

A thirty-six-inch double-bladed longsword to be exact, forged in Sheffield, England, and embossed with jewels.

On the second day of the Tehran Conference, in a large conference room in the Soviet embassy, the Prime Minister, on behalf of King George VI of the United Kingdom, presents the commemorative sword to the Soviet Premier, to honor the people of Stalingrad for the heroic defense of their city in the face of the Nazi invasion. In both Russian and English, the sword bears the inscription:

To the Steel-Hearted Citizens of Stalingrad,
the Gift of King George the Sixth,
in Token of Homage of the British People

A light brass band plays in the background as Churchill solemnly presents the sword—it will soon be known as the Sword of Stalingrad—to the Soviet leader. Stalin, clearly moved, holds up the sword and kisses the scabbard.

It's a magical moment that's nearly ruined when Stalin, while showing the weapon to the others, briefly tilts the scabbard in the wrong direction and the sword slides out to the floor. General Kliment Voroshilov, accompanying Stalin, lunges and catches it just before it hits the ground.

After the ceremony, the Big Three move to the embassy's front portico, where American, British, and Soviet war photographers are waiting.

At the top of the stairs, the three leaders—wearing their finest for both the ceremony and the photo—take three adjacent seats.

It's a moment captured for the ages: at the height of the war, the three Allied leaders meeting for the first time.

In a few days—when the conference is officially made known to the public—the photographs will transmit around the world.

If Winston Churchill's face bears something of a scowl in most of the photographs, it might be because he knows he's headed for a tough afternoon. Roosevelt and Stalin are newly aligned on the issue

Allied leaders Joseph Stalin, Franklin Roosevelt, and Winston Churchill, aka the Big Three, sit for photographs just outside the Soviet embassy in Tehran, Iran, on November 29, 1943. (Courtesy of History / Bridgeman Images)

they all know will once again dominate the day's session: the plan for Operation Overlord.

Churchill and his team come ready to fight. Like before, they insist that additional operations east of the Mediterranean will have real value, and that they only want flexibility on the date of the cross-Channel attack—maybe extend it to July.

Stalin won't have it. Right away, he declares that "Overlord was the most important and nothing should be done to distract attention from that operation."

Roosevelt agrees.

From there, the pile-on continues, Roosevelt and Stalin insisting that the date be fixed in spring. Of the two of them, Stalin does more of the talking. As recorded in the minutes of the conference:

> MARSHAL STALIN said he would like to see OVERLORD undertaken during the month of May; that he did not care whether it was the 1st, 15th or 20th, but that a definite date was important.
>
> THE PRIME MINISTER said . . . The British Government was anxious to begin OVERLORD as soon as possible but did not desire to neglect the great possibilities in the Mediterranean merely for the sake of avoiding a delay of a month or two.
>
> MARSHAL STALIN said that the operations in the Mediterranean have a value but they are really only diversions.

On and on it goes. Roosevelt steps in to bolster the Soviet position, not to defend Churchill.

Churchill and his team keep fighting. For hours, they approach the topic from various directions. Everyone's frustrated. The argument gets heated.

Toward the end of the session, Stalin even crosses a line into the personal. Leaning forward, he says that he "wished to ask Mr. Churchill an indiscreet question, namely, do the British really believe in Overlord or are they only saying so to reassure the Russians?"

For Churchill, it's an attack on his integrity.

The Prime Minister is clearly offended.

Roosevelt can see that things have gone too far and suggests they adjourn for dinner. Even when they do, the tension hangs in the air.

When they reconvene—for Soviet-hosted cocktails and dinner—Churchill's mood remains sour. He's losing the argument, and as the drinks start flowing, the energy in the room stays sharp.

During dinner, the leaders shift to other subjects rather than Overlord. But as Harriman later recalled, even on these "Stalin kept needling Churchill without mercy."

The Soviet leader has a soft-spoken but biting tone that always seems aimed at the Prime Minister. According to Harriman, "Several times through the evening [Stalin] plainly implied that the Prime Minister" was "nursing some secret affection for the Germans."

The bad feelings reach a pinnacle as they discuss the possible fate of postwar Germany. Stalin worries that even a defeated Germany would be "bound to rise up again in a matter of fifteen or twenty years" unless the Allies take tough measures to contain them.

Using some very Russian humor, Stalin suggests, as a possible solution, "that some 50,000 or possibly 100,000 German military officers should be liquidated."

Maybe Churchill didn't see Stalin's "sardonic smile"—the Premier really was only joking—but either way, he's had enough.

"The British Parliament and public will never tolerate mass executions!" Churchill thunders back at Stalin. "The Soviets must be under no delusion on this point."

"Fifty thousand must be shot," Stalin counters, waving his hand casually and sticking with the joke.

"I would rather be taken out into the garden here and now and be shot myself than sully my own and my country's honor by such infamy!" the Prime Minister roars.

Roosevelt, startled by the exchange, tries to diffuse the tension. "Not fifty thousand should be shot, but only forty-nine thousand," he says, making his best attempt at humor.

The President's quip doesn't help matters. Churchill is tired of being needled and ganged up on. Minutes later, he storms out, heading for the back garden.

Chomping on his cigar and standing in the garden, he's still fuming—but as he gazes out into the night, he feels a hand on his shoulder.

It's Stalin.

He and Molotov have come out to reassure Churchill that it was all just a joke. They want to make amends.

Churchill calms down, and they walk back in together. Yet the Prime Minister is still offended that they said he was being soft on Germany. Back in the dining room, he declares to the two Soviet leaders, "I'd like to go to your front, and I'm in my seventieth year!"

The vodka flows for a few more hours. Gradually, the participants make their way home.

For Winston Churchill, it's been a brutal two days. His closest ally seems aligned against him . . . his integrity's been questioned . . . it's all been a mess.

Thankfully, tomorrow is his birthday.

That alone should make it better.

64

—— · ——

The NKVD have the Nazis in their crosshairs.

There are six Nazis in total, working out of a secret nearby safehouse and using a radio transmitter to send encrypted messages back to Berlin.

It's Vartanian's account of these tense few days that provides the few details we currently have about how the NKVD were secretly decrypting the Nazi's radio signals.

As the Soviets already told the Americans and the British, the Nazis are planning the "assassination or abduction of the Big Three." These six hidden Germans are the advance team, while the real commandos to come are "to be led by Skorzeny."

For the Soviets, this is the fork in the road. Time to make a choice.

The NKVD can continue to surveil the radio operators, purposely allowing the mission to proceed, or, with their advanced knowledge of what's to come, they can intercept, overwhelm, and capture or kill the team—including their mythic leader.

"It was tempting to seize Skorzeny himself," Vartanian later admitted, knowing the accolades this would bring.

The problem is, passively awaiting the arrival of a well-armed team of Nazi commandos is extremely dangerous.

"The Big Three had already arrived in Tehran and we could not afford the risk," Vartanian later explained. If Skorzeny's team manages to harm the Allied leaders, or even if they fail but still take out some Allied soldiers along the way, the responsibility would fall squarely on the shoulders of the NKVD agents who let them come.

One option is to simply storm in and kill the agents—or throw them in some Soviet prison—but that wouldn't be of much help. Under that scenario, the Soviets lose their one way to track Skorzeny as well as his team's arrival and whereabouts.

Instead, they come up with something a bit more nuanced. On November 28 or 29—according to Vartanian, it's somewhere within the first two days of the conference—the NKVD bursts into the house and arrests the six Nazi agents.

"We deliberately gave a radio operator an opportunity to report the failure of the mission," Vartanian later explained.

It's a clever strategy. After raiding the premises, the Soviets force one of the Germans to make a radio report to Berlin that they've been captured, and that the operation was compromised.

Once Berlin hears the news that the mission was discovered, hopefully they'll call it off.

The only question is, will the Germans believe it?

65

---·---

November 30, 1943

It's Winston Churchill's birthday, and for the third day in a row, the sun is shining in Tehran.

Overall, Roosevelt can feel his grand plan working. He's got at least some of Stalin's trust, and together they put maximum pressure on Churchill.

But he also saw that at last night's dinner, Churchill had nearly reached his breaking point. The President wanted to reach out to his friend, but he didn't want any nearby Russian seeing the two of them talking in private. That would immediately get reported to Stalin and set things back.

Instead, after the dinner, Roosevelt sent his close friend Harry Hopkins, whom Churchill was fond of, to speak candidly to the Prime Minister.

There's no record of the exact words that Hopkins said to Churchill, but the message, in a kindly tone, was this: Churchill was "fighting a losing battle in trying to delay the invasion of France," that "there was really little Churchill could do," and that the Prime Minister should "yield with grace."

Thankfully, as the bright sun hangs in the clear sky, Churchill seems to be yielding.

"Whether Hopkins's visit or something else did the trick is not known," Roosevelt's interpreter Charles Bohlen later recalled, "but apparently Churchill made his decision that night." By the end of the morning the Prime Minister is on board, and on board completely. He'll accept a set date for the cross-Channel attack.

Now, everyone can really get to work. The Americans and British military leaders conduct small meetings in different combinations to work through the details.

Meanwhile, the President and Prime Minister invite Stalin for a lunch meeting. There, Roosevelt announces that the Combined Chiefs of Staff have forged a plan for Overlord—and that the Americans and British fully agree on it.

The President reads the top line of the report for Stalin. "We will launch Overlord during May, in conjunction with a supporting operation against the South of France on the largest scale that is permitted by the landing craft available at the time."

Finally, a guarantee of a cross-Channel invasion. They'll pick a fixed date in May without delay, and will promise that the Mediterranean operations will not interfere.

Ambassador Harriman is at the table, watching the Soviet Premier's reaction. "Stalin, who had waited two years to hear those words, showed great satisfaction," Harriman later recalled.

Right there, the summit gets the burst of energy it needs. At long last, everyone is in sync.

At the 4 p.m. full staff meeting in the main conference room, Roosevelt repeats his commitment for Operation Overlord to launch in May. He makes the additional promise, per Stalin's request, that he will name a commander for the mission within a week.

Yet it's Churchill who seems to be the excited one. His sore throat is gone, and his sour mood has lifted.

"Now that the decision had been taken," he declares to the room, he believes "that Overlord should be delivered with *smashing force*."

Looking directly at the Soviet Premier, Churchill insists that in preparing this enormous mission, "it was important that close and intimate contact be maintained with Marshal Stalin." In other words, they need to coordinate their attacks on Nazi forces—and as Churchill goes on to explain, "In closing in on the wild beast all parts of the narrowing circle should be aflame with battle!"

Stalin agrees heartily and says that he will help. He thinks it likely that Hitler will try to "transfer troops from the Eastern front to oppose Overlord." As a result, he promises that "the Red Army would launch simultaneously with Overlord large scale offensives in a number of places for the purpose of pinning down German forces and preventing the transfer of German troops to the west."

Now that they're aligned, the ideas are flowing. The Soviet leader describes the strategies his armies have employed to conceal their missions, creating decoy military operations that lure the Nazi generals in the wrong direction.

Roosevelt and Churchill agree to create a "cover plan . . . in order to confuse and deceive the enemy as to the real time and place of our joint blows."

At this point, Churchill starts speaking extemporaneously, delivering one of his many famous phrases. Fake operations will be created alongside the real mission, he declares, because "truth deserves a bodyguard of lies!"

The energy couldn't be more different than yesterday. Forget two *days* . . . it's been two *years* of tension on this issue, but here they are, all moving in lockstep.

The feelings are so positive, the leaders agree to end the session early. There are plenty of other topics to discuss beyond Overlord, but they'll cover those during the final daytime meetings tomorrow.

For now, it's time to celebrate.

66

From the moment Churchill said he would host his own birthday party, his staff has scrambled around the clock. The menu, the silverware, the music, the drinks—everything has to be perfect.

Unlike the previous dinners, this one is held at the British embassy, a few hundred yards from the Soviet embassy across a cordoned-off street. Since the front entrance involves a steep flight of stairs, Churchill even has his staff build a ramp alongside the building to accommodate Roosevelt's wheelchair.

In addition, the security teams are also extra busy. The U.S. Secret Service detail, led by Mike Reilly, does a full survey of the grounds and interior. They comb every shrub outside, and every piece of furniture inside, searching for bombs, explosives, any evidence of enemy activity.

They find nothing.

When the American team finishes, the Soviet security team takes over and repeats the process.

As dinner approaches, the Prime Minister is in fine form greeting the arriving guests outside. Spotting the American Secret Service team—mostly young men with crew cuts—forming a long straight line, Churchill knows that the President is coming, but he still makes a joke, asking if they're preparing to sing a chorus.

Just before 8:30 p.m., Roosevelt arrives, his son Elliott pushing his wheelchair.

The two leaders greet each other. For three days, Roosevelt has been cagey with Churchill, keeping him at arm's length in order to establish equal footing with Stalin, while applying pressure to the British. Now, the gamesmanship is gone.

Roosevelt even made sure he brought a special birthday gift for the Prime Minister, sending Ambassador Harriman to pick it up: a twelfth-century Persian vase.

"May we be together for many years," Roosevelt says, handing his friend the antique bowl.

Stalin's entrance, a few minutes later, isn't so smooth.

After he and Molotov climb the front stairs, a young member of the British staff sees that the Premier is wearing a cape. The young man innocently approaches to help take it off. In an instant, the NKVD agents posted in the hall close in. One of them grabs the young man, another sticks a pistol in his ribs, and they drag him off roughly down the hall.

After the scuffle, the various guests make their way to a grand room where a banquet table has been prepared. Greetings are exchanged, seats are taken, and the three Allied leaders sit side by side at the head. The birthday host sits between the other two.

For dinner, Churchill decides that instead of making speeches, they'll follow the Russian tradition of giving plentiful toasts. So as the guests start eating, the toasts start flowing—as do the accompanying glasses of vodka, whiskey, and wine.

Roosevelt starts with a ceremonial toast to King George VI of the United Kingdom.

Churchill follows with a toast to the President. Roosevelt, he says with feeling, is "a man who had devoted his entire life to the cause of defending the weak and helpless, and to the promotion of the great principles that underlie our democratic civilization."

Next, he toasts Stalin for his leadership of the Soviet armies. In the Russian tradition he should be known as "Stalin the Great," Churchill says, getting a few laughs.

Stalin goes next, raising his glass in response. But, he says of Churchill's compliments, "the honors which had been paid him really belong to the Russian people."

Roosevelt raises his glass again, to say happy birthday to the Prime Minister and to express "his joy in the friendship which had developed between them in the midst of their common efforts in this war."

Each toast gets a warm round of applause. It all seems entirely sincere. Tonight, Bohlen later reflected, "probably represented the high-water mark of Anglo-American-Soviet collaboration during the war."

The toasts continue through dinner, with many joining in.

Once the plates are cleared, a waiter places a massive cake in front of Churchill, containing sixty-nine candles shaped in a "V" for victory. It takes a few tries, but Churchill eventually blows them out.

Yet as the party goes on, there's one person who's clearly not enjoying himself. Mike Reilly. All evening, he stands along the wall, eyes darting, trying to study every part of the room at once.

For three days, Reilly has been on edge, constantly worried about the President's safety. For him, the conference began with news of Nazi parachutists and hidden assassins. Rightfully, he hasn't been able to relax since.

As dinner ends and everyone's about to get up, Roosevelt asks to give one more toast.

Raising his glass, he toasts the people of the three countries: the United States, the United Kingdom, and the Soviet Union. Looking around the room, he says, "We have differing customs and philosophies and ways of life. Each of us works out our scheme of things according to the desires and ideas of our own peoples. But we have proved here at Teheran that the varying ideals of our nations can come together in a harmonious whole, moving unitedly for the common good of ourselves and of the world."

This gets the biggest applause of the night. The gathered guests rise from their seats, cocktails in hands, to mill around the room. With smiles and laughter, these visitors from three different countries continue to mingle.

At one point, the music swells a little and Churchill, now officially sixty-nine years old, begins to demonstrate some dance moves. Before anyone can stop him, he starts kicking up his short legs, his rendition of a traditional Scottish dance called the hornpipe.

Even Mike Reilly, exhausted as he is, notices this. He's the one who'll later share the story for the world to remember. But in the moment, he can't possibly enjoy it. He's still a nervous wreck.

If Reilly could see just a little into the future, he'd know that the evening will end just fine.

By 2 a.m. or so, all the guests will be safely back in their quarters.

Whatever potential assassins are out there, they never make it to tonight's celebration. Within thirty-six hours, the three Allied leaders are all gone from the city, without incident.

Of course, Reilly doesn't know this yet. So here at the party, he can't possibly be at ease.

But there's someone else in the room who is: the American President, Franklin Roosevelt.

This summit was Roosevelt's vision, more than anyone else's. For more than a year, he fought for it, overcoming every imaginable obstacle. At many points, it seemed like it would never take place.

But it did.

Here, in the city of Tehran, the three Allied leaders gathered for the world to see—and in a few days, the photographs of them together will spread across the globe, creating a surge of confidence on the Allied side.

It's not just the photographs, though. The Allied leaders, representing their three countries, set aside their differences and forged a plan, one to end this terrible war and destroy the tyrannical Nazi regime that started it.

Yet at this moment, the war is still raging all over the world. The horrors continue, never seeming to let up. For the Allies, the road ahead is long, and there are many dark and difficult days to go.

Still, tonight, in this room, there are some hopeful moments to savor.

Roosevelt's grand vision for a Big Three summit has been realized.

The Allied leaders have avoided an assassination plot.

And Winston Churchill is dancing.

PART V

Aftermath

67

Washington, D.C.

December 17, 1943

President Roosevelt has been gone for more than a month.

Now, at 4:15 p.m., he steps to the podium in front of the press corps gathered in a tightly packed room in the West Wing of the White House.

He arrived back in Washington, D.C., at 9:15 this morning, so he's only been home seven hours. The Tehran Conference concluded two weeks ago. After Tehran, he and Churchill went back to Cairo for more conferences, then the President made a few stops along the Mediterranean to visit troops before finally coming home.

This is his first time talking to the White House press corps about the trip. "I thought it was in every way a success," he begins, keeping it brief, "not only from the point of view of the conduct of the war, but also . . . based on the general thought that when we win the war, we don't want to have another one as long as this generation is alive."

When a reporter asks him about his "personal impressions" of Joseph Stalin, Roosevelt is similarly brief. "The actual fact of meeting him lived up to my highest expectations. We had many excellent talks."

The answers seem canned, the reporters probably assuming that Roosevelt is exhausted. He has reason to be—the journey took him through a dozen countries spanning three continents. Mike Reilly, who's standing by FDR's side during the press conference, later estimates that on the trip to Cairo and Tehran, the President traveled "by land, sea, and air" a total of 17,442 miles.

Roosevelt doesn't say much about the trip beyond what the reporters already know, so they're quickly ready to move on and ask about domestic affairs.

Then the President gets a glint in his eye—as if he suddenly remembers an amusing detail. He starts describing his initial arrival at the U.S. legation in Tehran.

"That night, late, I got word from Marshal Stalin that they had got word of a German plot."

A German plot? The reporters start scribbling.

"Everybody was more or less upset, Secret Service, and so forth," Roosevelt explains. Stalin, he adds, "pleaded with me to go down to the Russian Embassy, they have two or three different buildings in the compound, and he offered to turn one of them to me . . . and that would avoid either his, or Mr. Churchill's, or my having to take trips through the streets to see each other."

All of it's a surprise to the White House press corps.

"Of course, in a place like Tehran there are hundreds of German spies, probably," Roosevelt continues. He pauses, and then, with a little smile, "I suppose it would make a pretty good haul if they could get all of us going through the street."

This gets a laugh. The reporters don't ask many follow-up questions, and Roosevelt moves on to other topics.

The next day, *The New York Times* prints the headline STALIN BARED PLOT AGAINST PRESIDENT. The story explains, "President Roosevelt disclosed today what the Russians said was a plot endangering his life at Tehran, the knowledge of which caused him to move his residence from the American legation to the Soviet embassy." There are no details beyond what the President told the reporters, and it gets no follow-up in the press.

If Roosevelt wasn't very talkative about Tehran, it might've been because by the time he finally returned home, the story of the Big Three summit had already been shared all over the world.

In terms of impact, the summit achieved exactly what Roosevelt had hoped. It was a global sensation and dominated headlines. The timing couldn't have been better, making it the perfect cap to the military successes of the summer and fall. It made clear that the Allies have the momentum. The iconic image of the three leaders side by side will galvanize the war effort for the coming year.

The spirit of cooperation at the conference filled Roosevelt with enormous optimism—not just about the Allied war effort, but also the world peace that will follow victory. On December 1, just before leaving Tehran, the three leaders signed a "Declaration of the Three Powers," which a few days later they shared with the press.

The declaration promises that the Allies will "make a peace which will command the good will of the overwhelming mass of the peoples of the world, and banish the scourge and terror of war for many generations." At war's end, the declaration states, "we shall seek the cooperation and the active participation of all nations, large and small, whose peoples in heart and mind are dedicated, as are our own peoples, to the elimination of tyranny and slavery, oppression and intolerance."

In addition to these grand sentiments, the Big Three's declaration asserts that "we have concerted our plans for the destruction of German forces" and that "our attack will be relentless and increasing." The leaders state that "the common understanding which we have here reached guarantees that victory will be ours."

These promises of victory dominate the news. PRESIDENT ROOSEVELT, PRIME MINISTER WINSTON CHURCHILL, AND SOVIET PREMIER JOSEPH STALIN ARE NOW PREPARING PLANS TO CRUSH GERMANY FINALLY AND PREVENT HER FROM EVER AGAIN SCOURGING THE WORLD WITH WAR, a typical American headline declared on December 2, two days after the conference.

While the leaders' official statement provides no military specifics, the press starts digging and soon reports that in Tehran, Roosevelt, Churchill, and Stalin agreed upon operations that the Allied world has long awaited: an Anglo-American attack against Nazi forces in Western Europe. And it will come in the spring of 1944.

Roosevelt's ambition for the conference—in addition to the grand symbolism of the Big Three meeting in person—had always been to forge a clear and binding military plan for 1944. After much back and forth, this goal was finally achieved.

Roosevelt and Churchill made their promise to Stalin. In that promise came a promise to the world.

Now comes the hard part.

They have to deliver.

68

Spring 1944

For two years they've discussed it, debated it, dissected it, revised it, renamed it, and—repeatedly—postponed it.

Operation Overlord. The cross-Channel attack.

By the time Roosevelt returns to the United States in late December, planning is already in high gear.

Just as the three Allied leaders discussed in Tehran, a key component of the plan will be deceit. The war planners craft a complex series of decoy missions, complete with elaborate command structures, aircraft and naval movements, ghost armies, and radio traffic.

The organization of these dummy missions is such a big undertaking, it gets its own name, Operation Bodyguard—a homage to Churchill's statement in Tehran that "truth needs a bodyguard of lies."

As for the real mission, Operation Overlord's supreme commander, U.S. General Dwight D. Eisenhower, considers several options for the most advantageous amphibious landing site. He ultimately settles on a long stretch of windswept beaches in the Normandy region of northern France, east of the port city of Cherbourg.

The planning is complex and all-consuming. It will be the largest combined-arms operation in the history of warfare.

The first wave alone involves 5,300 ships, 1,500 tanks, 12,000 aircraft, and a total of 150,000 soldiers. That's just for the initial landing. A total of one million troops are at the ready to join the mission in successive waves.

Although it's being led by an American, Overlord is a joint operation between the U.S. and British commands. At one point in the planning, Prime Minister Churchill declares that he will personally accompany the British officers as they lead the mission. He wants to be on one of the seacraft that land on the beaches.

Eisenhower wisely convinces him otherwise.

Due primarily to weather conditions, the operation is delayed for several weeks past the agreed-upon May deadline. Anticipation mounts, not just in the Allied armed forces, but all over the world.

The Nazi leadership are aware that the Americans and British are coming—that they'll attack Western Europe sometime in spring, probably in France. What they don't know is exactly where or when.

Hitler had long thought that the Pas-de-Calais peninsula was the most likely landing spot for the Allies, and that's where the Wehrmacht concentrates its forces. But the German's "Atlantic Wall" defense, organized by Field Marshal Erwin Rommel, is designed to be flexible, and the Wehrmacht's fearsome tank and infantry divisions will be able to move along the coast to meet the enemy whenever they arrive.

By the beginning of June, the tension is excruciating.

Then, in the early hours of June 6, German soldiers in northern France spot a few Allied paratroopers in the skies.

This is it.

The invasion is coming.

69

---·---

June 6, 1944

"The deciding day of this war has dawned," Nazi Minister of Propaganda Joseph Goebbels writes in his diary early that morning, just after the first report reaches him.

The Allied forces aren't coming quite where the Germans expected, so the Wehrmacht commanders start racing infantry divisions along the Normandy coast to meet the incoming invasion.

In Moscow, in Washington, D.C., in London, and in cities all over the world, the early breathless rumors and hints arrive that the long-awaited invasion is underway. All anyone can do is wait.

In preparation for the attack, the Allied Combined Chiefs of Staff divided the roughly fifty-mile stretch of the Normandy beaches into five adjacent zones. Each zone has its own code name: Utah, Omaha, Gold, Juno, and Sword.

In the early light of dawn, the initial landing craft approach the Normandy shores. On Utah, the westernmost beach, the landing U.S. troops meet only minor resistance from the enemy. Likewise on Gold and Sword, British and Canadian troops make their landings with moderate casualties.

But on Omaha, the beach east of Utah, everything goes wrong.

Here, the storm-swept waters of the Channel are much rougher than expected. The landing craft encounter sandbars and can't get close enough to shore. Enemy artillery starts to rain down on the boats, creating chaos.

In the early botched attempts to land, panicking soldiers tumble from the craft and drown in the freezing waters. Several tanks also slide off the landing craft prematurely and sink in the Channel, taking their crews with them.

The soldiers who don't drown find themselves in frigid neck-deep water. Carrying twenty pounds of gear underwater, they slowly push toward shore with rifles held over their heads. As the first wave of GIs stumble onto the beach, they're instantly cut down by German machine guns and artillery firing at them from the bluffs and sand dunes. Many soldiers, especially those who have never experienced combat before, simply panic. Some dive to the ground, immobilized by terror at the carnage around them.

"There were men crying with fear, men defecating themselves," one young American private later recalled. "I lay there with some others, too petrified to move . . . At one point something hit me in the arm. I thought I'd taken a bullet. It was somebody's hand, taken clean off by something."

In several hours of fighting during the Omaha beach landing, eight hundred U.S. soldiers die. But while the bodies pile up along the shore, the ships and soldiers keep coming.

By midday, they've established a footing—and by afternoon, some soldiers have reached the bluffs.

Casualties along the beaches continue to mount throughout the long day and evening. At nightfall, the Americans have suffered roughly 2,400 deaths—but have landed 34,000 troops.

Each of the beaches has its own story. Yet in total, by midnight of June 7, over 150,000 troops have landed on the Normandy coast, and the Allies have established beachheads in each of the five zones.

In the first twenty-four hours, the total number of U.S., British, and Canadian casualties is roughly 10,000, with a similar number on the German side. These numbers are small compared to the cataclysmic battles on the Eastern front; strategically, however, the consequences of the landing are enormous. Now Anglo-American forces have a clear and protected entry point into Western Europe.

As much as the first day of the Normandy landings will later be memorialized, the fighting inland in the subsequent days is equally fierce. Here, Allied forces encounter the Wehrmacht's vaunted tank divisions. But with a large numerical advantage and superior airpower, the Allies keep pressing forward.

By the end of June, after three weeks of combat, the Anglo-American forces have a secure foothold in northwestern France. From here, they can start to move, slowly but steadily, across the French countryside in the direction of Berlin.

Hitler and his commanders would have liked to throw the entire might of the German army at the approaching American and British ground forces in northern France.

Yet they can't—because thousands of miles away, the massive Soviet forces along the Eastern front are also on the move. They're pushing relentlessly toward Germany from the other side.

For the remainder of the war, Nazi ground forces will be divided.

There are still many dark days and terrible battles ahead.

But for the Allies, the end is in sight.

70

Berlin, Germany

April 30, 1945

A pistol and a cyanide pill.

The Führer, Adolf Hitler, carries these with him to the *Führerbunker*, his underground study beneath the Reich Chancellery Garden in Berlin. Much of the city above him is in ruins from American bombs and Soviet artillery.

Five months earlier, in November 1944, he fled the Wolf's Lair when the Red Army reached East Prussia.

He now sits on a small couch in the study. Seated beside him is Eva Braun, his longtime romantic partner. Yesterday, they finally got married in the middle of the night in a tiny underground ceremony. Following Nazi regulations, in their wedding vows they each affirmed their pure Aryan origins.

A few hours after the ceremony, Hitler dictated to his personal secretary a final testament.

In it, he named his successors to lead the Reich. He also included a final screed. "Centuries will pass away," the testament declares, but "the hatred will ever renew itself against . . . [the] international Jewry."

Now, he and his new bride sit together on this tiny couch. Outside the closed door, a uniformed soldier stands guard. At roughly 3:15 p.m., according to plan, Braun puts the cyanide pill in her mouth and bites down on it—while Hitler raises the pistol to his right temple and pulls the trigger.

The Führer is dead.

He was, in Winston Churchill's words, "the repository and expression of the most virulent hatreds that have ever corroded the human breast."

But it wasn't just Hitler.

It was an entire regime. It was a hateful ideology that began decades earlier, festering and growing. First, it gripped a political party, then it spread to a nation.

It's easy to hate one man—but every one of Hitler's appalling decisions was supported by countless enablers and collaborators within a vast, powerful political and cultural movement.

In the hours after Hitler's death, one of those who races to handle the Führer's remains is Joseph Goebbels, the Nazi Propaganda Minister. Goebbels and a few others use gasoline to cremate Hitler's and Braun's bodies in the Chancellery gardens above the bunker.

The following evening, Goebbels also kills himself. That same night, Goebbels's wife, Magda, instructs an SS doctor to put cyanide pills in the mouths of her six youngest children, aged four to twelve, before taking her own life.

In the coming days and weeks, American and Soviet forces will overtake Berlin. The Nazi Party is done. The Allies will scour all of Germany and former Axis territories to find and arrest the remaining Nazi officials who are not already captured or dead.

It's a daunting task to locate, identify, and seize these thousands of officials and military officers who had composed the Reich's leadership.

Among those the Allies apprehend during this time is Walter Schellenberg, the former Nazi foreign intelligence leader. In June 1945, roughly two months after the fall of Berlin, the British capture him in Denmark, where he'd been trying to arrange his own arrest.

In the several months prior, behind Hitler's back, Schellenberg had been secretly collaborating with SS leader Heinrich Himmler to try and negotiate peace terms with the Allies. As a bargaining chip, Schellenberg was ready to offer to arrange for the release of thousands of Jewish prisoners from concentration camps.

By doing so, Schellenberg had convinced Himmler that they had a chance to salvage some elements of the German government and stop the Allies from destroying Berlin.

This last-ditch effort was doomed to fail. The idea that the Allies would ever negotiate in good faith with Himmler—the founder of the all-powerful SS, a key architect of the death camps, and the person many believed would succeed Hitler—was preposterous. As Roosevelt had promised at the Casablanca Conference in early 1943, the Allied policy was unconditional surrender. They weren't going to negotiate with Himmler, or Schellenberg, or any other Nazi leader.

Upon his arrest, Schellenberg, always a cagey operator, tried to position himself as a friend to the Allies. He had no part in planning the war, he tells them, and was not personally responsible for the atrocities committed by Nazi leadership. Yet, with his intimate knowledge of the inner workings of the party, he has much knowledge to offer them.

To some extent, this posture works. Allied intelligence files describe Schellenberg in flattering terms: "Handsome and extremely well-groomed . . . has well-manicured hands . . . soft voice, very well spoken."

After learning more about his position as head of foreign intelligence for the SD, the British request that he be transferred to London for extensive interrogation because he "is undoubtedly in possession of information of the highest importance."

For the next two years, the Allies interrogate Schellenberg extensively. Ultimately they charge him with a few relatively modest crimes.

Eventually, he testifies at the Nuremberg trials. He's forthcoming with information that implicates others, but careful to avoid implicating himself. Unlike many of his former colleagues of similar or higher rank, Schellenberg is spared the death penalty.

Instead, on November 4, 1949, the Court sentences Schellenberg to six years in prison. He serves two years of the sentence then obtains a release due to ill health. He spends his last two years in Switzerland and then Italy, where he devotes himself to writing a lengthy memoir about his life and career within the Nazi Party. He dies on March 31, 1952, at the age of forty-two.

Another Nazi official caught in the Allies' dragnet shortly after Berlin's fall is Waffen-SS Lieutenant Colonel Otto Skorzeny, the infamous rescuer of Mussolini.

In the final year of the war, Skorzeny had become one of Hitler's favorite military officers, receiving increasingly prestigious military commands. He led German forces in Western Europe, as well as in battles against the Soviets during the Red Army's final push through Eastern Europe to Berlin.

Unlike Schellenberg, Skorzeny has no interest in forging peace with the Allies. He's a military man and Nazi soldier to the core. In early April 1945, as the Allies close in, he embarks on a high-risk scheme to airlift dozens of Special Forces units to the snowy Austrian mountains, where he plans to lead a three-thousand-strong paramilitary resistance against the occupying Allied troops.

Skorzeny and some of his men make it to Austria, but they have little in the way of supplies and organization. In the wake of Hitler's suicide and the fall of Berlin, the situation appears increasingly hopeless. Like many Nazi officials and officers, he has a decision to make.

He could arrange for aircraft to lift him and a few others from the mountains and make an escape to a neutral country. But to take this option, Skorzeny considers, "would mean good-bye to everyone and everything—home, family, and comrades."

There's also the grim option taken by Hitler, Goebbels, and several other Nazi officials. Skorzeny considers it, but wavers. "As for suicide, many have felt that it was the only way out, but I considered it my duty to stand by my men and share their fate. I had done nothing wrong and had nothing to fear from our former enemies."

He and his remaining commandos descend from the Austrian alps and, after establishing communication with local U.S. commanders, Skorzeny turns himself in on May 16.

At first, the American authorities don't quite realize who they have in their midst. They treat him like a typical captured enemy officer—until they discover who he really is. Minutes later, Skorzeny later describes, "a dozen submachine-guns were pointing at me and the interpreter asked me to hand over my pistol, which I did . . . Then I was frisked and stripped naked." The local command sends him away for higher-level interrogations.

For the next two years, U.S. and British officials transfer Skorzeny from city to city and from prison to prison. Intelligence authorities interrogate him dozens of times. He occasionally endures rough treatment, including solitary confinement and sleep deprivation.

His most famous act—the rescue of Mussolini—is not strictly a war crime, but he faces charges for other activities during several other phases of the war, including the alleged murder of Allied POWs.

Ultimately, a Nuremberg tribunal acquits him of all charges, but he still faces lengthy detention as part of the Allied "denazification" program. He also faces potential charges in Denmark and Czechoslovakia for his wartime activities in those countries.

In 1948, he manages to escape from Allied detention in a complex plot in which three German friends dress as U.S. officers and secure his release. Since Skorzeny was never charged with a crime, international authorities don't waste more resources to track him down.

After that, he embarks on a postwar life that takes him throughout Europe and South America. Leaning on his mythic reputation from the war, he contracts himself to various governments and other entities as a Special Forces expert. He aligns himself with a range of right-wing militia groups and movements. At one point, he forms a shadowy company, the Paladin Group, that offers clandestine services and Special Ops expertise.

In one of history's amazing ironies, Skorzeny—lifelong Nazi and formerly one of Adolf Hitler's favorite military officers—even works as a contractor for Israel's Mossad intelligence organization.

Skorzeny, like Schellenberg, writes memoirs of his life during and after the war. In them he presents himself as a true patriot and soldier for Germany—someone who only wanted to serve his country. He expresses no contrition that he fought for a regime that committed some of the worst atrocities in history.

In the end, though, there's one last thing that Skorzeny has in common with Schellenberg. Despite all the interrogations that they both endured in Allied custody, neither ever says a word—nor is asked, apparently—about the alleged plot to kill Roosevelt, Stalin, and Churchill at the Tehran Conference in November 1943.

In the sweep of world-changing events that followed the summit, the entire episode was seemingly forgotten.

But that doesn't mean it completely disappeared.

71

In the months and years following the Big Three conference in Tehran—and in the months and few years immediately following the end of the war—not much was publicly said or written about the assassination plot of November 1943.

Behind the scenes, however, there were rumblings questioning some of the details, and even questioning the plot itself.

Shortly after FDR gave his December 17 press conference—where he said that if the plot succeeded, it would've been "a pretty good haul"—at least one person back in Tehran made it clear that they didn't appreciate it.

Joe Spencer, the head of British intelligence services in the region, thought that the President was irresponsible to spread unverified information to the public. Spencer claimed the story of the plot was unreliable because Spencer himself had not seen any evidence of it. He also didn't like Roosevelt's mention of "hundreds of German agents" in Tehran because Spencer's team believed they had successfully cleared the city of most, if not all, German agents.

Naturally, Spencer wasn't about to pick a public fight with the President of the United States—especially in the months just before

Operation Overlord—but he did issue an internal memo to the British services in the region.

The memo takes a slightly sarcastic tone. "While agreeing with Mr. Roosevelt that the assassination of the three leaders would have been 'a pretty good haul,' it must be pointed out that, as far as this office is aware, there is no truth whatsoever in the reports given in the press or on the radio." In the classic manner of intelligence professionals, Spencer criticizes the press for running with the story. "Such careless reporting and broadcasting is harmful," he scolds.

Spencer oversaw British intelligence in the region before and during the conference, so his opinion shouldn't be ignored. Yet, it's also true that Spencer didn't know everything about Nazi activities in Iran. In fact, he couldn't have.

At the time, security and intelligence in Iran was divided between the British and the Soviets, with the British in charge of the southern half of the country, and the Soviets in charge of the northern. Tehran was a shared effort. Because every report of the assassination plot came from the Soviet side—the NKVD—it's possible or even likely that British intelligence wouldn't have known about the German agents that the Soviets were tracking.

Compounding this, the Soviet intelligence services were—and the Russian spy services still are—infamous for being the most secretive in the world. Unlike the American and British agencies, the NKVD and its successors rarely, if ever, release records to the public or share them with other governments. Although the Soviets and British were allies during the war, the relationship was characterized by rivalry and distrust.

Spencer's comments also reflect his own self-interest. As the person charged with knowing about enemy activity in Iran, he might've been embarrassed to learn that the Soviets discovered thirty-eight Nazi paratroopers and a plot so dangerous that it caused the Americans to move across the city. Certainly, it wasn't a good look for Spencer to have another agency warn the Big Three in advance. His dismissal of the plot may have been simply a way to save face and protect the reputation of his agency.

Spencer isn't the only one to privately throw some cold water on the assassination details, however. Averell Harriman, Roosevelt's ambassador to the Soviet Union, who first reported the plot to the President based on the account from Soviet Foreign Minister Molotov, left the conference with nagging questions about what had transpired.

Soon after the summit, Harriman found himself in a room with Molotov and decided to ask the Foreign Minister, candidly, how serious the plot really was. "When the conference was over, I specifically asked Molotov if there had been a plot," Harriman later recalled. "He said they had taken precautions because of rumors. He never said there was a specific plot."

The conversation left Harriman unsure whether a real Nazi plot existed.

Harriman's skepticism—and Molotov's apparent uncertainty of the evidence—was counterbalanced by others who attended the conference and believed that the plot was most definitely real.

Churchill himself asserted afterward that he was sure there was a plot to kill the Big Three—and his certainty was matched and outdone by his personal head of security during the conference, police detective Walter H. "Tommy" Thompson. Thompson later claimed that he personally learned on the ground, presumably through conversations with NKVD agents, of at least sixty German parachutists who had landed in or near Tehran on the eve of the conference, and that many of those captured were armed with guns and explosives.

Which brings us back to Mike Reilly, Roosevelt's head of security. Of all the Americans who were in Tehran at the time, Reilly learned the fullest and most comprehensive version of the plot from Soviet sources.

Reilly's entire job and purpose was to determine credible threats to the President—and separate them from the rumors and fakes. He had a lot of experience at this, during both peace and war, and he found the NKVD reports to be entirely legitimate. It's why he personally convinced Roosevelt to get into an elaborate fake motorcade and move to the Soviet embassy. Reilly never doubted the veracity of the NKVD's claims about the plot, even years later when he wrote his memoir.

In the years following the end of the war, the initial murkiness of

the assassination plot was made murkier by the fact that the only people who would know for certain the extent and details of the plot—
namely, the Nazis who planned it—would never, ever admit to it.

By the late 1940s, Nuremberg prosecutors were pushing aggressively to charge and convict former Nazi officials with war crimes.
The tribunals eventually sentenced a total of thirty-seven former Nazi
officials to the death penalty and sentenced many more to long prison
terms.

For any former Nazi official or German military officer to reveal
participation in a plot to kill the Allied leaders—or even to reveal secret
knowledge of such a plot—might be, literally, suicide.

For this reason, the emerging lack of witnesses or any paper trail
on the German side is unsurprising and doesn't prove much either
way. Someone like Walter Schellenberg, who would almost by defi-
nition have been involved in any assassination plot in Tehran—he
was in charge of foreign intelligence and oversaw all the other secret
missions to Iran the year before the conference—would've remained
totally silent about it and eliminated any evidence.

Still, the lack of any real evidence on the Nazi side, and the refusal
of the Soviets at the time to share more concrete information, left
some with lingering questions.

A skeptical view of the plot—generally championed by the
British—began to take hold.

Yet, even for the top skeptics, it's impossible to ignore one simple
detail.

If there wasn't a real, verified Nazi assassination plot against the Big
Three, why would the Soviets invent one? Or to ask it in a different
way: Why would they scramble to notify the Americans at midnight
the night before the start of the conference, urging Roosevelt to move
his entire delegation across the city?

The answer, it turns out, adds a brand-new mysterious wrinkle to
the story.

72

He was still just a kid.

In November 1943, at the time of the Big Three conference, Sergo Beria had recently turned nineteen years old. He was in Tehran with his father, Lavrentiy Beria, the notorious head of the NKVD, who'd traveled with Stalin to the meeting.

According to Sergo's account many years later, on that first morning in Tehran, Stalin asked to meet with him. Because young Sergo knew how to speak and read English, Stalin gave him a special assignment. Every morning, Stalin instructed, Sergo should translate from English to Russian some secret recordings from the night before.

The source of these recordings? Audio obtained from secret microphones planted within the American villa at the Soviet embassy. Where Franklin Roosevelt was staying.

In other words, the Soviets were bugging FDR's quarters.

"I want to entrust you with a mission that is delicate and morally reprehensible. You are going to listen to the conversations that Roosevelt will have with Churchill, with the other British, and with his own circle," the younger Beria later recalled Stalin telling him.

Why? "It is now that the question of the second front will be settled. I know that Churchill is against it. It is important that the Americans support us in this matter," Stalin explained.

The young man followed orders and, every morning at 6 a.m., busily listened to, translated, and transcribed the recordings of the President talking to his aides the night before. At precisely 8 a.m., he shared the transcripts with Stalin.

The younger Beria's account of the bugging has not been proven and is probably not provable. But it is plausible. Stalin was famous for secretly recording enemies and allies alike.

Over time, some have argued that if Beria's account is true, Roosevelt was gullible to allow his private conversations to be heard by a foreign leader at an event of such critical importance. But it's also possible, as others have suggested, that FDR and his team were experienced enough with Stalin that they would've assumed any room within the Soviet embassy was bugged, and that FDR would've intentionally only said things that he wanted Stalin to hear. In this way, they'd be using the fact that their rooms were bugged as a tool to manipulate the Soviets.

If this was true, there's another big layer of complicated gamesmanship going on during the Tehran summit beyond what transpired in the conference rooms.

In any event, the possibility that Stalin bugged Roosevelt's room is fodder for the skeptical view of what really happened. The theory is simple: The Soviets made up the Nazi plot so that they could eavesdrop on FDR. In the words of former British intelligence officer Kenneth Strong, "I still assume that the Russians wanted precisely what they got. They used the plot to persuade Roosevelt to move into a villa in the compound of the Russian embassy in Teheran. And you may be sure that was well bugged."

Countering this, in the postwar years, some Russian journalists and researchers studied the alleged plot from a different angle. They would generally take the NKVD's initial claims at face value, and then fill in details with a mix of research and speculation. Over time, a host of theories began emerging, most of them interesting but unverifiable.

At one point, the CIA even opened a short file devoted to tracking postwar Soviet stories about the Tehran plot. Maybe they're a form of propaganda, the CIA theorized, deciding that the U.S. should therefore be aware of any Soviet efforts that might shape the historical narrative.

As more time passed, the history of the assassination plot became colored by the Cold War. In this era of rising hostilities between the West and the Soviet Union, the Americans and British couldn't allow the Soviets to be the heroes who saved the day. Instead, it must be that the plot was all a hoax to deceive and manipulate Roosevelt.

The Soviets, meanwhile, had the opposite agenda. Feeling unjustly vilified by the Western democracies, they had to praise the Motherland in the face of such criticism. In their framing, it was the Soviet intelligence services who heroically thwarted a Nazi plot that could've killed the Allied leaders. For this, the Western world owes the Soviet Union a debt of gratitude.

These diverging views of the plot reflected increasing tensions between the East and West about how the war was remembered. The Soviets began to resent the United States and the United Kingdom for downplaying, or simply forgetting, the dominant role of the Soviets in defeating Nazi Germany. Soviet critics could point to many Western mass media portrayals of the war—Hollywood movies, newsreels, radio programs, and even history textbooks taught in schools—in which the United States and Great Britain heroically saved the world from Hitler, while the USSR is barely mentioned, if at all.

These grievances came from a deep place. By any measure, the Soviet Union did more of the fighting against Nazi Germany than any of its allies. According to one tally, roughly three-quarters of all German soldiers lost in war died facing Soviet troops. Military aid from the United States certainly helped, but on the battlefield, it was Soviet troops that did most of the fighting against Nazi armies.

The numbers are even more skewed when it comes to the war's death toll. Throughout the yearslong conflict—including the entire Pacific theater and every other theater of combat—the United States suffered an estimated 419,000 war-related deaths. The United Kingdom suffered an estimated 451,000 war-related deaths. Those are certainly large numbers, but within the same time frame, the Soviet Union lost at least *24 million* lives to the war—over twenty-five times more than the U.S. and U.K. combined. In terms of sheer sacrifice, there's simply no comparison.

As nations grappled with their memories of the larger war, depictions of the Tehran plot took on intriguing new dimensions.

In the 1960s, a renewed public appetite for World War II espionage stories led to several sensationalized and semifictionalized treatments of the plot. During this time, an anecdote emerged that the Nazi planners had a special name for the assassination mission: Unternehmen Weitsprung, or "Operation Long Jump." This became the official terminology for the plot in the press and the popular literature—and still is to this day—although there's no clear evidence that this name was ever used by the Germans or anyone else at the time.

It was also during this period that Otto Skorzeny, famed rescuer of Mussolini, came forward to respond to journalists who'd reached out to him about the story. His name had been mentioned repeatedly in conjunction with the plot, and he wanted to set the record straight. He would also address rumors of the plot in some of his memoirs, soon to be published at the time.

The first thing Skorzeny did was blame his old Nazi rival for the whole business. "I believe that Walter Schellenberg was enthusiastic about the idea of planning an action against the 'big three' enemies of Germany," he asserted.

Yet in seeking to distance himself from the plot, Skorzeny also revealed a remarkable detail: that he and Schellenberg met with Hitler at the Wolf's Lair in early November 1943, specifically to talk about the possibility of assassinating the Big Three in Tehran.

Nevertheless, Skorzeny claimed that he wanted nothing to do with such an operation. He said that at the time he reviewed the available intelligence on Tehran and decided that "the plan was simply impractical," and declined to participate.

It's hard to see why Skorzeny would make up the story of the meeting, especially so long after the fact. But his denial of any involvement in the plot is inconclusive. Former Nazi war criminals were still not immune from prosecution, and the last thing Skorzeny would've wanted was a potential new charge against him.

His denial, then, could've been his way of taking any remaining suspicion off himself, and instead putting it on someone who was already dead. Also, he never did like Walter Schellenberg.

In 1967, after these intriguing remarks from Skorzeny, a French-Hungarian journalist named Laslo Havas threw another log on the fire by writing the first book-length account of the Tehran assassination plot.

Called *The Long Jump,* Havas's book is populated with colorful characters and exciting plot twists. Havas claimed that to research the book, he tracked down and personally interviewed several persons with firsthand knowledge of the plot, including former Nazi agents who participated in it.

There's one big problem. There are no other records of most of the individuals whom Havas claims to have interviewed. As such, their statements can't be verified—in fact, their very existence can't be verified. Havas's book is also sprinkled with historical inaccuracies that put his larger claims in doubt. Nevertheless, some authors and journalists have accepted that Havas's interviewees are authentic and have incorporated their statements into other histories of the plot, often intermixing them with verified historical figures and genuine evidence.

All of this has made for a very confusing picture. By the end of the Cold War, the story of the alleged plot to kill the Big Three in Tehran remained murkier than ever. Would there ever be clarity on what really happened?

From the start, the Soviets were the ones who first revealed the story. So it's probably fitting, then, that as the twenty-first century begins, it's the Russians who get the surprising last word.

73

Moscow, Russia

November 18, 2003

No one sees it coming.

In 2003, on the sixtieth anniversary of the Tehran Conference, the Kremlin International News arranges and broadcasts a special press conference featuring a panel of former members of the Russian Foreign Intelligence Service.

In addition to commemorating the conference, the plan is to announce the publication of a new Russian-language book called *Tehran 43*, written by Iurii Kuznets, that among other things will supposedly reveal new declassified information about the alleged Nazi plot to kill the Big Three.

One of the first to speak is a former Deputy Chief of the KGB— the successor agency to the NKVD—named Vadim Kirpichenko.

"There is endless discussion on whether there was a 'Long Jump' or not," the former spy leader says, wanting to set the record straight. "I want to say that there were preparations for the assassination of the heads of three states . . . The assassination had been prepared and there is no doubt about that."

After a few statements like these, the presenters promise that this new book will finally reveal to a new generation the full true story of the assassination that could've changed the course of world history.

Unfortunately, the book doesn't quite do what the presenters promise. It provides some interesting new details about Soviet preparations for the conference, but as far as the Nazi assassination plot goes, it ends up mostly repeating the same details that were already known. The promised newly declassified intelligence files never materialize.

None of this really matters, though, because the star of this unusual press conference turns out not to be the *book,* but rather one of the other men seated on the panel, who at first is quiet. Finally, the moderator introduces him.

He's seventy-nine years old. A lifelong agent of the Russian intelligence services.

His name is Gevork Vartanian.

Vartanian explains that he was there in Tehran during the summit— as an NKVD agent. He was nineteen years old at the time. And most important, he was riding a bike.

"Many say that no such [assassination] attempt had been made," he states at the press conference. "All this is rubbish. An attempt had been made, and we provided the security of the conference and we knew what was going on."

Vartanian goes on to tell the colorful story of the Light Cavalry, and of his efforts to track and arrest Nazis in Tehran through the summer and fall of 1943.

He also confirms some rumored details, namely, that the Nazi plotters intended to get to the Soviet embassy via the water pipes, and that the Soviets believed the assassins would try to strike on the night of November 30, Churchill's birthday. He even relays the story of the six parachutists whom the NKVD tracked from Qom to the Tehran safehouse, describing how the NKVD monitored their radio signals, then forced them to call off the departure of the second team that would've been led by Otto Skorzeny.

Vartanian is the most memorable character at the press conference, and his story gets additional news coverage, both in Russia and abroad. In the coming months, he receives honors and accolades, not just for his role thwarting the 1943 plot, but for a lifetime of service to Russia, from the Soviet era to the present.

One person who also takes notice? Winston Churchill's grand-daughter, Celia Sandys.

In 2007, four years after the press conference, Sandys travels to Russia—with a documentary crew following her—to meet Vartanian. She wants to thank him personally for saving the life of her grand-father. This story, too, gets some international attention.

In 2012, Gevork Vartanian dies in Moscow at the age of eighty-seven. Russian President Vladimir Putin attends his funeral and pays Vartanian's widow, Goar, who is also a former Soviet spy, his personal respects.

That seems to be the end of it. A respected intelligence official with firsthand knowledge finally fills in the details and, more importantly, confirms that there really was a Nazi plot. Case closed, right?

Not exactly.

On further inspection, Vartanian's story doesn't entirely hold up. Some parts of it seem real—like his general depiction of the Light Cavalry, and his overall picture of Nazi activity in Tehran in the months and weeks prior to the conference. Other details are plausible but not provable, like the plan to use the water pipes and the focus on Churchill's birthday.

Yet, in Vartanian's multiple tellings of the story—all of which are verbal rather than written—some facts keep changing, and he some-times contradicts himself. Some of his claims seem highly unlikely: For example, that some time prior to the conference, Otto Skorzeny personally came to Tehran on a scouting mission.

Perhaps most significantly, he says he distinctly remembers that one of the six Nazi radio operators in the safehouse was Corporal Werner Rockstroh.

The problem is, that isn't possible, because Rockstroh was one of the Operation Franz radio operators whom British agents arrested back in August 1943, *before* the Big Three had even agreed to meet.

Sure, Vartanian is an older man, so he could just be jumbling a few facts. Maybe he's conflating the Operation Franz mission with the assassination mission. He was involved in monitoring both groups, and both involved exactly six Nazi agents operating wireless transmitters. If he's conflating the missions, which details apply to which? And if some facts are wrong, can we trust other aspects of his story?

Vartanian's account ends up being a fascinating addition to the story of the plot to kill the Big Three—but given the inconsistencies, still isn't definitive.

In a way, it may be the most fitting possible conclusion to the complicated story—that our final understanding of it is through the hazy memories of a seventy-nine-year-old lifelong Russian spy.

Yet all of this raises the question: What should we ultimately think about the plot? More important, how close did we really get to a calamitous event that would have changed the course of history?

Historians have their own theories.

74

Researchers and authors who've studied the 1943 Tehran plot tend to fall into two camps: those who skeptically believe it was a hoax on the part of the Soviets, and those who accept the more sensational claims about the story as promulgated by Laslo Havas and others, which have found their way into popular culture.

In the end, we believe that there's a middle ground between these camps—one that takes the known facts of the story, mixes them in with educated guesses, and adds, perhaps most important, some basic common sense.

One thing we know for certain is that in the fall of 1943, the Germans were desperate to turn the tide of the war. That year, Nazi armies had experienced a series of brutal defeats on the battlefield. The Wehrmacht remained a mighty force, but it was growing steadily weaker as the Allied forces grew stronger. Nazi Germany's only real "victory" during this period was Skorzeny's rescue of Mussolini in early September—but this rescue, however remarkable, would hardly influence the military course of the war.

It's hard to imagine, in these circumstances, that the Nazi leadership *wouldn't* try to seize the opportunity to strike against the Big Three during their proposed summit. The cost of failure would be minimal—the loss of a few dozen men, maybe—but the rewards of success would be immense. Assassinating Roosevelt, Stalin, and Churchill on the world stage, or even assassinating just one of them, would've been so earth-shattering, and such a huge blow to the Allies, that the war would change overnight in ways almost impossible to fathom.

Furthermore, once the Nazi intelligence services learned of the summit's probable location—Tehran, Iran—the idea of launching a clandestine assassination mission would have been almost irresistible. The SD's foreign office, run by Walter Schellenberg, happened to already have an infrastructure in place for parachuting armed commando teams into Iran that included, so they still believed, an on-the-ground network of Nazi agents and sympathizers in Tehran ready to support any such operation.

So what do we make of Stalin's desire to eavesdrop on Roosevelt during the summit? Sergo Beria's account of his instructions from Stalin does seem credible—there's no particular reason to doubt it—and it may well be the case that the Soviets successfully bugged the President's quarters throughout his stay at the Soviet embassy in Tehran. If so, does this prove that the Soviets made up the assassination plot to lure Roosevelt into an eavesdropping trap?

The answer is no. Because, quite simply, two things can be true at once.

On the one hand, the NKVD could have been genuinely worried about a Nazi plot to kill the Big Three and believed that Roosevelt should move to the Soviet embassy to avoid the three leaders repeatedly crossing through the city in daylight. At the very same time, Stalin could have realized there was a great opportunity to eavesdrop on Roosevelt once the idea was raised—and the decision soon made—for the President to move to the Soviet embassy. One truth does not cancel the other; in fact, both make sense based on everything known about the Soviets and their preparations for the summit.

There's another key point to consider. In the fall of 1943, Stalin wanted one thing above all else: for the United States and the United Kingdom to launch a cross-Channel attack into Western Europe. He had reason to doubt whether his allies would ever come through on this. Given the enormous stakes at play for the Soviet Union, would Stalin really have risked destroying his credibility and alienating his allies by flagrantly lying to the Americans and playing an elaborate hoax on Roosevelt on the eve of the very conference during which the cross-Channel attack was the dominant issue?

After all, if the Americans had somehow learned that the Soviets were lying to their faces—and trying to play a humiliating trick on the President—the summit could've easily fallen apart before it even started. Would Stalin really have potentially jeopardized something so important for the relatively small gain of being able to eavesdrop on Roosevelt?

Stalin was nothing if not shrewd. If the Soviets played an elaborate hoax on their ally at this particular moment, it would have been a very large risk for a minor reward.

Above all else, if the plot was simply a Soviet hoax, it's a hoax that was repeated and supported in the weeks, months, years, and decades to come. For the plot to be such a hoax, successive Soviet and Russian governments and intelligence agencies spanning many decades—from the NKVD, to the KGB, to today's modern organizations—would all have had to be party to it, and been willing to repeat it, despite knowing it wasn't true.

That means that a full sixty years after the fact, in 2003, the Russian Foreign Intelligence Service—a post-Soviet organization that was totally removed from Stalin's long-ago government and had no direct connection to it—would have still been making the effort to hold a false press conference and launch a media blitz based on what they knew was a lie told a half century earlier.

Put another way, to believe the plot was a Soviet hoax is to believe in a sixty-year conspiracy held together by generations of Russian intelligence services, all of whom are covering up a lie told by a former leader to whom they no longer have any allegiance. Why go to such trouble? This version of it starts to seem absurd.

As we've noted earlier, the lack of a paper trail on the German side doesn't prove or disprove much of anything, because the SD destroyed every sensitive document.

One detail that's certain, however, is the Nazis' willingness to employ assassination as an act of war. Schellenberg himself later recounted a plot that Hitler contemplated in 1944 to assassinate Stalin in Moscow. A high-level Nazi emissary, possibly Heinrich Himmler, would enter the Kremlin on a supposed top secret diplomatic mission and then—as soon as he was in a room with Stalin—pull out a concealed pistol and shoot the Man of Steel before being gunned down by the Soviet guards.

The existence of this later plot, apparently conceived by Hitler himself, removes any suggestion that the Führer or his leadership had any qualms or reluctance on principle when it came to killing the Allied leaders. Assassination was fair game in this war—as both sides had demonstrated.

Based on all of this, we believe that the available evidence, and common sense, lead to the conclusion that on the night before the conference, Soviet intelligence services meant what they said to American officials: The NKVD *had* been tracking Nazi paratroopers who touched down in or near Tehran, and that the lives of the Big Three *were* in danger.

Unlike some other accounts, however, we believe that many of the more sensational details of the plot that appear in popular culture are either unlikely or unverifiable, and that some aspects of the story will probably always be uncertain. New evidence could always come to light if researchers are ever allowed access to the complete archives of the Russian Foreign Intelligence Service, but even then some details will probably remain unclear.

Did Nazi commandos really have a plan to enter the Soviet embassy through the water pipes, as Vartanian claimed? It's possible, but for now it's hard to know for sure. Was the Nazi strategy really to strike on the night of Churchill's birthday? That's also plausible—and similarly unknown.

Finally, there's the question of Skorzeny. We know he oversaw training and outfitting missions to Iran in the summer and fall of 1943, both before and after his mission to rescue Mussolini. But was he the one personally in charge of a plan to assassinate the Big Three and, as later claimed by Vartanian, ready to board a plane bound for Iran to lead the assassination team on the night of November 30,

1943? Or is Skorzeny's own story—that he met with Hitler and Schellenberg in early November to discuss the possibility of assassinating the Big Three, and declined to participate—the one we should trust?

In the end, the answer may come down to whether you choose to believe a former Soviet spy or an ex-Nazi.

While researchers can continue to debate the details, there's one conclusion upon which the most skeptical *and* the most sensational accounts of the plot usually agree: Its ultimate failure rested in large part on the shoulders of one person.

Paradoxically, it's a person who did not even know the plot existed: Franz Mayr.

Any Nazi attempt to assassinate the Big Three during the Tehran Conference would've required local intelligence and support on the ground—which is what Mayr and his clandestine network were supposed to provide.

Once the British apprehended and arrested Mayr in August 1943, Nazi capabilities in Tehran were severely crippled—and any future assassination mission was probably doomed. Of course, Nazi intelligence didn't know this at the time because they didn't learn of Mayr's arrest until much later. The SD's belief that their man in Tehran was still up and running may have been what led Nazi planners in Berlin to think the difficult mission was still possible.

Yet that raises the question, whatever became of Franz Mayr?

Like Skorzeny and Schellenberg, he spent a lot of time after his arrest in a very uncomfortable place: the interrogation room. According to his British captors, Mayr "at first resisted interrogation with considerable energy," but soon succumbed to the pressure and offered up all he knew, including the whereabouts of the remaining members of Operation Franz.

In late 1943, the British transferred Mayr from Tehran to Cairo, Egypt, where he was held as a prisoner of the Allies for the rest of the war. At one point, the Germans suggested his name as part of a potential prisoner exchange, but the plan never materialized.

After the war, Mayr remained in Allied custody, but he proved to be just as resourceful when the fighting was done as when it was raging. In 1946, he successfully escaped from Allied quarters in Egypt and made his way to Switzerland. Swiss authorities arrested him for illegal entry and sent him, under Allied jurisdiction, to occupied Germany—where he promptly escaped again.

From there, Mayr began a long period of moving from place to place, with years spent in Austria, Switzerland, Italy, Spain, Portugal, Lebanon, Egypt, and Syria. Utilizing his international contacts, he found success managing an import-export firm based in Hamburg, Germany. His business may have also been a front for political activities, including the recruitment of former SS officers to work for Middle Eastern governments.

Little is known of Mayr's life beyond that point, and it's not clear when or where he died.

However, records of Mayr's initial interrogations reveal a particularly interesting moment during his captivity. Shortly after his arrest, he asked the British authorities, just as he had once asked his German superiors, for permission to marry his girlfriend in Tehran, Lili Sanjari.

Even as a prisoner, Franz Mayr was still in love.

It's not clear how he expected his British captors to honor this unusual request. In any case, they refused, and Franz Mayr probably never saw Lili Sanjari again.

As for Sanjari herself, nothing more is known about her, beyond the fact that she remained in the capital city. After Mayr was arrested the British authorities simply lost interest in her, and she presumably resumed a civilian life after the war.

The Germans came and went, and the Allies came and went—but Lili Sanjari simply stayed in Tehran.

75

---·---

April 12, 1945

The President never gets to see the end.

As the Allies began their long march through France, some military leaders thought the war in Europe might end quickly. Germany's position was clearly hopeless. The Wehrmacht was battered, its forces depleted. The largest and most powerful military units in the world were closing in on either side.

Hitler's refusal to surrender at this point was one of the many incalculable tragedies of the war. Armies on both sides had to keep fighting, battle after battle, with senseless casualties mounting for all involved.

In this later phase of the war, the suffering of innocent populations never ceased; if anything, the toll inflicted on civilians grew worse.

Prior to invading the Normandy beaches, the Allies had begun aerial bombing raids on interior France to destroy bridges, roads, factories, and other targets useful to occupying German troops. The raids were successful—and caused over forty thousand civilian deaths.

As Soviet troops surged westward through Eastern Europe, they exacted brutal revenge on local populations or groups they suspected of earlier collaboration with the Germans. This continued a vicious cycle of mass retaliatory violence in the region, in which innocent civilians were often the victims.

On the other side of the globe, Allied naval forces pushed steadily across the ocean toward Japan, securing island after island, gradually overwhelming the resistance of dug-in Japanese troops. The military death toll was enormous, but so was that of civilian and native populations in the region, both of them caught in the cross fire of combat or ravaged by war-related famine. Entire indigenous populations were decimated in a war they had nothing to do with.

By the summer of 1944, it's clear that although Allied victory may eventually be assured, it will be a long and bloody road to get there.

Meanwhile, election season is coming in the United States—and President Roosevelt faces a decision.

He has no desire to run for a fourth term. To put it plainly, he's exhausted. His health has not been well. Many family members and close friends, worried for his safety, beg him not to run again.

He promises that he won't—so long as the European war is over.

Yet by the late summer, it's not over. It's still dragging on. The Pacific war drags on too, although Japan's position is as hopeless as Germany's. Both countries continue to send hundreds of thousands of their own soldiers to certain death, drawing out the suffering, even when losing is inevitable.

Weighing his options, Roosevelt decides that the country and the world still need him. He can't drop out just yet.

"Reluctantly, but as a good soldier . . . I will accept and serve this office," he writes on July 11 to the Democratic Party chairman, the weariness practically dripping from the message.

Roosevelt has plenty of political enemies on domestic issues, but when it comes to the war, the country is almost completely behind him. At this point his knowledge, his leadership, and his relationships across the world are simply irreplaceable.

As the American Presidential primaries get underway, Soviet troops advance steadily westward into occupied Poland, pushing Nazi forces back toward Germany.

On the night of July 22, 1944, a handful of Red Army soldiers march into the Lublin district—and as they approach what at first appear to be a series of barracks, they are soon horrified by what they find.

They've entered the Majdanek death camp, vacated by the SS only a few days ago as the Soviets approached.

The camp is mostly empty now, but the evidence of unimaginable atrocities is still there—including the zigzagging trenches where, only eight months earlier, SS guards massacred and buried eighteen thousand Jewish prisoners during Operation Erntefest.

Majdanek is the first Nazi death camp to be discovered and liberated by Allied forces. Many more are soon to come. As researchers, journalists, and forensic experts begin to study the camps, the overwhelming scope and horror of the Nazi death program becomes sickeningly clear.

Back in the United States, Roosevelt eventually wins reelection in a landslide, 432 electoral votes to 99. The country still stands behind the President, but the long Presidential campaign exhausts him—and takes a further toll on his health.

By the time it's over, he's lost nineteen pounds. Dr. Bruenn, his loyal physician, now stays by his side almost every day, monitoring his weight, his diet, his blood pressure, and other vital signs.

Everyone can see that he looks different—paler, more gaunt, with bags under his eyes.

On a frigid Inauguration Day, January 20, 1945, with the war still ongoing, he's sworn in for the fourth time. Roosevelt dispenses with the usual parade and instead gives a speech on the south portico of the White House.

"We have learned that we cannot live alone at peace, that our own well-being is dependent on the well-being of other nations far away," he declares. "We have learned to be citizens of the world. We have learned . . . 'The only way to have a friend is to be one.'"

Inside, after the speech, the President nearly collapses. "I felt certain he was going to die," a friend later recalled.

Roosevelt's idealism for the coming peace is what still drives him. After fighting this long and terrible war—and with victory over fascism so near—he desperately wants to implement his ideals for lasting postwar harmony.

It's this impulse that brings the Big Three leaders—Roosevelt, Churchill, and Stalin—together one last time.

Like before, it's Roosevelt who once again urges a conference, this time for early 1945.

Despite Roosevelt's poor condition, Stalin again insists that the other leaders travel across the world to meet him. Ironically, he cites his own health as the reason he can't travel far.

Roosevelt agrees to the condition and urges Churchill to do the same. Once again, he feels that a face-to-face conference is too important to miss.

The long journey takes him by ship to Malta—an island in the Mediterranean—for preliminary discussions with Churchill. Then, together, they fly to Yalta, a resort town on the Black Sea, where Stalin awaits.

On February 4, the three leaders meet again. By this time, it has been five and a half years since the start of the war in Europe. Over fifty million lives around the world have been lost.

All three leaders have aged since Tehran, but Roosevelt most of all. He looks pale for much of the Yalta Conference, wearing a heavy shawl around his shoulders as his aides push him from place to place.

Nonetheless, his energy rises to the occasion. Gradually, the three leaders start working through the enormous complexities of a postwar Europe, many parts of which have been decimated by a half decade of destruction, famine, and mass murder.

The issues are impossible to solve in a few days. They come away with only partial agreements. But once again, the symbolism is enormous. The Big Three are together again, side by side. And this time, they don't call it a war conference—it's a peace conference.

Upon his return to the United States, Roosevelt is exhausted and weak.

He's scheduled to address a Joint Session of Congress after the trip, and for the first time in his presidency, he speaks to the chamber sitting down rather than propping himself at the podium.

He receives a standing ovation.

On March 30, 1945, Roosevelt goes with family and close aides to his favorite place in the world: Warm Springs, Georgia.

It's the place where, decades earlier, in the outdoor springs, he'd undergone his recovery from polio. He later turned it into a large, welcoming outdoor facility for others afflicted with polio to recuperate. Every time he visits, it's an inspiration to the patients who are there, struggling against their ailment. They draw strength from him—and he draws strength from them.

This time, he plans to stay for a long visit to recover his energy and health.

Yet after a few days, he looks no better.

Mike Reilly is there with him, as usual. Following their regular routine, Reilly always transfers the President from his wheelchair to the car, but now, he feels something has changed. Normally, Roosevelt always feels light in his arms. Not anymore.

"He was absolutely dead weight," Reilly later recalled.

At this point, Allied troops are in Germany, coming from multiple directions, all heading for Berlin. The circle is getting smaller. Victory is so close.

Hitler won't stop fighting. Rather than surrender Berlin, he orders the Hitler Youth corps, composed of boys and teenagers, to join what's left of the battered German armies defending Berlin. It's a hopeless cause—a suicide mission—and when Allied tanks and troops storm the burning capital city to defeat the last Nazi troops, thousands of German youths, some as young as twelve, will die in the carnage.

On April 12, still in Warm Springs, Roosevelt begins the day hoping for rest and recovery. Although the weather is warm, he feels a chill and asks for a cape to put over his shoulders. He also complains of a headache and neck stiffness, but it seems to get better after a massage.

Before lunch, he sits for a portrait. The artist, Elizabeth Shoumatoff, notices that he has some color back in his face. He's in a chair at a card table that serves as a makeshift desk, reading the newspaper and writing some letters as Shoumatoff paints.

At roughly 1 p.m., he looks at his watch. "We have fifteen more minutes to work," he says.

Then, suddenly, his head droops forward and he puts a hand on the back of his neck. "I have a terrific pain in the back of my head," he says and slumps to the floor.

A few minutes later, he's upstairs. His close friends and family surround him in bed, gasping with horror. He's lost consciousness—and will never regain it.

At 3:35 p.m., the doctor pronounces President Franklin Delano Roosevelt dead.

All over the country, radios and television stations stop their broadcasting to report the tragedy.

Within minutes of the announcement, the story reaches London.

"I felt as if I had been struck by a physical blow," Winston Churchill later recalled. For months, he'd been dreaming of the day when he and Roosevelt, together, would celebrate the coming victory in Europe. Instead, he is "overwhelmed by a sense of deep and irrefutable loss."

It isn't just the heads of state who are devastated.

The next morning, in rainy southern Germany, behind enemy lines, a small group of American prisoners of war walk along a muddy road near a field of long grass. Nazi guards are marching them from one place of detention to another.

In less than a month, Berlin will fall, and Hitler will be dead. But these soldiers don't know that yet. From their perspective, they may soon face their own deaths at the hands of their captors.

Earlier that morning, a German guard heard the news and told some of the prisoners, President Roosevelt is dead.

At noon, when the Germans halt the group to rest, an officer among the POWs pulls the bugle sergeant by the arm and walks up a small grassy hill to address his fellow soldiers.

"I have been told . . . that President Roosevelt died yesterday, April 12th," he says.

The bugler, following the officer's signal, starts to play *Taps*.

"The sound was clear and pure," a young private later recalled. It was "the saddest song I ever heard."

Soon, the bugler finishes.

"We all stood silently with our heads bowed, and I heard the unabashed weeping of a soldier among us," the private remembered. "Then we marched on."

That same morning, back in Georgia, the President's family is making last-minute arrangements for his body to travel to Washington, D.C.

The Warm Springs Rehabilitation facility has a longstanding tradition that at the end of one of Roosevelt's many visits, the other camp attendees, many of them children afflicted with polio, would gather outside the main hall near the camp's entrance to say goodbye to him in person.

Today, they gather again, this time to say goodbye for good. Sitting in wheelchairs and leaning on arm braces, they watch as an open hearse carrying a flag-draped coffin slowly drives past.

"The child patients were sobbing," the President's secretary, Grace Tully, later recalled. "The adults sobbed too."

A few soldiers and musicians from nearby Fort Benning had been sent to join the small makeshift procession. As the hearse passes by, one of Roosevelt's favorite musicians, a Chief Petty Officer named Graham W. Jackson, steps forward with an accordion and plays a piece called "Going Home." He, too, has tears streaming down his face.

Several hours later, the Presidential train arrives in Washington, D.C., bearing the coffin. Here, another procession is waiting, but this one isn't small. It's a crowd of five hundred thousand people, gathered at the National Mall, many of whom had traveled from all over the country to pay tribute.

He had led the nation through the darkest days of war. Now peace is coming, and the President, Franklin Delano Roosevelt, is finally, truly, at rest.

Acknowledgments

From Brad

This book became far more personal than we expected. So let me start by thanking the one person whose point of view so deeply matches my own, Josh Mensch. When it comes to writing a book together, it helps to share ideas—but it's far more helpful when you also share a similar worldview and values. Josh and I have been working together for nearly a decade now, which means that my original impression was absolutely correct: He is one of the kindest, most thoughtful people I've ever encountered—and one of the most thorough researchers and writers, committed to sourcing every bit of history that's packed into these pages. Yet, as with each book we do together, something new emerges, and here, it was his dedication to making sure that the victims of this war—from the Jews in the Holocaust to the civilians who were starved and plowed over—were never excluded from the story. As a Jewish writer myself, I'd grown up learning about the Holocaust, but as the research took us deeper, we were both still humbled to see this new view of the decimation, including the utterly bureaucratic process that empowered and enabled the Nazi horrors. *How did this happen?* we still ask today. Sadly, the answer is: *Quite easily.* So, Josh, thank you for always seeing what's vital—both today and yesterday. I'm honored to call you and Mary my friends. This book would never exist without you.

I also owe massive thanks to the following: My first lady, Cori, who has helped me find, redefine, and build my own history. Jonas, Lila, and Theo are my own Big Three, the reason for it all. They are a united front against their parents, and I hope it'll always be that way. I'm writing these acknowledgments after the passing of my friend and agent, Jill Kneerim, the single most important person in my professional life. No words are enough. I love and miss you dearly. Friend and agent Jennifer Rudolph Walsh built this nonfiction universe—and Jay Mandel at WME has run so beautifully with it. Special thanks to Hope Denekamp, Lucy Cleland, and all our friends at the Kneerim & Williams agency.

I want to also thank my sister, Bari, who knows my history like no one else. Also to Bobby, Ami, Adam, Gilda, and Will, for always looking out for us.

My Secret Service holds my life in their hands: Noah Kuttler, Ethan Kline, Dale Flam, Matt Kuttler, Chris Weiss, and Judd Winick are always there to keep me honest—and every page is improved by it. Additional thanks go to Chris Eliopoulos, Katy Greene, Marie Grunbeck, Nick Marell, Staci Schecter, Liz Sobel, Caryn Stumpfl, Pansy and Rob Price, Jason Sherry, Jim Day, Denise Jaeger, Katriela Knight, and Maria Venusio.

For research and historical support, we are so grateful to have Jeff Alexander on our Allied front. His insights and expertise are interwoven throughout these pages. Thank you, Jeff, for guiding us along the way. Special thanks to our incredible researchers, Benjamin Diehl and Garret McDonald, who are our true secret weapons.

Massive love to our family at *Lost History*, and at HISTORY and Left/Right, for bringing Josh and I together all those years ago: Nancy Dubuc, Paul Cabana, Mike Stiller, Ken Druckerman, Mike Mezaros, Mary Robertson (who is also family!), and Lee White; and to Rob Weisbach, for being the first to say yes.

I also want to thank everyone at Flatiron and Macmillan: our leader and friend Don Weisberg, Jon Yaged, Kristen Bonanno, Marlena Bittner, Aileen Boyle, Nancy Trypuc, Vincent Stanley, Emily Walters, Donna Noetzel, Jeremy Pink, and Keith Hayes, as well as Astra Berzinskas, Malati Chavali, Leigh George, Jenn Gonzalez, Jonathan Hollingsworth, Laura Pennock, Brad Wood, Jeanette Zwart, plus Jasmine Faustino, Lauren Bittrich, and the entire sales force who fight on the front lines everyday. I'll never say it enough: They're the real reason this book is in your hands.

I need to add a special thank-you to the unstoppable Louis Grilli, who kept the trains running, then put the trains on his back and carried us into the final station, saving us on a nearly daily basis. Especially toward the end. Thank you, Louis! Finally, I want to thank our true Commander in Chief, Bob Miller. As we've said in other books, leadership isn't about being in charge—it's about taking care of those in your charge. Bob, you constantly take care of us. Your friendship and passion brought this series to fruition. I owe you forever for this chapter of my life. Thank you, Bob, for your faith.

From Josh

First, I want to thank Brad Meltzer. Brad and I have worked together for a decade now, and the stories we've told have spanned centuries. Brad, it's been a remarkable journey writing with you, and your emphasis on kindness and generosity in work and life remains an inspiration. Thank you, truly, for being a great collaborator and friend. As always, Mary and I send our love to you and Cori and your wonderful family.

Brad and I owe an enormous debt of gratitude to Bob Miller at Flatiron Books. From the beginning, Bob's support, encouragement, and commitment has been the engine that drives us. We also owe thanks to many other great people at Flatiron who make our work possible. At the top of this list is Louis Grilli, who contributed so much to this book from start to finish. Louis, we couldn't have done this without you! Thanks also to Nancy Trypuc, Marlena Bittner, Katherine Turro, and the many great folks on the sales team, the marketing team, the audiobook team, and so many others. Shout out also to Jasmine Faustino and Lauren Bittrich, whose work was so important to our earlier books.

I want to give a very special thank-you to my agent, Lisa Grubka, at Fletcher & Company. During a difficult and stressful time, Lisa provided much-needed guidance and wisdom. Lisa, thank you for your patience and encouragement every step of the way.

When it came to helping unravel the strands of this enormously complicated story, two people were essential: researchers Benjamin Diehl and Garret MacDonald. Ben, thank you for helping me navigate the dense maze of conflicting sources in the early stages of the process; and Garret, thank you for your outstanding input, organization, and guidance in the final stretch. This story is ours together. I also must thank our wonderful editor, Jeff Alexander, whose sure-handed input made this book so much better. Thanks also to my brother, James Freeman, for providing some excellent translations from Russian to English. Working together with such smart and dedicated people was one of the absolute highlights of this project.

As authors of nonfiction history, we rely completely on the organizations that preserve and document historical materials for public and scholarly use. For this project I want to thank, among many other institutions, the Franklin D. Roosevelt Presidential Library at Marist College, the United States Holocaust Memorial Museum, the National World War II Museum, and the New York Public Library.

I also want to thank my extended family. The writing of this book coincided with a painful time for us, and I'll forever associate the work with this difficult period. Despite the loss, we found together a camaraderie and generosity with one another that I'll never forget. In that spirit I want to thank Greg Patnaude, Pamela Mensch, Elizabeth Mensch, Jonathan Mensch, Jacob Mensch, Joseph Mensch, James Freeman, Jeremy Freeman, Libby Mensch, and Claire Mensch. I also want to thank Anna Acunto, John Acunto, London Acunto, Mila Acunto, and August Acunto, Lynn James, Daeon James, and Denae James.

My deepest gratitude of all is for my two children, Malcolm and Maxine, who bring new laughter and joy every single day. You make me the proudest father in the world. Finally, throughout every trial and every triumph, one person has remained my foundation: my wife, Mary Robertson. Thank you for being my best friend and soul mate. I love you forever.

Notes

Prologue

1 *The President is hiding . . . the capital of Iran*: For the details of Roosevelt's travel from the American embassy to the Soviet embassy on this day, see Michael F. Reilly, *Reilly of the White House* (New York: Simon & Schuster, 1947), 178–79; and Gary Kern, "How 'Uncle Joe' Bugged FDR," *Studies in Intelligence* 47, no. 1 (March 2003).

1 *Here in late November 1943 . . . state of commotion*: See Keith Sainsbury, *The Turning Point: Roosevelt, Stalin, Churchill, and Chiang Kai-shek, 1943: The Moscow, Cairo, and Tehran Conferences* (New York: Oxford University Press, 1985), 218–19.

1 *The event was . . . revealed to the public*: On the secrecy of the conference, see Iurii Kuznets, *Tehran 43* (Moscow: Eskimo, 2003), 194.

2 *The President is traveling . . . Prime Minister of the United Kingdom*: Sainsbury, *Turning Point*, 218–19.

2 *This conference . . . complicated security considerations*: Ibid., 137–50.

2 *The real President . . . through the winding streets*: Reilly, *Reilly of the White House*, 178–79; and Kern, "How 'Uncle Joe' Bugged FDR."

3 *Right here in Tehran . . . attempt to assassinate the "Big Three*: Our book will closely examine some debates and controversy surrounding the story of this assassination plot, including theories that the plot was exaggerated by the Soviet intelligence services. See our chapters 71–74. For examples of introductory sources about the story that are reliable according to our research, see Reilly, *Reilly of the White House*, 178–88; Nikolai Dolgopolov's *Vartanian: zhizn' zamechatel'nykh liudei* (Moscow: Molodaia gvardiia, 2014), 25–73; and Kuznets, *Tehran 43*, 7–10.

3 *For nearly four years . . . too numerous to count*: See Ian Kershaw, *To Hell and Back: Europe 1914–1949* (New York: Penguin, 2015), 346–47.

3 *The driving force of the war . . . cult of personality around a narcissistic leader*: For overview of this ideology see ibid., 228–32.

3 *Under the influence . . . unleashed this calamitous war*: Ibid., 294.

3 *The clash of world military powers . . . the world to fully comprehend*: Ibid., 356–73.

4 *To fight back . . . suffering around the world*: For the general significance of the 1943 Tehran Conference to the Second World War, see for example

Sainsbury, *Turning Point*; and Keith Eubank, *Summit at Teheran: The Untold Story* (New York: William Morrow & Co., 1985).

Chapter 1

7 *The ships have been traveling . . . prepares to change course*: See Walter Lord, *Day of Infamy: The Bombing of Pearl Harbor* (New York: Open Road Media, 2021), 73–89.

7 *There's no land in sight . . . aboard and mobilized*: Ibid., 394.

7 *3,500 miles*: Jean Edward Smith, *FDR* (New York: Random House, 2007), 532.

7 *The rest accelerate . . . carrier decks*: Ibid., 534.

8 *At 6:05 a.m. . . . . flagship carrier*: Antony Beevor, *The Second World War* (New York: Little, Brown & Co., 2012), 250.

8 *183 planes*: Ibid.

8 *Ninety minutes later, at roughly 7:40 a.m.*: Ibid.

Chapter 2

9 *It's 8:45 a.m . . . tray of food in front of him*: Nigel Hamilton, *The Mantle of Command: FDR at War, 1941–1942* (New York: Houghton Mifflin Harcourt, 2014), 44. If Roosevelt was in the middle of "having his breakfast" when the fourteenth decrypt arrives at 9 a.m., we assume he had started the breakfast by 8:45 a.m.

9 *He often starts the day . . . begin the day*: Roosevelt's typical morning White House routine, including his 8:30 a.m. breakfast-and-work in bed habit, is described in Conrad Black, *Franklin Delano Roosevelt: Champion of Freedom* (New York: PublicAffairs, 2003), 284.

9 *Earlier that evening . . . according to a prepared timeline*: Hamilton, *Mantle of Command*, 43–44.

9 *The Navy's intercept . . . war against Nazi Germany*: Jean Edward Smith, *FDR* (New York: Random House, 2007), 506–40.

10 *At roughly 9:30 a.m., . . . received, decrypted, and translated*: Hamilton, *Mantle of Command*, 48–49.

10 *"efforts towards . . . with further negotiations"*: Quoted from David L. Roll, *The Hopkins Touch: Harry Hopkins and the Forging of the Alliance to Defeat Hitler* (Oxford: Oxford University Press, 2013), 158–59.

10 *Minutes later . . . to terminate their offices*: Ibid., 158–59.

10 *They agree that Japan . . . interests in Southeast Asia*: Hamilton, *Mantle of Command*, 48–49.

11 *As his advisors debate . . . or with their families*: Roll, *Hopkins Touch*, 162.

11 *"The President wants you . . . to pick you up"*: Grace Tully, *F.D.R.: My Boss* (Chicago: People's Book Club, 1949), 255.

11 *"like a fireman"*: Grace Tully interview, December 15, 1970, as quoted in James M. Scott, *Target Tokyo: Jimmy Doolittle and the Raid That Avenged Pearl Harbor* (New York: W.W. Norton and Co., 2015), 16.

11 *"I was disappointed . . . could possibly join us"*: Eleanor Roosevelt, *This I Remember* (New York: Harper, 1949), 232.

11 *Then, at 1:47 p.m. . . . Secretary of the Navy*: Hamilton, *Mantle of Command*, 53.

11 *"picked up a radio . . . 'no drill'"*: Robert E. Sherwood, *Roosevelt and Hopkins: An Intimate History* (New York: Harper and Brothers, 1948), 430–31.

11 *"like the Japanese have attacked Pearl Harbor"*: Knox as quoted in Smith, *FDR*, 536.

12 *"I expressed the belief . . . not attack in Honolulu"*: As quoted in Roll, *Hopkins Touch*, 160.

12 *"I could hear . . . as he talked to me"*: Tully, *F.D.R.: My Boss*, 255.

12 *She puts him on . . . the results are catastrophic*: Roll, *Hopkins Touch*, 160–61.

12 *This will be the worst day of Roosevelt's presidency*: Roosevelt never specifically stated that Pearl Harbor was the worst day of his life or of his presidency, but the notion has been widely accepted by historians and scholars. See for example Paul M. Sparrow, "Day of Infamy," https://fdr.blogs.archives.gov/2016/12/02/day-of-infamy/. See also Hamilton, *Mantle of Command*, 45.

12 *"near hysteria . . . expression of his mouth"*: Tully, *F.D.R.: My Boss*, 254–55.

12 *Indeed, the terrible news . . . were sitting ducks*: John Toland, *The Rising Sun: The Decline and Fall of the Japanese Empire, 1936–1945* (New York: Modern Library, 2003), 213.

12 *"battleship row"*: Lord, *Day of Infamy*, 395–96.

12 *The attacking aircraft . . . carefully aimed torpedoes*: Beevor, *Second World War*, 251.

12 *Minutes later . . . four hundred sailors and crew to their deaths*: Ibid.

13 *Within an hour . . . nineteen years old*: Lord, *Day of Infamy*, 395–96.

13 *Amid the chaos . . . Tully*: Tully, *F.D.R.: My Boss*, 256.

13 *For the past few hours . . . every word counts*: See Roll, *Hopkins Touch*, 162; and Hamilton, *Mantle of Command*, 66–67.

Chapter 3

15 *isolationism . . . crippling depression*: Susan Dunn, *1940: FDR, Willkie, Lindbergh, Hitler—the Election amid the Storm* (New Haven, CT: Yale University Press, 2013), 58–70.

15 *nearly a quarter of U.S. citizens were unemployed*: See, for example, Ben S. Bernanke, ed., *Essays on the Great Depression* (Princeton, NJ: Princeton University Press, 2004), esp. chapter 7; and Abigail Trollinger, *Becoming Entitled: Relief, Unemployment, and Reform during the Great Depression* (Philadelphia, PA: Temple University Press, 2020), esp. chapter 1.

16 *"The test of our progress . . . those who have too little"*: FDR inaugural address, January 20, 1937, https://millercenter.org/the-presidency

/presidential-speeches/january-20–1937-second-inaugural-address, visited May 23, 2022.

16 *In 1939 America's army ranked only nineteenth*: United States Army Center of Military History, *Biennial Reports of the Chief of Staff of the United States Army to the Secretary of War: 1 July 1939–30 June 1945* (Washington, D.C.: U.S. Government Printing Office, 1996), v.

16 *Nevertheless, the U.S. watched . . . he was in total control*: Kershaw, *To Hell and Back*, 208–14.

16 *At his huge rallies . . . and foreign influence*: Ibid., 228–32.

16 *"one strong new idea . . . Germany great again"*: Adolf Hitler speech of February 1940, as quoted in *St. Louis Star and Times*, February 24, 1940.

16 *Hitler and other party leaders . . . hardworking people*: Kershaw, *To Hell and Back*, 118–19.

17 *"ruined our race, corrupted our morals"*: Nazi pamphlet from 1932. Source: Joseph Goebbels and Mjölnir, *Die verfluchten Hakenkreuzler. Etwas zum Nachdenken* (Munich: Verlag Frz. Eher, 1932).

17 *"Nuremberg Laws" . . . stripped Jews of citizenship rights*: Ibid., 283–90.

17 *"enemy of all law, all liberty, all morality, all religion"*: FDR, fireside chat, September 11, 1941. FDR Presidential Library and Museum, http://www.fdrlibrary.marist.edu/_resources/images/msf/msf01445.

17 *Meanwhile, Hitler launched . . . right belonged to "the Fatherland"*: Kershaw, *To Hell and Back*, 316–25.

17 *Roosevelt thought Nazism . . . public who supported them*: Dunn, *1940*, 58–70.

17 *"I have said . . . any foreign wars"*: FDR campaign speech in Boston, Mass., October 30, 1940, quoted from Doris Kearns Goodwin, *No Ordinary Time: Franklin and Eleanor Roosevelt: The Home Front in World War II* (New York: Simon & Schuster, 1994), 187.

18 *According to the 1930 U.S. Census . . . German Americans*: U.S. Department of Commerce and U.S. Bureau of the Census, *Fifteenth Census of the United States: 1930* (Washington, D.C.: Government Printing Office, 1933), 2:264.

18 *While Hitler's rise . . . wearing Nazi armbands*: For the Christian Front, see Stephen H. Norwood, "Marauding Youth and the Christian Front: Anti-Semitic Violence in Boston and New York During World War II," *American Jewish History* 91, no. 2 (2003): 233–67. For the German American Bund, see Leland V. Bell, "The Failure of Nazism in America: The German American Bund, 1936–1941," *Political Science Quarterly* 85, no. 4 (1970): 585–99.

18 *On February 20, 1939 . . . with an audience of twenty thousand*: Dunn, *1940*, 235.

18 *"if George Washington . . . friends with Adolf Hitler"*: J. Wheeler-Hill speech at Madison Square Garden in New York, NY, February 20, 1939. The night's speeches were compiled in a pamphlet called "Free America:

The German American Bund at Madison Square Garden," published and distributed by the German American Bund. The pamphlet, which does not contain page numbers, is viewable here: https://ia804500.us.archive .org/2/items/FreeAmerica_0/FA_PDF_1.pdf.

18 *"fight for a Gentile America . . . Jewish Marxist elements"*: Bell, "Failure of Nazism in America," 594.

19 *"we look to Heinrich Ford . . . translated and published"*: Dunn, *1940*, 60–61.

19 *"one of those . . . Yellow, Black, and Brown"*: Charles Lindbergh quoted in Max Wallace, *The American Axis: Henry Ford, Charles Lindbergh, and the Rise of the Third Reich* (New York: St. Martin's Press, 2003), 212.

19 *Lindbergh became a prominent spokesperson . . . to challenge Roosevelt*: Dunn, *1940*, 72.

20 *At the same time . . . at the forefront*: An example was the endorsement by the American Jewish Congress of an economic boycott on Germany. See Richard Breitman and Allan J. Lichtman, *FDR and the Jews* (Cambridge, MA: Harvard University Press, 2013), 57.

20 *On November 9, 1939 . . . police looked on indifferently*: Dunn, *1940*, 29.

20 *Jerry Siegel and Joe Shuster, gave birth to Superman*: See, for example, Roy Schwartz, *Is Superman Circumcised?: The Complete Jewish History of the World's Greatest Hero* (Jefferson, NC: McFarland, 2021).

20 *depicted a musclebound red-white-and-blue hero*: See Joe Simon and Jack Kirby, *Captain America #1*. March, 1941. Reprinted in *Captain America: The Classic Years*, ed. Bob Harras (New York: Marvel Entertainment Inc., 1991). For more on the history of comic books please see Jean-Paul Gabilliet, *Of Comics and Men: A Cultural History of American Comic Books*, trans. Bart Beaty and Nick Nguyen (Jackson: University Press of Mississippi, 2010).

20 *The truth . . . entered the conflict*: Dunn, *1940*, 57–70.

21 *"Lend-Lease"*: Ibid., 288.

22 *"Lending war equipment . . . You don't want it back"*: Ibid., 286.

22 *81 percent of Americans were opposed to the U.S. entering the conflict*: Gallup Poll, April 28, 1941. Survey #234K, Question #8a.

Chapter 4

23 *The transport plane's cabin . . . the sky is black*: For descriptions of this parachute drop, see Dolgopolov, *Vartanian*, 25–73; Kuznets, *Tehran 43*, 7–10; Reilly, *Reilly of the White House*, 178–88.

23 *Apart from the steady howl . . . breathing is near impossible*: For information on the flight experience of German parachutists preparing to drop into Iran, see Adrian O'Sullivan, *Nazi Secret Warfare in Occupied Persia (Iran): The Failure of the German Intelligence Services, 1939–45* (New York: Palgrave Macmillan, 2014), 172–75.

24 *outside the city of Qom*: Iurii Plutenko and Gevork Vartanian, "Tegeran-43:

'My byli ne takie! . . . ,'" *Zavtra* (October 31, 2007), accessed September 30, 2021, https://zavtra.ru/blogs/2007–10–3122.

24 *Ju 290 cargo craft*: See, for example, O'Sullivan, *Nazi Secret Warfare*, 167.

24 *The pilot is not . . . the German air force*: Ibid., 92, 173. Also see Howard Blum, *Night of the Assassins: The Untold Story of Hitler's Plot to Kill FDR, Churchill, and Stalin* (New York: HarperCollins, 2020), 255–57.

Chapter 5

25 *In the 1930s . . . into colonial subjects*: Toland, *Rising Sun*, 56.

25 *Yet, while Japan spoke . . . they deemed inferior*: Ibid., 450–51.

26 *By the 1930s . . . a "puppet state" called Manchukuo*: Ibid., 8.

26 *slaughtered as many as two hundred thousand Chinese civilians*: Ibid., 50–51.

26 *Japan's aggression was met . . . condemned Japan's military aggression*: Ibid., 48.

26 *"The Western powers . . . took up contract bridge"*: Matsuoka Yosuke, as quoted in Thomas W. Burkman, *Japan and the League of Nations: Empire and World Order, 1914–1938* (Honolulu: University of Hawaii Press, 2008), 215.

26 *Be that as it may . . . hostile military conquest*: Roosevelt's anti-colonialist views were often in conflict with his counterpart Winston Churchill. For context, see Toland, *Rising Sun*, 634–35.

26 *Japan signed the Tripartite Pact*: Toland, *Rising Sun*, 63–64.

27 *"in the coming age . . . common spiritual foundations"*: Gen. Tomoyuki Yamashita as quoted in *Time* magazine, "Foreign News: Troubled Tokyo," June 30, 1941.

27 *Spirituality aside . . . Japanese naval operations*: Toland, *Rising Sun*, 85.

27 *"It would not do . . . harm to get into war"*: FDR to Japanese ambassador Adm. Kichisaburo Nomura, quoted in Smith, *FDR*, 513.

27 *No surprise . . . upper hand in the Pacific*: Toland's chapter "Then the War Will Be a Desperate One" covers the logic of Japanese strategy toward the United States as it developed throughout 1941. See Toland, *Rising Sun*, 54–86.

27 *With the element . . . the Pacific for good*: Ibid.

27 *"Our empire stands . . . glory or oblivion"*: Japanese War Minister Gen. Hidecki Tojo quoted in Max Hastings, *Inferno: The World at War, 1939–1945* (New York: Random House, 2011), 191.

28 *On November 26, 1941 . . . to the Hawaiian island of Oahu*: Smith, *FDR*, 532.

Chapter 6

29 *"WAR! OAHU BOMBED BY JAPANESE PLANES"*: "War! Oahu Bombed By Japanese Planes!," *Honolulu Star-Bulletin*, 1st Extra, De-

cember 7, 1941, 1. Available online at https://www.newspapers.com/clip/35778414/war-oahu-bombed-by-japanese-planes/.

29 *By Monday . . . flood of new details*: See Michael E. Ruane, "'WAR!' How a Stunned Media Broke the Pearl Harbor News," *Washington Post,* December 6, 2011, accessed August 28, 2021, https://www.washingtonpost.com/local/war-how-a-stunned-media-broke-the-pearl-harbor-news/2011/12/06/gIQABzFtaO_story.html.

29 *The attack on Pearl Harbor . . . Wake Island, and Guam*: Toland, *Rising Sun,* 230–35.

29 *At 12:30 p.m . . . a standing ovation*: Roll, *Hopkins Touch,* 164.

30 *When it comes to speeches . . . any other public figure*: Smith, *FDR,* chapter 10.

30 *Today is different . . . catching their breath*: Roll, *Hopkins Touch,* 164.

30 *"Yesterday, December 7, 1941 . . . between the United States and the Japanese Empire"*: Franklin D. Roosevelt, *"Day of Infamy" Speech: Joint Address to Congress Leading to a Declaration of War Against Japan,* December 8, 1941, SEN 77A-H1, Records of the United States Senate, Record Group 46, National Archives, https://www.archives.gov/historical-docs/day-of-infamy-speech.

31 *"I do not think . . . of the whole people"*: Robert E. Sherwood quoted in Hamilton, *Mantle of Command,* 77.

31 *The Senate votes 82–0; the House of Representatives votes 388–1*: Roll, *Hopkins Touch,* 164.

31 *"This may have been . . . history of our country"*: Lowell Thomas CBS radio broadcast on Dec 8, 1941. Compiled in Lowell Thomas, *History as You Heard It* (New York: Doubleday, 1957), 182.

Chapter 7

32 *Sixty-eight years old . . . occupation of Nazi Germany*: Martin Gilbert, *Churchill: A Life* (London: Pimlico, 2000), 645–50.

32 *To friends . . . midday bath and brandy*: Ibid., 62.

32 *Churchill was born . . . and other subjects*: For other thorough accounts of Churchill's life and background, please see Paul Addison, *Churchill: The Unexpected Hero* (New York: Oxford University Press, 2005); Robert Blake and Wm. Roger Louis, *Churchill: A Major New Assessment of His Life in Peace and War* (New York: Oxford University Press, 1993); and Paul Johnson, *Churchill* (New York: Penguin, 2010).

33 *By the 1930s . . . annex nearby territories*: Gilbert, *Churchill,* 480.

34 *"hopes that if he feeds . . . will eat him last"*: Churchill radio broadcast January 20, 1940, https://winstonchurchill.org/resources/speeches/1940-the-finest-hour/the-war-situation-house-of-many-mansions/.

34 *Hitler invaded Poland in late 1939*: Kershaw, *To Hell and Back,* 349.

34 *Churchill's prescient understanding . . . as the war was beginning*: Ibid.

34 *"I felt as if . . . for this trial"*: Winston Churchill, *The Second World War,* abridged edition (London: Bloomsbury, 2013), 220.

34 *"You ask, what is our policy . . . toil, tears and sweat"*: The full text of this speech is available online; please see Winston Churchill, "Blood, Toil, Tears and Sweat: First Speech as Prime Minister to the House of Commons, May 13, 1940," International Churchill Society, accessed September 10, 2021, https://winstonchurchill.org/resources/speeches/1940-the-finest -hour/blood-toil-tears-sweat/.

34 *The problem was . . . around the Mediterranean*: Hastings, *Inferno*, 52–76.

35 *Only the British remained . . . existence was in doubt*: Ibid., 77–102.

35 *His great hope . . . America into the war*: Winston Churchill, *The Second World War*, vol. 3, *The Grand Alliance* (New York: Houghton Mifflin Co., 1985), 478–80.

35 *Now, tonight . . . and his aides are confused*: Roll, *Hopkins Touch*, 161.

35 *The designation "Pearl Harbor" isn't well known*: See Cita Stelzer, *Dinner with Churchill: Policy-Making at the Dinner Table* (New York: Pegasus Books, 2013).

35 *In true British fashion . . . by the butler*: Churchill, *Second World War*, 3:538.

36 *The United Kingdom's role . . . invading the Soviet Union*: Hastings, *Inferno*, chapter 6.

36 *Operation Barbarossa*: Kershaw, *To Hell and Back*, 350–31.

36 *With ruthless speed . . . approaching Leningrad and Moscow*: Hastings, *Inferno*, chapter 6.

36 *When the invasion first began . . . was a complicated business*: Churchill, *Second World War*, 3:340–347.

36 *"No one has been . . . to Russia and the Russian people"*: Churchill radio broadcast on the Soviet-German war, June 22, 1941. For the complete speech, see https://www.jewishvirtuallibrary.org/churchill-broadcast-on -the-soviet-german-war-june-1941.

36 *the Soviets had in fact been collaborating with Hitler*: See Hastings, *Inferno*, chapter 1.

37 *Unlike previous communist leaders . . . his personal ruthlessness*: Ibid., chapter 6.

37 *For the Prime Minister . . . "I guess we're in the same boat now"*: Roll, *Hopkins Touch*, 161–62.

38 *"the greatest joy . . . saved and thankful"*: Churchill quoted in Smith, *FDR*, chapter 23.

Chapter 8

39 *"The Wolf's Lair"*: Ian Kershaw, *Hitler, 1936–1945: Nemesis* (London: W. W. Norton & Co., 2000), 395–98.

39 *It's probably . . . Führer, Adolf Hitler*: Ibid., 442.

39 *Hitler's personal office . . . discover its whereabouts*: Ibid., 395–98.

39 *The Lair . . . rather than the Führer*: Ibid., 694–95. See also, Colin Schultz, "Meet the Woman Who Taste-Tested Hitler's Dinner," *Smithso-*

nian Magazine, April 29, 2013, https://www.smithsonianmag.com/smart -news/meet-the-woman-who-taste-tested-hitlers-dinner-44682990/.

40 *Lately, rather than . . . was logistically overwhelming*: Kershaw, *To Hell and Back,* 350.

40 *Meanwhile, Stalin . . . from the Soviet line*: Beevor, *Second World War,* 230–46.

41 *Now, with the winter . . . must wait until spring*: Kershaw, *To Hell and Back,* 352.

41 *Germany still has . . . worse than that*: Kershaw, *Hitler,* 445–47.

41 *"a bolt from the blue"*: Joseph Goebbels, quoted in Beevor, *Second World War,* 278.

41 *"slapped his thighs . . . brought to him"*: Hamilton, *Mantle of Command,* 88.

41 *"It was as if a . . . everyone around him"*: Ibid.

42 *"caught up in an ecstasy of rejoicing"*: Ibid.

42 *"jumping for joy . . . on the United States"*: Ribbentrop's reaction as reported by Italian Foreign Minister Galeazzo Ciano, ibid.

42 *By chance, Hitler . . . more time to prepare*: Kershaw, *Hitler,* 442–46.

42 *Hitler angrily rejects . . . full of lesser races*: Klaus P. Fischer, *Hitler and America* (Philadelphia: University of Pennsylvania Press, 2011), 10.

42 *"country of Negroes and Jews"*: Benito Mussolini as quoted in Hastings, *Inferno,* 193.

43 *"A great power . . . it declares war itself"*: Foreign Minister Joachim von Ribbentrop, quoted in Beevor, *Second World War,* 278.

43 *Without consulting . . . be buried or forgotten*: Kershaw, *Hitler,* 446.

43 *"that man who . . . more united than today"*: Jewish Virtual Library, "Adolf Hitler: Speech Declaring War Against the United States (December 11, 1941)," Speeches and Declarations, https://www.jewishvirtuallibrary .org/hitler-s-speech-declaring-war-against-the-united-states.

45 *It's no accident . . . Germany's grand mission*: Personal animosities were a product of the deeply personalized vision taken by Hitler during his rule. See Kershaw, *Hitler,* xliii-xliv.

Chapter 9

49 *With some exceptions . . . Iranian security forces*: O'Sullivan, *Nazi Secret Warfare,* 1.

49 *But like many . . . under Allied control*: The Allied invasion of Iran took place in August 1941, several months before this chapter's depiction of Tehran. For a description of the invasion see ibid., 25–29.

49 *Franz Mayr*: Security Service, KV 2/1479–3, 51, National Archives, United Kingdom.

50 *Four years earlier . . . the Nazi cause*: O'Sullivan, *Nazi Secret Warfare,* 3–4.

50 *He initially trained . . . Nazi intelligence organization*: Security Service, KV 2/1479–3, 51.

50 *Unlike Germany's traditional military . . . answered only Adolf Hitler*:
David Kahn, *Hitler's Spies: German Military Intelligence in World War II*
(New York: Macmillan, 1978), 6–7.

50 *Within the entry-level . . . on behalf of Germany*: Security Service, KV
2/1479–3, 51.

50 *"The S.D. were . . . Instructions would follow"*: Security Service, KV
2/1479–1, 48.

51 *Those instructions . . . in the city*: Security Service, KV 2/1479–3, 51–52.

51 *Hitler responded favorably . . . superior Aryan race*: Blum, *Night of the
Assassins,* 72–74.

51 *Hitler's true motivations . . . to the Caspian Sea*: O'Sullivan, *Nazi Secret
Warfare,* 10–12.

51 *Once Hitler attacked . . . with the Allies*: Ibid., 25–27.

52 *The Soviets . . . to the Soviet Union*: For more on Lend-Lease see George
C. Herring, Jr., *Aid to Russia, 1941–1946: Strategy, Diplomacy, the Origins
of the Cold War* (New York: Columbia University Press, 1973); Warren F.
Kimball, *The Most Unsordid Act: Lend-Lease, 1939–1941* (Baltimore, MD:
Johns Hopkins University Press, 1969); Vladimir Kotelnikov, *Lend-Lease
and Soviet Aviation in the Second World War* (Warwick, UK: Helion and
Company, 2018); and Albert L. Weeks, *Russia's Life-Saver: Lend-Lease Aid
to the U.S.S.R. in World War II* (Lanham, MD: Lexington Books, 2004).

52 *"The situation inside . . . punishment for this"*: Franz Mayr diary entry,
June 28, 1942, Security Service, KV 2/1482–2, 8.

52 *"the life of an enemy . . . every day and every night"*: Franz Mayr diary
entry, September 11, 1942, Security Service, KV 2/1482–2.

52 *In this environment . . . to neutral Turkey*: O'Sullivan, *Nazi Secret Warfare,* 132–33.

52 *Mayr, though, refused . . . to get things done*: Security Service, KV
2/1479–3, 51–56. For the main members of the Melliun circle, see KV2
1479–2, 51–52.

52 *"Slowly but surely . . . with the people"*: Franz Mayr diary entry, July 2,
1942, Security Service, KV 2/1482–2.

53 *For most of 1942 . . . were on to him*: Security Service, KV 2/1482–1, 14.

53 *Yet through these . . . her family at risk*: O'Sullivan, *Nazi Secret Warfare,*
118–21.

53 *"I should so much . . . like to see you"*: Security Service, KV 2/1482–4, 23.

Chapter 10

55 *The press conference . . . country of Morocco*: For more on the Anfa Hotel
and the process of selecting it as the site of the Casablanca Conference, see
Reilly, *Reilly of the White House,* 148–49.

55 *"The entire area . . . and barbed wire"*: *New York Times,* January 27,
1943.

56 *"He wore a . . . in a long holder"*: Ibid.

56 *"Prime Minister Churchill . . . in his mouth"*: Ibid.

57 *"I think it can . . . by Germany, Italy, and Japan"*: FDR and Churchill

press conference, January 24, 1943, in Casablanca, Morocco. Full transcript is from *The Public Papers and Addresses of Franklin D. Roosevelt: 1943, The Tide Turns* (New York: Harper & Brothers Publishers, 1950), 37–45.

58 *"I was standing . . . a surprise to him"*: Recollection of Joel McCrea, quoted in Nigel Hamilton, *Commander in Chief: FDR's Battle with Churchill, 1943* (New York: Houghton Mifflin Harcourt, 2016), 128–129.

58 *"does not mean . . . subjugation of other people"*: FDR and Churchill press conference, January 24, 1943, in Casablanca, Morocco, *1943, The Tide Turns*, 37–45.

58 *"one thing . . . we work together"*: Ibid.

59 *one of the few foreign leaders to address the United State Congress*: The Marquis de Lafayette holds the position of the first foreign leader to address the House of Representatives, appearing before them on December 10, 1824, while Louis Kossuth, the exiled governor of Hungary, first addressed the U.S. Senate on January 5, 1852. The first time a foreign leader addressed a joint meeting of Congress occurred when King Kalakaua of Hawaii visited Washington, D.C., in 1874. Almost a decade prior to Churchill, French Ambassador Andre de Laboulaye addressed a joint session of Congress to mark the centennial of the death of the Marquis de Lafayette (May 20, 1934).

59 *"the forces ranged . . . and in peace"*: The full text of the speech is available online; see Winston Churchill, "Address to Joint Session of US Congress, 1941," America's National Churchill Museum, accessed September 10, 2021, https://www.nationalchurchillmuseum.org/churchill-address-to-congress.html.

59 *"Now Fields . . . sleep at night"*: Churchill to Alonzo Fields, as quoted in Joseph E. Persico, *Roosevelt's Centurions: FDR and the Commanders He Led to Victory in World War II* (New York: Random House, 2013), 115.

60 *"stark naked . . . President of the United States"*: This anecdote is widely attributed to Harry Hopkins; see for example Robin Renwick, *Fighting with Allies: America and Britain in Peace and War* (London: Biteback Publishing, 2017), chapter 5.

61 *"Even when there is . . . into storm and ruin"*: Roosevelt and Churchill press conference, January 24, 1943, in Casablanca, Morocco, *1943, The Tide Turns*, 37–45.

Chapter 11

64 *Nazi "Hunger Plan"*: For more information on the "Nazi Hunger Plan," see Lizzie Collingham, *The Taste of War: World War II and the Battle for Food* (New York: Penguin Press, 2013), esp. chapter 9; Alex J. Kay, "Germany's Staatssekretäre, Mass Starvation and the Meeting of 2 May 1941," *Journal of Contemporary History* 41, no. 4 (2006): 685–700; Alex J. Kay, "'The Purpose of the Russian Campaign Is the Decimation of the Slavic Population by Thirty Million': The Radicalization of German Food Policy in Early 1941," in *Nazi Policy on the Eastern Front, 1941: Total War, Genocide,*

and Radicalization, eds. Alex J. Kay, Jeff Rutherford, and David Stahel (Rochester, NY: University of Rochester Press, 2012), 101–29; and Gesine Gerhard, "Food and Genocide: Nazi Agrarian Politics in the Occupied Territories of the Soviet Union," *Contemporary European History* 18, no. 1 (February 2009): 45–65.

64 *"The whole field . . . train moved on"*: Alexander Tvardovsky as quoted in Beevor, *Second World War,* 196.

65 *instructions to execute any of their own soldiers who retreated*: This order came on July 28, 1942, as Order No. 227, often known by its infamous proclamation "Not one step back!" See Soviet Order No. 227 in S. V. Stepashin and V. P. Iampol'skii, *Organy Gosudarstvennoy Bezopasnosti SSSR v Velikoy Otechestvennoy Voyne: Sbornik documentov* (Moscow: Kniga i biznes, 1995–2014), vol. 3, bk. 2, doc. 1027, 76–80.

65 *seven hundred thousand Soviet soldiers and civilians*: Andrew N. Buchanan, *World War II in Global Perspective, 1931–1953: A Short History* (Hoboken: John Wiley & Sons, 2019), 74.

65 *The German army . . . during the same period*: For casualties on the Eastern front, please see Donald Niewyk and Francis Nicosia, *The Columbia Guide to the Holocaust* (New York: Columbia University Press, 2003), 421. For Soviet casualties, please see Chris Bellamy, *Absolute War: Soviet Russia in the Second World War* (New York: Vintage Press, 2008), 476; and G. F. Krivosheev, ed. *Soviet Casualties and Combat Losses in the Twentieth Century,* trans. Christine Barnard (Philadelphia, PA: Stackpole Books, 1997).

66 *"The Führer is . . . large urban population"*: Adolf Hitler's directive of September 29, 1941, to Army Group North. Quoted from Anna Reid, *Leningrad: Tragedy of a City Under Siege, 1941–44* (London: Bloomsbury, 2011), 135.

67 *crime of cannibalism*: On cannibalism cases in Leningrad and elsewhere, see Richard Overy, *Russia's War: A History of the Soviet War Effort, 1941–1945* (New York: Penguin, 1998), 107, 183; and Reid, *Leningrad,* 280, 286–92, 408.

67 *nine hundred thousand residents*: On civilian casualties in the siege of Leningrad, see Richard Bidlack, *The Leningrad Blockade, 1941–1944: A New Documentary History from the Soviet Archives,* trans. Marian Schwartz (New Haven, CT: Yale University Press), esp. 1, 36; David M. Glantz, *The Siege of Leningrad 1941–44: 900 Days of Terror* (Osceola, WI: Zenith Press, 2001), 179; and Reid, *Leningrad,* 3–4.

67 *"We have only to kick . . . crashing down"*: As quoted in Beevor, *Second World War,* 190.

68 *Still, in the fall of 1942 . . . planting tank mines*: On the battle of Stalingrad, please see Anthony Beevor, *Stalingrad: The Fateful Siege, 1942–1943* (New York: Penguin, 1999); and Jochen Hellbeck, *Stalingrad: The City That Defeated the Third Reich,* trans. Christopher Tauchen and Dominic Bonfiglio (New York: PublicAffairs, 2015).

69 *"war of extermination"*: Hitler quoted in Beevor, *Second World War,* 189.

Chapter 12

70 *Nazi spy Franz Mayr . . . received his message*: O'Sullivan, *Nazi Secret Warfare*, 216–21.

71 *The odds of . . . seemingly forgotten mission*: Ibid., 67.

71 *"by the end . . . English are concerned"*: Adolf Hitler as stated to Albert Speer, quoted in Ashley Jackson, *Persian Gulf Command: A History of the Second World War in Iran and Iraq* (New Haven, CT: Yale University Press, 2018), 254.

72 *Mayr has shared . . . whereabouts a secret*: For Mayr's trust and reliance on Sanjari, see O'Sullivan, *Nazi Secret Warfare*, 111, 114.

72 *No doubt . . . Merrick continued to do*: Ibid., 118–21.

Chapter 13

74 *"the most unprecedented . . . of the century"*: United Press International news wire story as printed in, e.g., *Richmond Times-Dispatch,* January 27, 1943. The *Times-Dispatch*'s headline was typical: "Roosevelt Flies to Africa to Talk War with Churchill: Allied Leaders Map Full 1943 Campaign to Eliminate Axis."

75 *"I know you will . . . will continue to do so"*: FDR to Churchill, March 18, 1942, in Beevor, *Second World War,* 281.

75 *"Mr. Brown"*: Smith, *FDR,* 557.

76 *"The more I consider . . . talk with you"*: Roosevelt to Stalin, December 2, 1942, in Susan Butler, ed., *My Dear Mr. Stalin: The Complete Correspondence of Franklin D. Roosevelt and Joseph V. Stalin* (New Haven, CT: Yale University Press, 2006), 42.

77 *"I welcome the idea . . . relaxed in January"*: Stalin to Roosevelt, December 6, 1942, in ibid., 43.

77 *"I am deeply disappointed . . . North Africa about March 1"*: Roosevelt to Stalin, December 8, 1942, in ibid., 43.

77 *"I, too, express deep . . . shall not differ"*: Stalin to Roosevelt, December 14, 1942, in ibid., 44.

78 *"I am very sorry . . . understand your position"*: Roosevelt to Stalin, December 21, 1942, in ibid., 45.

Chapter 14

79 *280 men in 1929 to 52,000 in 1933*: numbers are from the United States Holocaust Memorial Museum, "The SS," Holocaust Encyclopedia, accessed on September 2, 2021, https://encyclopedia.ushmm.org/content/en/article/introduction-to-the-holocaust.

80 *"like a nursery . . . of the SS"*: Heinrich Himmler quoted in Anthony Read, *The Devil's Disciples: Hitler's Inner Circle* (New York: W.W. Norton & Co., 2003), 179.

81 *"I walked out . . . the Third Reich"*: Walter Schellenberg, *Hitler's Secret Service,* trans. Louis Hagen (New York: Harper & Row, 1971), 29–30.

82 *"the offensive force . . . against the Jews"*: Leslie Alan Horvitz and

Christopher Catherwood, *Encyclopedia of War Crimes and Genocide* (New York: Facts on File, 2006), 199.

82 *"Untouched by any pangs . . . extreme cruelty"*: Schellenberg, *Hitler's Secret Service,* 30.

Chapter 15

84 *Einsatzgruppen, or "Operation Groups"*: For the activities of the Einsatzgruppen, please see Christopher R. Browning, *Ordinary Men: Reserve Police Battalion 101 and the Final Solution in Poland* (New York: Harper Perennial, 2017); Helmut Langerbein, *Hitler's Death Squads: The Logic of Mass Murder* (College Station: Texas A&M University Press, 2003); and Richard Rhodes, *Masters of Death: The SS-Einsatzgruppen and the Invention of the Holocaust* (New York: Vintage Press, 2003).

86 *Bila Tserkva . . . ninety Jewish children aged six or younger*: The episode described here and below is fully recounted in Richard J. Evans, *The Third Reich at War* (New York: Penguin Books, 2008), 229–230.

86 *"I shall never forget . . . before they died"*: Ibid., 230.

Chapter 16

88 *It's no ordinary train . . . case of emergency*: Details of the train are from Edward G. Lengel, "Franklin D. Roosevelt's Train Ferdinand Magellan," White House Historical Association, accessed on September 8, 2021, https://www.whitehousehistory.org/franklin-d-roosevelt-rsquo-s-train-ferdinand-magellan.

89 *"The communications car . . . wished to send"*: William Rigdon as quoted in Hamilton, *Commander in Chief,* 181–82.

90 *"From Solomon Defense . . . RXZ at 0800"*: Ibid., 182.

90 *"We've hit the jackpot . . . to get Yamamoto"*: Ibid., 183.

92 *"They shot any man . . . hogs and cows"*: From the diary of Father Wendelin Dunker, a Catholic missionary stationed in the region. Quoted from James M. Scott, "The Untold Story of the Vengeful Japanese Attack after the Doolittle Raid," *Smithsonian Magazine,* April 15, 2015, https://www.smithsonianmag.com/history/untold-story-vengeful-japanese-attack-doolittle-raid-180955001/.

93 *"raped time after time . . . by venereal disease"*: Diary of Rev. Frederick McGuire, quoted from ibid.

93 *"These Japanese troops . . . in those areas"*: Gen. Chiang Kai-shek cable to FDR, April 28, 1943, in Otto David Tolischus, *Through Japanese Eyes* (New York: Reynal & Hitchcock, 1945), 197.

93 *Today, historians continue . . . headlines in America*: Arguments for the Doolittle Raid's importance for Allied military strategy include Robert B. Kane, "The Doolittle Raid—75 Years Later," *Air & Space Power Journal* 31, no. 1 (spring 2017): 72–80; and David G. Styles, "Towards a Place in History," *Air Power History* 50, no. 3 (fall 2003): 34–41.

95 *"The brutality of the Germans . . . in broad daylight"*: Winston Chur-

chill, *The Second World War, vol. 4, The Hinge of Fate* (London: Cassell & Co., 1951), 742.

Chapter 17

96 *Heinrich Müeller . . . Reich Security Main Office*: The original documents from the Wannsee Conference, including the full list of attendees, was after the war obtained by the U.S. government, translated, and presented as evidence in the trials at Nuremberg. The paperwork, known as the "Wannsee Protocol," is archived online by the University of Pennsylvania at https:// www.writing.upenn.edu/~afilreis/Holocaust/wansee-transcript.html, accessed August 12, 2021.

97 *"In the course of . . . new Jewish revival"*. Ibid. No page numbers are indicated in the documents as translated.

100 *"Since it is opportunity . . . stupid and idiotic"*: Adolf Hitler as quoted in Callum MacDonald, *The Killing of Reinhard Heydrich: The SS "Butcher of Prague"* (New York: Da Capo Press, 1989), 182.

Chapter 18

104 *"bolt from the blue"*: O'Sullivan, *Nazi Secret Warfare*, 66.

104 *He had provided Berlin directions and coordinates . . . oversight*: Ibid., 217.

105 *Operation Franz*: See ibid., 167–76.

105 *Not only had they failed . . . in Washington, D.C.*: Goodwin, *No Ordinary Time*, 401–2. For a more detailed account of the "casa blanca" mishap and Walter Schellenberg's role in it, see Ladislas Farago, *The Game of the Foxes: The Untold Story of German Espionage in the United States and Great Britain During World War II* (New York: Bantam Books, 1973), 722–24.

106 *"tough callous ox"*: Schellenberg, *Hitler's Secret Service*, 328.

106 *"From the first . . . petrify its prey"*: Ibid., 328.

106 *"quota of one . . . glasses of wine"*: Ibid., 330.

Chapter 19

107 *The weapons hit . . . is just beginning*: O'Sullivan, *Nazi Secret Warfare*, 176.

Chapter 20

109 *"an Irishman . . . than brain"*: Reilly, *Reilly of the White House*, 7.

110 *On the day . . . the White House*: Ibid., 6.

111 *"The big bugaboo . . . any of these"*: Ibid., 15.

111 *And it was Reilly . . . car route, and hotel*: Reilly details his and the Secret Service's advance measures in preparation for Roosevelt's trip to Casablanca in ibid., 142–47.

111 *"I could outwit . . . nightmares in bed"*: Ibid., 8.

113 *"engaged in combat . . . a war plane"*: "Japanese Admiral Killed in Combat," *New York Times*, May 21, 1943.

113 *"Q: Mr. President . . . Gosh! (laughter)"*: Presidential press conference in the

Executive Office of the President, May 21, 1943, FDR Library, Marist College, http://www.fdrlibrary.marist.edu/_resources/images/pc/pc0149.pdf.

Chapter 21

115 *After the midnight . . . to do is follow*: O'Sullivan, *Nazi Secret Warfare,* 176.

Chapter 22

118 *Gevork Vartanian*: For the most complete biography of Vartanian see Nikolai Dolgopolov's *Vartanian: zhizn' zamechatel'nykh liudei* (Moscow: Molodaia gvardiia, 2014). For short, English-language biographies of Vartanian and his activities in Tehran, see Nikolai Dolgopolov, "How 'the Lion and the Bear' Were Saved," *Russia Beyond The Headlines,* November 29, 2007, accessed September 30, 2021, https://www.rbth.com/articles /2007/11/29/lion_and_bear.html; "Gevork Vartanyan," *The Telegraph,* January 11, 2012, accessed September 30, 2021, https://www.telegraph.co .uk/news/obituaries/9008287/Gevork-Vartanyan.html; and "Russian Spy Who 'Changed the Course of History,' Goar Vartanyan, Dies Aged 93," Reuters/ABC, November 28, 2019, accessed September 30, 2021, https:// www.abc.net.au/news/2019–11–28/female-russian-spy-goar-vartanyan -dies-age-93/11745228.

119 *"As a child . . . for the Motherland"*: Plutenko and Vartanian, "Tegeran-43."

119 *"My first task . . . to my group"*: Dolgopolov, *Vartanian,* 53–54.

120 *rumors of enemy paratroopers*: Numerous German airdrops took place over Iran in the spring of 1943, and no fewer than thirty-four unidentified aircraft sightings were reported and officially documented by the British over Iran and northern Iraq during that summer. See O'Sullivan, *Nazi Secret Warfare,* 190n3.

Chapter 23

125 *Schellenberg's spacious corner office . . . dies a year later*: Reinhard R. Doerries, *Hitler's Intelligence Chief: Walter Schellenberg* (New York: Enigma Books, 2009), 164n332. A memorial plaque commemorating Alexander Beer's life and death is now on this building, which still stands on Berkaer Strasse in Berlin.

126 *"There were times . . . block every exit"*: Schellenberg, *Hitler's Secret Service,* 214, 218.

129 *"a man who . . . thought he was"*: Otto Skorzeny, *My Commando Operations: The Memoirs of Hitler's Most Daring Commando,* trans. David Johnston (Atglen, PA: Schiffer Publishing, 1995), 91.

Chapter 24

131 *"My Dear Mr. Stalin . . . meet this summer"*: Roosevelt to Stalin, May 5, 1943, in *Foreign Relations of the United States: Diplomatic Papers: The Conferences at Cairo and Tehran, 1943* (Washington, D.C.: United States Government Printing Office, 1961), 3–4.

132 *"Three is a crowd . . . take care of that"*: Elizabeth Kimball MacLean, *Joseph E. Davies: Envoy to the Soviets* (Westport, CT; Praeger, 1992), 100.

132 *"Africa is out . . . of Bering Straits"*: Roosevelt to Stalin, May 5, 1943, in *Conferences at Cairo and Tehran*, 4.

Chapter 25

134 *In the weeks . . . August of 1942*: Gordon A. Harrison, *The European Theater of Operations: Cross-Channel Attack* (Washington, D.C.: U.S. Army Center of Military History, 1993), 12.

135 *Although the idea . . . "second front" in 1942*: Notes on White House meeting cited in Sherwood, *Roosevelt and Hopkins*, 563.

135 *"it does not seem . . . will be possible"*: United States Department of State, *Foreign Relations of The United States, The Conferences at Washington, 1941–1942*, accessed on April 6, 2022, https://history.state.gov /historicaldocuments/frus1941-43/d115.

137 *"he would get along . . . Churchill's absence"*: W. Averell Harriman and Elie Abel, *Special Envoy to Churchill and Stalin, 1941–1946* (New York: Random House, 1975), 216.

138 *"We, both of us . . . with Marshal Stalin"*: Churchill address to the House of Representatives, May 19, 1943, *Congressional Record*, vol. 89, pt. 4, 4621.

Chapter 26

139 *"Azerbaijan East should . . . advancing troops"*: Security Service, KV 2/1482–5, 76.

140 *"The Managing Committee . . . traitorous ministers"*: Security Service, KV 2/1482–6, 40**.

Chapter 27

143 *"unequivocally devoted . . . Why?"*: Eubank, *Summit at Teheran*, 80–81.

144 *"You are doing . . . Good luck!"*: Roosevelt to Stalin, May 5, 1943, in *Conferences at Cairo and Tehran*, 5.

144 *"I think your President . . . as he suggests"*: Eubank, *Summit at Teheran*, 82.

145 *"seemed to be . . . cordially received"*: Davies to Roosevelt, May 21, 1943, in *Conferences at Cairo and Tehran*, 5.

146 *"I agree with you . . . Mr. Davies personally"*: Stalin to Roosevelt, May 26, 1943, in ibid., 6–7.

146 *"Joe, you have done a grand job"*: Eubank, *Summit at Teheran*, 88.

148 *"In the Mediterranean . . . Spring of 1944"*: Roosevelt and Churchill to Stalin, June 2, 1943, in Butler, *My Dear Mr. Stalin*, 136–38.

Chapter 28

149 *For a while . . . water-borne bacteria*: O'Sullivan, *Nazi Secret Warfare*, 176.

150 *"We had to cut . . . cases and rucksacks"*: Ibid., 119.

150 *As Mayr originally . . . to the next location*: Security Service, KV 2/1478–4, 34.

Chapter 29

152 *"Your decision creates . . . course of the war"*: Stalin to Churchill and Roosevelt, June 11, 1943, in Ministry of Foreign Affairs of the U.S.S.R., *Correspondence Between the Chairman of the Council of Ministers of the U.S.S.R. and the Presidents of the U.S.A. and the Prime Ministers of Great Britain During the Great Patriotic War of 1941–1945, vol. 2* (Moscow, U.S.S.R.: Foreign Languages Publishing House, 1957), 70-71.

153 *"I quite understand . . . the Soviet armies"*: Churchill to Stalin, June 19, 1943, in Butler, *My Dear Mr. Stalin*, 141-42.

154 *"You say that you . . . armies are insignificant"*: Stalin to Churchill, June 24, 1943, in *Correspondence, vol. 2*, 74–76.

155 *"we British were left . . . leave me unmoved"*: Churchill to Stalin, June 27, 1943, in Ministry of Foreign Affairs of the U.S.S.R., *Correspondence Between the Chairman of the Council of Ministers of the U.S.S.R. and the Presidents of the U.S.A. and the Prime Ministers of Great Britain During the Great Patriotic War of 1941-945, vol. 2* (Moscow, U.S.S.R.: Foreign Languages Publishing House, 1957), 140–41.

155 *Churchill, always temperamental . . . over for good*: See, for example, Eubank, *Summit at Teheran*, 96.

Chapter 30

156 *"difficult assignment from . . . emphasize his disappointment"*: Harriman and Abel, *Special Envoy*, 216–17.

157 *"low point in the history of the alliance"*: Ibid., 213.

157 *"Averell told me . . . and alarmed thereby"*: Churchill to Roosevelt, June 25, 1943, in *Conferences at Cairo and Tehran*, 10–11.

158 *"I did not suggest . . . trust between them"*: Roosevelt to Churchill, June 28, 1943, in ibid., 11.

Chapter 31

159 *"These meetings . . . my service"*: Schellenberg, *Hitler's Secret Service*, 354.

159 *the Forschungsamt*: Kahn, *Hitler's Spies*, 55.

160 *"Brown Sheets"*: Ibid., 181.

160 *"I have received . . . meet Stalin somewhere"*: Joseph Goebbels, *The Goebbels Diaries: 1942–1943*, trans. Louis P. Lochner (Garden City, NY: Doubleday & Company, 1948), 333.

161 *"news has reached . . . meet Stalin soon"*: Ibid., 381.

161 *"Through collaboration . . . the United States"*: Schellenberg, *Hitler's Secret Service*, 359.

161 *One night in late July . . . German spymaster*: The depiction of this evening is from Howard Blum, *Night of the Assassins*, chapter 14.

162 *Hitler, according to Canaris . . . where it is*: Ibid.

Chapter 32

164 *"In addition to . . . the same period"*: Roosevelt to Stalin, June 16, 1943, in Butler, *My Dear Mr. Stalin*, 141.

165 *"Two years ago . . . so heroically making"*: Roosevelt to Stalin, June 22, 1943, in ibid., 144.

165 *"Everything was enveloped . . . slaughterhouse of tanks"*: Statement of Vasilii Bryukhov, Russian T-34 Commander, as quoted in Lloyd Clark, "The Largest Tank Battle in History Began 75 Years Ago Today—Here's How it Changed WWII," *Military Times,* July 5, 2018, accessed on October 8, 2021, https://www.militarytimes.com/veterans/military-history/2018/07/05/the-largest-tank-battle-in-history-began-75-years-ago-today-heres-how-it-changed-wwii/.

166 *two hundred thousand Germans and around eight hundred thousand Soviets*: These casualties include those of Operation Citadel, the Battle of Kursk, and the subsequent Soviet counterattacks. For a breakdown of these statistics, please see Karl-Heinz Frieser, *Die Ostfront 1943/44: Der Krieg im Osten und an den Nebenfronten* (München: Deutsche Verlags-Anstalt, 2011), 153–54, 197–201; and Krivosheev, *Soviet Casualties,* 124–32.

166 *"Although I have no . . . you and me"*: Roosevelt to Stalin, July 15, 1943, in *Conferences at Cairo and Tehran,* 16.

168 *population of 114,000 is now only 30,000*: Figures are from Butler, *My Dear Mr. Stalin,* 149.

168 *"Sincere congratulations . . . heroic accomplishments"*: Roosevelt to Stalin, August 5, 1943, in ibid., 149.

168 *"Thank you for . . . objections to this"*: Stalin to Roosevelt, August 8, 1943, in *Conferences at Cairo and Tehran,* 18.

Chapter 33

170 *"Schellenberg was a talker . . . Prague the year before"*: Otto Skorzeny, *My Commando Operations,* 91.

170 *"I must say . . . this commando post"*: Ibid., 203.

171 *Operation Anton . . . mostly alone*: For more on Berthold Shulze-Holthus's activities in Iran, see O'Sullivan, *Nazi Secret Warfare,* chapter 10; for more on Operation Anton see ibid., chapter 13.

171 *"I had drawn up . . . handling of motorboats"*: Otto Skorzeny, *Skorzeny's Special Missions: The Memoirs of Hitler's Most Daring Commando* (Minneapolis: Zenith Press, 2011), 82.

171 *He has just finished . . . calls to check in*: Ibid., 101.

171 *"wild excitement . . . nothing at all"*: Ibid., 101–2.

172 *"Could it be connected . . . not probable"*: Ibid., 102.

172 *"What [is] in store . . . I knew nothing"*: Ibid., 103–4.

173 *"I'll take you to the Führer . . . every limb"*: Ibid., 109.

Chapter 34

174 *"Now I was to meet . . . bow was correct"*: Skorzeny, *Skorzeny's Special Missions,* 110–11.

175 *"His word . . . extraordinary power"*: Skorzeny, *My Commando Operations,* 230.

175 *"What do you think . . . stay, Captain Skorzeny"*: Skorzeny, *Skorzeny's Special Missions,* 113.

175 *"Mussolini was betrayed . . .* Duce *depends on it!"*: Skorzeny, *My Commando Operations,* 229–30.

176 *"The longer Hitler spoke . . . deeply moved"*: Skorzeny, *Skorzeny's Special Missions,* 115.

176 *"I have full confidence . . . best of luck"*: Skorzeny, *My Commando Operations,* 230.

176 *"I fully understand . . . do my best"*: Skorzeny, *Skorzeny's Special Missions,* 115.

Chapter 35

177 *For months they've been . . . [wireless transmitter] operator"*: Security Service, KV 2/1478–4, 2.

178 *So right now . . . discovery of the night*: O'Sullivan, *Nazi Secret Warfare,* 118.

Chapter 36

182 *"do not enable . . . 'Bunnyhug' or 'Ballyhoo'"*: Memo from Winston Churchill to Gen. Hastings Ismay (undated). After the war a copy of the Prime Minister's memo landed in the archives of the Central Intelligence Agency in the United States. In 1952 Allen Dulles, then Deputy Director of the CIA, forwarded Churchill's memo to an agency colleague with a small note saying: "I send for your amusement . . . and I suggest we take into account the wise comments made in connection with the designation we give to our projects." Both Dulles's note and Churchill's original memo are from https://www.cia.gov/readingroom/docs/CIA -RDP80M01009A000701010051–5.pdf.

183 *"We wish to emphasize . . . more your consideration"*: Roosevelt and Churchill to Stalin, August 18, 1943, in *Conferences at Cairo and Tehran,* 20–21.

183 *"I entirely share . . . point as Fairbanks"*: Stalin to Roosevelt and Churchill, August 24, 1943, in ibid., 22.

184 *"I hope you have seen . . . held very soon"*: Roosevelt to Churchill, August 26, 1943, in ibid., 23.

184 *"A large scale buildup . . . effort against the Axis"*: Roosevelt and Churchill to Stalin, August 25, 1943. Ministry of Foreign Affairs of the U.S.S.R., *Correspondence Between Stalin, Roosevelt, Truman, Churchill and Attlee During World War II* (Honolulu: University Press of the Pacific, 2001), 150–51.

184 *"Nothing is nearer . . . the Hitlerite tyranny"*: This speech is reprinted at length in the Australian newspaper *The Morning Bulletin.* Please see "Broadcast by Churchill from Quebec: 'Drive On Until We Have Finished the Job,'" *Morning Bulletin,* September 2, 1943, 1, 4. Available at https:// trove.nla.gov.au/newspaper/article/56288916/5448880. The speech can also be listened to at the International Churchill Society website, https://winstonchurchill.org/resources/speeches/1941–1945-war-leader /broadcast-from-quebec/.

185 *"I still hope . . . and December fifteenth"*: Roosevelt to Stalin, September 4, 1943, in *Conferences at Cairo and Tehran*, 23.

185 *"As to our personal . . . for instance, Iran"*: Stalin to Roosevelt, September 8, 1943, in ibid., 24.

Chapter 37

189 *"Pick fifty men—only the best"*: Skorzeny, *Skorzeny's Special Missions*, 120.

190 *"We learned that . . . no real clue"*: Ibid., 134.

191 *elevation of 7,200 feet*: Skorzeny, *My Commando Operations*, 254. Skorzeny indicates the hotel's altitude as 2,212 meters; the nonmetric equivalent is 7,257 feet.

191 *September 8*: Date of aerial reconnaissance is from "Operation Eiche: The Rescue of Benito Mussolini," *Veritas* 11, no. 1 (2015): 35.

192 *"It was certain . . . one and only chance"*: Direct quote is from the manuscript: Otto Skorzeny, "My Rescue of Mussolini, 12 September 1943," Mataxis Collection, USASOC History Office Classified Files, Fort Bragg, NC.

192 *A dozen lightweight DFS 230 gliders*: "Operation Eiche," 37.

192 *"Helmets on!"*: Skorzeny, *Skorzeny's Special Missions*, 189.

192 *"The pilot turned . . . out of the question"*: Ibid.

193 *"Crash landing . . . you can get"*: Ibid., 191.

Chapter 38

196 *"I am delighted . . . made for our convenience"*: Roosevelt to Stalin, September 11, 1943, in *Stalin's Correspondence*, 92–93.

196 *"he would welcome . . . to provide facilities"*: Alexander C. Kirk to Roosevelt, September 10, 1943, in *Conferences at Cairo and Tehran*, 25.

196 *"I am pleased . . . defer to your wishes"*: Churchill to Stalin, September 10, 1943, in *Stalin's Correspondence*, 161.

197 *"As regards the meeting . . . is not yet represented"*: Stalin to Roosevelt and Churchill, September 12, 1943, in *Stalin's Correspondence*, 94.

197 *"I have been pondering . . . somewhat loosely-controlled area"*: Churchill to Stalin, September 27, 1943, in *Stalin's Correspondence*, 165.

197 *"Then perhaps only two . . . them to the President"*: Churchill to Stalin, October 1, 1943, in *Stalin's Correspondence*, 165–66.

198 *"I do not think . . . correspondence on the meeting"*: Stalin to Churchill, October 3, 1943, in *Stalin's Correspondence*, 170–71.

Chapter 39

199 *"I closed my eyes . . . last mighty heave"*: Skorzeny, *Skorzeny's Special Missions*, 190.

200 *"stick to him like glue"*: Ibid., 191.

200 *"A hasty kick sent . . . You are free"*: Ibid., 191–95.

201 *"I knew my friend . . . moments in my life"*: Skorzeny, *My Commando Operations*, 268.

202 *the plane accelerates . . . Gran Sasso mountains*: Details of the takeoff are from Skorzeny, *Skorzeny's Special Missions*, 202–3.

Chapter 40

204 *"You have performed . . . my friend Mussolini"*: Hitler's words to Skorzeny, as quoted in Skorzeny, *Skorzeny's Special Missions*, 202–3.

204 *Knight's Cross of the Iron Cross*: As described in ibid., 211.

205 *"Let us rejoice . . . touching a ceremony"*: Goebbels, *Goebbels Diaries*, 450–53.

205 *"Most Dangerous Man in Europe"*: See for example "Mussolini's Rescuers Flee Internment Camp," *Ottawa Journal*, September 30, 1948.

Chapter 41

208 *"decipher[ing] the American Naval codes"*: "Gevork Vartanyan," *The Telegraph*, January 11, 2012, accessed September 16, 2021, https://www.telegraph.co.uk/news/obituaries/9008287/Gevork-Vartanyan.html.

209 *"According to our . . . as soon as possible"*: The transmission is documented in British intelligence files; see Security Service, KV 1478–3, 6.

Chapter 42

212 *"had been left at large as a decoy"*: "Narrative of the Arrest of Franz Mayr," Security Service, KV 2/1478.

213 *"go-between between Mayr"*: Ibid.

213 *"The DSO . . . attempt to resist"*: Ibid.

213 *"Are you Franz Mayr? . . . Yes"*: Ibid.

Chapter 43

216 *The trick is . . . larger war*: For more information on the Soviet-Japanese Neutrality Pact, see Boris Slavinsky, *The Japanese-Soviet Neutrality Pact: A Diplomatic History, 1941–1945,* trans. Geoffrey Jukes (New York: Routledge, 2003). For the actual text of the pact, see "Soviet-Japanese Neutrality Pact," April 13, 1941, accessed January 25, 2022, https://avalon.law.yale.edu/wwii/s1.asp.

217 *"excellent buildings . . . American guards"*: Roosevelt to Stalin, October 14, 1943, in Butler, *My Dear Mr. Stalin*, 172–73.

217 *"we could put . . . seclusion and security"*: Churchill, *The Second World War, vol. 5, Closing the Ring* (London: Cassel & Co., Ltd., 1952), 273.

217 *"Unfortunately, not one . . . acceptable for me"*: Stalin to Roosevelt, October 19, 1943, in Butler, *My Dear Mr. Stalin*, 174.

217 *"I would have . . . generations to come"*: Roosevelt to Stalin, October 21, 1943, in ibid., 178.

217 *"It is very awkward . . . and preparations made"*: Churchill to Roosevelt, October 29, 1943, in *Conferences at Cairo and Tehran*, 35.

218 *"He proceeded to repeat . . . place but Tehran"*: Conrad Hull to FDR, October 21, 1943, in ibid., 35.

218 *"he did not see . . . cost thousands of lives"*: Conrad Hull to FDR, October 26, 1943, in ibid., 46.

219 *"the important factor . . . the Marshal himself"*: Conrad Hull to FDR, October 31, 1943, in ibid., 58.

219 *SEXTANT*: Churchill to Roosevelt, October 29, 1943, in ibid., 50.

Chapter 44

220 *"Cordell Hull . . . President I saw you"*: Reilly, *Reilly of the White House*, 160–63.

Chapter 45

224 *Operation Erntefest*: For figures and information on Operation Harvest Festival, see Yitzhak Arad, *The Operation Reinhard Death Camps: Belzec, Sobibor, Treblinka: Revised and Expanded Edition* (Bloomington: Indiana University Press, 2018), chapter 46; and Stefan Klemp, *"Aktion Erntefest": Mit Musik in den Tod: Rekonstruction eines Massenmords* (Münster: Geschichtsort Villa ten Hompel, 2013).

225 *"The Jews have richly deserved . . . for millennia by the Jews"*: Goebbels, *Goebbels Diaries*, 86.

226 *"We faced the question . . . from the earth"*: Heinrich Himmler quoted in Ian Kershaw, *Hitler*, 876–77.

226 *"The United Kingdom . . . these liberated countries"*: "Joint Four-Nation Declaration," October 1943, accessed January 25, 2022, https://avalon.law.yale.edu/wwii/moscow.asp.

Chapter 46

229 *"FIROUZ, after crossing . . . the dentist QUIDSI"*: Communication Istanbul to Prague dated October 20, 1943, Security Service, KV 2/1478, 2.

Chapter 47

231 *"The whole world . . . talk with you"*: Roosevelt to Stalin, November 8, 1943, in *Conferences at Cairo and Tehran*, 72.

231 *"I thank you . . . Iran, I accept"*: Stalin to Roosevelt, November 10, 1943, in *Conferences at Cairo and Tehran*, 78.

232 *"I now feel . . . have been involved"*: Churchill to Roosevelt, October 27, 1943, in *Conferences at Cairo and Tehran*, 47–48.

232 *"In view of . . . are deeply concerned"*: Ibid.

233 *"Postponement to midsummer . . . this particular problem"*: Henry Stimson to Harry Hopkins, November 10, 1943, in *Conferences at Cairo and Tehran*, 176.

234 *"Torpedo is coming . . . the starboard beam"*: Eubank, *Summit at Teheran*, 139.

Chapter 48

236 *"I could see . . . speak so eloquently"*: Schellenberg, *Hitler's Secret Service*, 333–34.

236 *the British ambassador's personal valet*: The valet's full name is Elyesa Bazna. Bazna, aka "Cicero," later wrote a memoir detailing his exploits; see Elyesa Bazna, *I Was Cicero* (New York: Harper and Row, 1962).

Chapter 49

238 *Accidentally, the torpedomen . . . a full investigation*: Kit Bonner, "The Ill-Fated U.S.S. William D. Porter," *Retired Officer Magazine*, March 1994, accessed November 9, 2021, https://web.archive.org /web/20080612075327/http://www.ussiowa.org/general/html/willie _d.htm.

239 *"must have been some damn Republican"*: Eubank, *Summit at Teheran*, 141.

Chapter 50

241 *Nikolai Kuznetsov*: Pavel Sudoplatov, Anatoli Sudoplatov, Jerrold Schecter, and Leona Schecter, *Special Tasks: The Memoirs of an Unwanted Witness—A Soviet Spymaster* (Boston: Little, Brown, 1994), 131.

242 *Ulrich von Ortel*: In some Russian accounts of this incident the name "von Ortel" is translated as "Oster" or "von Ostel." See Slava Katamidze, *Loyal Comrades, Ruthless Killers: The Secret Services of the USSR, 1920's to the Present* (New York: Brown Reference Group, 2003), 105; and Sudoplatov et al., *Special Tasks*, 130. In English language accounts the name is generally written as "von Ortel." See for example Blum, *Night of the Assassins*, 145; and Nigel West, *Encyclopedia of Political Assassinations* (Lanham, MD: Rowman & Littlefield, 2017), 144.

242 *"in Persian rugs"*: Katamidze, *Loyal Comrades, Ruthless Killers*, 105.

243 *"promptly reported to Moscow"*: Sudoplatov et al., *Special Tasks*, 130.

Chapter 51

244 *Mike Reilly is . . . back to Oran*: Reilly's travel itinerary is recounted in Reilly, *Reilly of the White House*, 163–66.

245 *"seething with unrest . . . President was in Cairo"*: Ibid., 164.

246 *"my opposite number"*: Ibid., 172. Reilly refers to the NKVD chief he meets as "General Artikov," but independent scholar Gary Kern suggests it was more likely Gen. Dmitri Arkadiev, who headed the NKVD's department of transportation and was apparently present at the conference. See Kern, "How 'Uncle Joe' Bugged FDR."

246 *roughly a mile and a half*: In his memoir Reilly incorrectly cites the distance as four miles. Ibid., 174.

246 *His next step . . . and Soviet embassies*: Not included in this account of Reilly's activities in Tehran is a trip he took to inspect the passenger railways that connect the city to Basra, Iraq. FDR's personal physician had suggested to Reilly that the President travel by train to Tehran rather than fly over the mountains at high altitude. Reilly, after inspecting the railroads, determined that travel by plane was still safer. For a full account of this, see ibid., 174–75.

Chapter 52

247 *"the Germans ha[ve] . . . for the parachutists"*: Reilly, *Reilly of the White House*, 175.

Chapter 53

250 *But the Germans . . . humans traversed them*: See Plutenko and Vartanian, "Tegeran-43."

Chapter 54

252 *"As we approached . . . solved more perfectly"*: Churchill, *Second World War*, 5:302.

Chapter 55

255 *The NKVD chief*: Reilly, *Reilly of the White House*, 177. In Reilly's account of the conversation, it is unclear whether he is speaking to General Arkadiev/Artikov or to some other NKVD official. Because Reilly refers to the speaker as the "NKVD chief," and because Arkadiev was the one who previously told him about the German parachutists, it seems likely that he would be the one to provide Reilly with this update.

255 *"captured some of . . . both heavily walled"*: Ibid., 177.

Chapter 56

258 *The bustle continues . . . difficult day ahead*: Times of day and locations are as reported in Harriman and Abel, *Special Envoy*, 263.

259 *"received bad news . . . looked comfortable enough"*: Ibid., 263–64.

Chapter 57

261 *3 p.m. on November 27*: "The President's Log at Tehran," in *Conferences at Cairo and Tehran*, 460.

261 *There are other advisors . . . room to room*: Based on the available records it is difficult to determine precisely who is in the room together with Roosevelt on this morning, who is speaking in the adjacent room, and when various personnel speak to Roosevelt either candidly or in front of others. The depiction herein is as detailed as can be ascertained from accounts later given by Harriman and Abel, *Special Envoy*, 263–64, and Reilly, *Reilly of the White House*, 177–78, and the account offered by the official "President's Log at Tehran" in *Conferences at Cairo and Tehran*, 462–463.

261 *"Teheran was filled . . . to each other"*: Harriman to FDR, as recorded in "President's Log at Tehran," 463.

262 *"the risk of assassination . . . [is] very real"*: Ibid.

262 *"would bring the three . . . drive about town"*: Ibid.

262 *"If we persisted . . . with President Roosevelt"*: Ibid.

262 *"it was Stalin . . . now to security"*: Harriman and Abel, *Special Envoy*, 264.

262 *"Stalin and Churchill . . . outside of town"*: Reilly, *Reilly of the White House*, 177–78.

263 *"If anything happened . . . not much difference, Sir"*: Ibid.

Chapter 58

264 *"I had no stomach . . . jumpers from Germany"*: Reilly, *Reilly of the White House*, 178.

265 *small group of three men*: Persons in car are indicated in Cairo/Tehran in "President's Log at Tehran," 487.

266 *"The Boss . . . amuse me much"*: Reilly, *Reilly of the White House*, 179.

Chapter 59

267 *"I'll talk to . . . indeed a shock"*: Reilly, *Reilly of the White House*, 179.

267 *"His hair was white . . . military escorts, notices"*: John L. Bates, "The 'Eureka' Conference: A Busy Time in Teheran," *Military Review* 66, no. 10 (October 1986): 78.

268 *"He was a small . . . across the room"*: Reilly, *Reilly of the White House*, 179–80.

268 *"At last . . . bring this about"*: Charles E. Bohlen, *Witness to History, 1929–1969* (New York: W.W. Norton & Co., 1973), 139.

268 *Whenever he meets . . . and filter holder*: Bates, "'Eureka' Conference," 78–80.

269 *"As the youngest . . . God-given opportunity"*: "Proceedings of the Conference, Sunday, November 28, First Plenary Meeting (Bohlen minutes)," in *Conferences at Cairo and Tehran*, 487.

269 *"I take pleasure . . . down to business"*: "Proceedings of the Conference, Sunday, November 28, First Plenary Meeting (Combined Chiefs of Staff minutes)," in ibid., 497.

Chapter 60

270 *"the plan adopted . . . May 1, 1944"*: "Proceedings of the Conference, Sunday, November 28, First Plenary Meeting (Bohlen minutes)," 489.

271 *"We cannot do . . . two or three"*: "Proceedings of the Conference, Sunday, November 28, First Plenary Meeting (Combined Chiefs of Staff minutes)," 499.

271 *"he and the Prime . . . Stalin on this point"*: Ibid.

271 *"The best method . . . northwestern France"*: "Proceedings of the Conference, Sunday, November 28, First Plenary Meeting (Bohlen minutes)," 490.

271 *"of great importance . . . defeat of Germany"*: "Proceedings of the Conference, Sunday, November 28, First Plenary Meeting (Combined Chiefs of Staff minutes)," 501.

271 *"had long agreed . . . should be undertaken"*: Ibid.

271 *"what could be done . . . months in Overlord"*: "Proceedings of the Conference, Sunday, November 28, First Plenary Meeting (Bohlen minutes)," 492.

272 *"Overlord be accepted . . . considered as diversionary"*: "Proceedings of the Conference, Sunday, November 28, First Plenary Meeting (Combined Chiefs of Staff minutes)," 505.

272 *"Stalin's aim . . . spring of 1944"*: Bohlen, *Witness to History*, 140.

272 *"all right . . . on the stomach"*: Joseph Stalin quoted in Simon Sebag Montefiore, *Stalin: The Court of the Red Tsar* (New York: Random House, 2003), 467.

Chapter 61

274 *"fourteen or sixteen hours per day"*: Plutenko and Vartanian, "Tegeran-43."

275 *"near the town . . . loaded with weapons"*: Dolgopolov, *Vartanian*, 36.

275 *"followed them to Tehran . . . by Skorzeny himself"*: Iurii Plutenko and Gevork Vartanian, "Tehran-43: Wrecking the Plan to Kill Stalin, Roosevelt and Churchill," *RIA Novosti*, October 16, 2007, accessed November 12, 2021, https://web.archive.org/web/20120629234011/http://en.rian.ru/analysis/20071016/84122320.html.

Chapter 62

277 *"accept rebuffs . . . it's my birthday"*: Averell Harriman's recollection of Churchill's words, quoted in Robert E. Sherwood, *The White House Papers of Henry Hopkins* (London: Eyre & Spottiswoode, 1949), 2:779.

Chapter 63

279 *It's a sword . . . embossed with jewels*: "Sword of Stalingrad," *New York Times*, December 7, 1943, 26.

279 *"To the Steel-Hearted . . . the British People"*: Ibid.

281 *"Overlord was the most . . . from that operation"*: "Proceedings of the Conference, Sunday, November 28, First Plenary Meeting (Bohlen minutes)," 537.

281 *"MARSHAL STALIN . . . really only diversions"*: Ibid., 538.

281 *"wished to ask . . . reassure the Russians"*: Ibid., 539.

282 *"Stalin kept needling Churchill without mercy"*: Harriman and Abel, *Special Envoy*, 273.

282 *"several times through . . . for the Germans"*: Ibid.

282 *"bound to rise up . . . should be liquidated"*: "Proceedings of the Conference, Monday, November 29, Tripartite Dinner Meeting (Bohlen minutes)," in *Conferences at Cairo and Tehran*, 553–54.

282 *"50,000 or possibly 100,000 . . . liquidated"*: Bohlen, *Witness to History*, 147.

282 *"The British Parliament . . . on this point"*: Harriman and Abel, *Special Envoy*, 274.

282 *"Fifty thousand must be shot"*: Churchill, *Second World War*, 5:330.

282 *"I would rather . . . by such infamy"*: Ibid.

283 *"I'd like to go . . . my seventieth year"*: Churchill quoted in Eubank, *Summit at Teheran*, 316.

Chapter 64

284 *"It was tempting . . . failure of the mission"*: Plutenko and Vartanian, "Tehran-43."

Chapter 65

286 *"fighting a losing . . . decision that night"*: Bohlen, *Witness to History,* 148.

287 *"Stalin, who had . . . showed great satisfaction"*: Harriman and Abel, *Special Envoy,* 274.

287 *"Now that the . . . with* smashing force*"*: "Third Plenary Meeting, November 30, 1943 (Bohlen minutes)," *Conferences at Cairo and Tehran,* 577.

287 *"it was important . . . aflame with battle"*: Ibid., 576.

288 *"transfer troops from . . . to the west"*: Ibid., 577.

288 *"cover plan . . . truth deserves a bodyguard of lies"*: Ibid., 578.

Chapter 66

289 *As dinner approaches . . . sing a chorus*: As described in Eubank, *Summit at Teheran,* 342.

290 *"May we be together for many years"*: Ibid.

290 *After he and Molotov . . . down the hall*: Ibid., 343.

290 *"a man who had devoted . . . our democratic civilization"*: "Tripartite Dinner Meeting, November 30, 1943 (Boettiger minutes)," in *Conferences at Cairo and Tehran,* 583.

290 *"Stalin the Great"*: Harriman and Abel, *Special Envoy,* 276.

291 *"the honors which . . . the Russian people"*: "Tripartite Dinner Meeting, November 30, 1943 (Boettiger minutes)," in *Conferences at Cairo and Tehran,* 583.

291 *"his joy . . . in this war"*: Ibid.

291 *"probably represented . . . during the war"*: Bohlen, *Witness to History,* 149.

291 *"We have differing . . . of the world"*: Ibid., 150.

Chapter 67

295 *"I thought . . . generation is alive"*: FDR press and radio conference, December 17, 1943, Executive Office of the President, accessed on November 2, 2021, http://www.fdrlibrary.marist.edu/_resources/images/pc/pc0155.pdf.

295 *"The actual fact . . . many excellent talks"*: Ibid.

296 *"by land, sea, and air"*: Reilly, *Reilly of the White House,* 188.

296 *"That night . . . through the street"*: FDR press and radio conference, December 17, 1943.

296 *"President Roosevelt disclosed . . . the Soviet embassy"*: "Stalin Bared Plot Against President," *New York Times,* December 18, 1943, 3.

297 *"we shall seek . . . will be ours"*: "Declaration of the Three Powers," in *Conferences at Cairo and Tehran,* 641.

297 *"President Roosevelt . . . world with war"*: Headline from *(Bradford, PA) Evening Star,* December 2, 1943, 1.

Chapter 68

299 *The first wave*: Figures from Hastings, *Inferno,* 516.

Chapter 69

301 *"The deciding day of this war has dawned"*: Joseph Goebbels diary entry June 6, 1944, quoted in Nigel Hamilton, *War and Peace: FDR's Final Odyssey, D-Day to Yalta, 1943–1945* (New York: Houghton Mifflin Harcourt, 2019), 265.

302 *"There were men crying . . . off by something"*: Hastings, *Inferno,* 517.

302 *total number . . . roughly 10,000*: See for example Sam Edwards, *Allies in Memory: World War II and the Politics of American Commemoration in Europe, c. 1941–2001* (Cambridge: Cambridge University Press, 2015), 85.

Chapter 70

304 *Yesterday, they finally got married*: Evans, *Third Reich at War,* 725.

304 *"Centuries will pass . . . international Jewry"*: For the complete and original German text of Hitler's final political testament, please see *Trial of the Major War Criminals before the International Military Tribunal: Nuremberg, 14 November 1945—1 October 1946,* vol. 41, Document Streicher-9 (Nuremberg: International Military Tribunal, 1947): 547–54.

305 *"the repository . . . human breast"*: Churchill, *Second World War, vol. 1, The Gathering Storm* (Boston: Houghlin Mifflin Company, 1948), 10.

305 *Goebbels's wife, Magda . . . her own life*: Evans, *Third Reich at War,* 727.

306 *"Handsome and extremely . . . very well spoken"*: "Notes on SS, SD and RSHA/MIL AMT, April 10, 1945," Security Service, KV 2/94–1, 60.

306 *"is undoubtedly . . . highest importance"*: "Interrogation of Franz Mayr," Security Service, KV 2/94–1, 9.

307 *Unlike Schellenberg . . . Allied troops*: Stuart Smith, *Otto Skorzeny: The Devil's Disciple* (New York: Bloomsbury USA, 2018), 231–32.

307 *"would mean good-bye . . . family, and comrades"*: Skorzeny, quoted in Ibid., 238.

307 *"As for suicide . . . our former enemies"*: Skorzeny, *Skorzeny's Special Missions,* 196.

307 *"a dozen . . . stripped naked"*: Skorzeny, *My Commando Operations,* 437.

308 *Allied "denazification" program*: For more information on "denazification," please see Andrew H. Beattie, *Allied Internment Camps in Occupied Germany: Extrajudicial Detention in the Name of Denazification, 1945–1950* (New York: Cambridge University Press, 2019); Perry Biddiscombe, *The Denazification of Germany: A History, 1945–1948* (London, UK: Tempus Publishing, 2006); and Frederick Taylor, *Exorcising Hitler: The Occupation and Denazification of Germany* (New York: Bloomsbury, 2011).

Chapter 71

311 *"While agreeing . . . broadcasting is harmful"*: "Defence Security Office, C.I.C.I. Persia, Counter-intelligence Summary No. 16, December 20, 1943," Security Service, KV 2/1480.

312 *"When the conference . . . a specific plot"*: Averell Harriman as quoted in Adrian O'Sullivan, *Espionage and Counterintelligence in Occupied Persia (Iran): The Success of the Allied Secret Services, 1941–45* (New York: Palgrave Macmillan, 2015), 182. See also Harriman and Abel, *Special Envoy,* 264–65.

312 *Thompson later claimed . . . guns and explosives*: See Walter Thompson's memoirs, Walter H. Thompson, *Assignment: Churchill* (Toronto: McLeod, 1955), esp. 283, and *Beside the Bulldog: The Intimate Memoirs of Churchill's Bodyguard* (London, UK: Apollo, 2003).

Chapter 72

314 *I want to entrust . . . in this matter"*: Sergo Beria, *Beria, My Father: Inside Stalin's Kremlin,* ed. Françoise Thom, trans. Brian Pearce (London, UK: Duckworth, 2001), 93.

315 *The younger Beria's . . . and allies alike*: For the full Beria account of Tehran, see ibid., 92–95. Beria further claims Stalin required him to do the same for the Yalta Conference, see ibid., 103–6. Another Soviet agent, twenty-three-year-old Zoya Zarubina, also claims she was assigned to gather information on Roosevelt and his entourage at Tehran and Yalta, playing the role of a hostess and furnishing Roosevelt's Tehran villa; see Inez Cope Jeffery, *Inside Russia: The Life and Times of Zoya Zarubina: Former Soviet Intelligence Officer and Interpreter During the Stalin Years* (Austin, TX: Eakin Press, 1999), 1–25. On Stalin and espionage more broadly, please see Hiroaki Kuromiya and Andrzej Peplonski, "Stalin, Espionage, and Counterespionage," in *Stalin and Europe: Imitation and Domination, 1928–1953*, eds. Timothy Snyder and Ray Brandon (New York: Oxford University Press, 2014), 73–91.

315 *"I still assume . . . was well bugged"*: Kenneth Strong quoted in O'Sullivan, *Espionage and Counterintelligence,* 183.

315 *At one point . . . the historical narrative*: The CIA has archived these files and they are viewable online, accessed October 15, 2021, https://www.cia .gov/readingroom/document/5197c264993294098d50e0b7.

316 *These diverging views . . . defeating Nazi Germany*: For accounts of the Soviet memory of the Second World War, see Jonathan Brunstedt, *The Soviet Myth of World War II: Patriotic Memory and the Russian Question in the USSR* (New York: Cambridge University Press, 2021), esp. chapter 5; and David L. Hoffman, *The Memory of the Second World War in Soviet and Post-Soviet Russia* (New York: Routledge, 2021). On competing memories of the war, please see Henry L. Roediger III et al., "Competing National Memories of World War II," *Proceedings of the National Academy of Sciences,* accessed February 2, 2022, https://www.pnas.org/content/116/34 /16678.

316 *Soviet critics . . . if at all*: Culturally, Soviet war films embraced Americans as allies immediately following the war, although often as unwitting individuals who initially sought to undermine the Soviet Union, only to discover it was much better than they thought. The first clear anti-American war movie came in 1949 with *Encounter at the Elbe,* which specifically portrays an American CIA agent conspiring with the Nazis. Among the Western Allies, especially in the United States, the memory of the war immediately capitalized how "we won the war," promoting nationalist narratives that downplayed the Soviet role. During the Cold War a general backlash toward Roosevelt's policies toward an alliance with the Soviets accompanied this trend. See John Bodnar, *The "Good War" in American Memory* (Baltimore, MD: Johns Hopkins University Press, 2010); Debra Ramsay, *American Media and the Memory of World War II* (New York: Routledge, 2015); Gennady Ustian, "Depicting Americans through the lens of Russian Cinema," *Russia Beyond,* March 4, 2017, accessed February 2, 2022, https://www.rbth.com/arts/movies/2017/03/04/depicting-americans-through-the-lens-of-russian-cinema_712646; and Vladislav M. Zubok, *A Failed Empire: The Soviet Union in the Cold War from Stalin to Gorbachev* (Chapel Hill: University of North Carolina Press, 2009), esp. chapters 1 and 2.

317 *"I believe that . . . enemies of Germany"*: Skorzeny, *My Commando Operations,* 204.

317 *"the plan was simply impractical"*: Ibid.

318 *Called* The Long Jump: Laslo Havas, *The Long Jump: The 1943 Plot to Assassinate the Big Three,* trans. Kathleen Szasz (London: Neville Spearman, 1967). In some editions the book has the alternate title *Hitler's Plot to Kill the Big Three.*

318 *Nevertheless, some authors . . . genuine evidence*: For a recent and thorough account of the plot that utilizes Havas's alleged characters and sources, see Howard Blum's *Night of the Assassins.*

Chapter 73

319 *"There is endless . . . was going on"*: "Press Conference with Veterans of the Russian Foreign Intelligence Service," Kremlin International News Broadcast, November 18, 2003.

321 *The problem is . . . agreed to meet*: As suggested in our text, it could be that Vartanian is actually discussing the events of August 1943, namely the pursuit and arrest of the Operation Franz agents. He concedes that after these arrests the assassination plot was canceled, but that the Soviets were not aware of this until after the war. See Dolgopolov, *Vartanian,* esp. chapter 2. This is further supported by another interview with Kirpichenko that originally appeared in the Russian newspaper *Gudok.* Kirpichenko, after reciting the standard Soviet version of events, claims the six German commandos included Rockstroh and that his diary, preserved in the Soviet intelligence archives, confirms the plot. The interview is available on the Russian Foreign Intelligence Service's

website: V. Loshkul, "Novoe o 'Tegerane-43,'" *Gudok,* November 28, 2003, accessed November 17, 2021, http://svr.gov.ru/smi/2003/11/gudok20031128.htm.

Chapter 74

323 *Researchers and authors . . . into popular culture*: For an example of the skeptical position regarding the existence of the plot, see Adrian O'Sullivan's *Espionage and Counterintelligence,* 170–94. For an example of a colorful account of the plot that incorporates the persons that Laslo Havas claims to have interviewed, see Blum, *Night of the Assassins.*

327 *"at first resisted interrogation"*: O'Sullivan, *Nazi Secret Warfare,* 124.

327 *In late 1943 . . . rest of the war*: Ibid., 121.

327 *Germans suggested his name . . . never materialized*: Ibid., 124.

327 *In 1946 . . . promptly escaped again*: Ibid., 248.

328 *From there . . . Middle Eastern governments*: Ibid., 248–49.

Chapter 75

329 *forty thousand civilian deaths*: The figure for the number of French civilian deaths caused by the 1944 Allied bombing raids has been a subject of some debate. French author and historian Henri Amouroux estimated the number was higher, at over fifty thousand. For his breakdown see Henri Amouroux, *La Grande histoire des Français sous l'Occupation,* vols. 7–8 (Paris: Robert Laffont, 1985–88).

329 *As Soviet troops . . . often the victims*: On the brutalities in the Soviet zone of occupation, pleases see Mikkel Dack, "Crimes Committed by Soviet Soldiers Against German Civilians, 1944–1945: A Historiographical Analysis," *Journal of Military and Strategic Studies* 10, no. 4 (Summer 2008): 1–33; Giles MacDonogh, *After the Reich: The Brutal History of the Allied Occupation* (New York: Basic Books, 2009); and Norman M. Naimark, *The Russians in Germany: A History of the Soviet Zone of Occupation, 1945–1949* (Cambridge, MA: Belknap Press, 1997), esp. chapter 2.

330 *"Reluctantly, but as . . . from the message"*: FDR letter to Robert Hannegan, July 11, 1944, American Presidency Project, accessed November 1, 2021, https://www.presidency.ucsb.edu/node/210899.

331 *"We have learned . . . is to be one"*: Roosevelt, "Fourth Inaugural Address," Saturday, January 20, 1945, in Yale Law School's *The Avalon Project: Documents in Law, History and Diplomacy,* accessed November 28, 2021, https://avalon.law.yale.edu/20th_century/froos4.asp.

331 *"I felt certain he was going to die"*: John Gunther quoted in Smith, *FDR,* 629.

332 *for the first time in his presidency*: Ibid., 632.

333 *"He was absolutely dead weight"*: Reilly, *Reilly of the White House,* 227.

333 *"We have fifteen more minutes to work . . . in the back of my head"*: Elizabeth Shoumatoff, *FDR's Unfinished Portrait: A Memoir* (Pittsburgh: University of Pittsburgh Press, 1990), 174–75.

334 *"I felt as if I had . . . deep and irrefutable loss"*: Churchill, *Second World War*, vol. 6, *Triumph and Tragedy* (Boston: Houghton Mifflin Co., 1953), 471.

334 *"I have been told . . . Then we marched on"*: Story and quotes are as recalled by the former private, Bill Livingstone; see Bill Livingstone "My Six Month Furlough," *World War II Magazine*, October, 2021, accessed November 2, 2021, https://www.historynet.com/he-jumped-out-of-a-burning-b-17-and-into-the-hands-of-the-germans/.

335 *"The child . . . sobbed too"*: Grace Tully, *F.D.R.: My Boss*, 369.

335 *one of Roosevelt's favorite musicians . . . down his face*: As described by Tully, Ibid. A photographer, Ed Clark, also captured a famous photograph of Jackson playing, accessed November 10, 2021, at https://www.life.com/history/mourning-fdr-in-a-classic-photo-the-face-of-a-nations-loss/.

Selected Bibliography

Bates, John L. "The 'Eureka' Conference: A Busy Time in Teheran." *Military Review* 66, no. 10 (October 1986): 74–82.

Bazna, Elyesa. *I Was Cicero*. Translated by Eric Mosbacher. New York: Harper and Row, 1962.

Beevor, Antony. *The Second World War*. New York: Little, Brown and Company, 2012.

Bell, Leland V. "The Failure of Nazism in America: The German American Bund, 1936–1941." *Political Science Quarterly* 85, no. 4 (1970): 585–99.

Beorn, Waitman Wade. *The Holocaust in Eastern Europe: At the Epicenter of the Final Solution*. London: Bloomsbury, 2018.

Beria, Sergo. *Beria, My Father: Inside Stalin's Kremlin*. Edited by Françoise Thom. Translated by Brian Pearce. London, UK: Duckworth, 2001.

Blandford, Edmund L. *SS Intelligence: The Nazi Secret Service*. Edison, NJ: Castle Books, 2001.

Bohlen, Charles E. *Witness to History, 1929–1969*. New York: W.W. Norton & Co., 1973.

Blum, Howard. *Night of the Assassins: The Untold Story of Hitler's Plot to Kill FDR, Churchill, and Stalin*. New York: HarperCollins, 2020.

Breitman, Richard, and Lichtman, Allan J. *FDR and the Jews*. Cambridge, MA: Harvard University Press, 2013.

Butler, Susan, ed. *My Dear Mr. Stalin: The Complete Correspondence of Franklin D. Roosevelt and Joseph V. Stalin*. New Haven, CT: Yale University Press, 2006.

Central Intelligence Agency. *C/CI/R&A: Soviet Book for Alleged Nazi Plot against Tehran Conference, December 23, 1968*. Freedom of Information Act Electronic Reading Room. https://www.cia.gov/readingroom/docs/TPMURILLO%20%20%20VOL.%201_0046.pdf.

———. *Situation Report No. 8: AMT VI of the RHSA, Gruppe VI C*. Eilitz, Herbert. Special Collection: Nazi War Crime Disclosure Act. FOIA/ESDN(CREST): 519a6b26993294098b511029. Washington D.C.: 2001/2006. https://www.cia.gov/readingroom/document/519a6b26993294098d511029.

Churchill, Winston. *The Second World War*. 6 vols. Boston: Houghton Mifflin Co., 1948–1954.

Doerries, Reinhard R. *Hitler's Intelligence Chief: Walter Schellenberg*. New York: Enigma Books, 2009.

———. *Hitler's Last Chief of Foreign Intelligence: Allied Interrogations of Walter Schellenberg*. London: Frank Cass, 2003.

Dolgopolov, Nikolai. "How 'the Lion and the Bear' Were Saved." *Russia Beyond The Headlines*, November 29, 2007. https://www.rbth.com/articles/2007/11/29/lion_and_bear.html.

———. *Vartanian: zhizn' zamechatel'nykh liudei*. Moscow: Molodaia gvardiia, 2014.

Dunn, Susan. *1940: FDR, Willkie, Lindbergh, Hitler—the Election amid the Storm*. New Haven, CT: Yale University Press, 2013.

Eubank, Keith. *Summit at Teheran: The Untold Story*. New York: William Morrow and Company, 1985.

Evans, Richard J. *The Third Reich at War*. New York: Penguin Books, 2008.

Farago, Ladislas. *The Game of Foxes: The Untold Story of German Espionage in the United States and Great Britain during World War II*. New York: D. McKay Company, 1972.

Foreign Relations of the United States: Diplomatic Papers: The Conferences at Cairo and Tehran, 1943. Washington, D.C.: United States Government Printing Office, 1961.

Gerwarth, Robert. *Hitler's Hangman: The Life of Heydrich*. New Haven: Yale University Press, 2011.

Gilbert, Martin. *Churchill: A Life*. London: Pimlico, 1991.

Goebbels, Joseph. *The Goebbels Diaries: 1942–1943*. Translated by Louis P. Lochner. Garden City, NY: Doubleday & Company, 1948.

Goodwin, Doris Kearns. *No Ordinary Time: Franklin and Eleanor Roosevelt: The Home Front in World War II*. New York: Simon & Schuster, 1994.

Hamilton, Nigel. *The Mantle of Command: FDR at War, 1941–1942*. New York: Houghton Mifflin Harcourt, 2014.

———. *Commander In Chief: FDR's Battle with Churchill, 1943*. New York: Houghton Mifflin Harcourt, 2016.

———. *War and Peace: FDR's Final Odyssey D-Day to Yalta, 1943–1945*. New York: Houghton Mifflin Harcourt, 2019.

Harriman, W. Averell, and Elie Abel. *Special Envoy to Churchill and Stalin, 1941–1946*. New York: Random House, 1975.

Harrison, Gordon A. *European Theater of Operations: Cross-Channel Attack*. Washington, D.C.: U.S. Army Center of Military History, 1993.

Hastings, Max. *Inferno: The World at War, 1939–1945*. New York: Random House, 2011.

Havas, Laslo. *Hitler's Plot to Kill the Big Three*. Cowles Book Company: New York, 1967.

———. *The Long Jump: The 1943 Plot to Assassinate the Big Three*. Translated by Kathleen Szasz. London: Neville Spearman, 1967.

Hett, Benjamin Carter. *The Death of Democracy: Hitler's Rise to Power and the Downfall of the Weimar Republic*. New York: Henry Holt and Company, 2018.

Hohne, Heinz. *Canaris: Patriot im Zwielicht.* Munich: C. Bertelsmann Verlag, 1976.

Irving, David, ed. *Breach of Security: The German Secret Intelligence File on Events Leading to the Second World War.* London: William Kimber, 1968.

Jackson, Ashley. *Persian Gulf Command: A History of the Second World War in Iran and Iraq.* New Haven, CT: Yale University Press, 2018.

Jewish Virtual Library. "Adolf Hitler: Speech Declaring War Against the United States (December 11, 1941)." Speeches and Declarations. https://www.jewishvirtuallibrary.org/hitler-s-speech-declaring-war-against-the-united-states.

Jörgensen, Christer. *Hitler's Espionage Machine: German Intelligence Agencies and Operations during World War II.* Staplehurst, UK: Spellmount Ltd., 2004.

Kahn, David. *Hitler's Spies: German Military Intelligence in World War II.* New York: Macmillan, 1978.

Katamidze, Slava. *Loyal Comrades, Ruthless Killers: The Secret Services of the USSR, 1920's to the Present.* New York: Brown Reference Group, 2003.

Kern, Gary. "How 'Uncle Joe' Bugged FDR." *Studies in Intelligence* 47, no. 1 (March 2003).

Kershaw, Ian. *Hitler, 1936–1945: Nemesis.* London: W. W. Norton & Co., 2000.

———. *To Hell and Back: Europe 1914–1949.* New York: Penguin, 2015.

Kimball, Warren F. "A Different Take on FDR at Teheran: Raising Questions." *Studies in Intelligence* 49 no. 3 (2005).

———. *Forged in War: Roosevelt, Churchill, and the Second World War.* New York: William Morrow and Company, 1997.

Kuznets, Iurii. *Tehran-43.* Moscow: Eskimo, 2003.

Lord, Walter. *Day of Infamy: The Bombing of Pearl Harbor.* New York: Open Road Media, 2021.

MacLean, Elizabeth Kimball. *Joseph E. Davies: Envoy to the Soviets.* Westport, CT: Praeger, 1992.

Mader, Julius. *Hitlers Spionagegenerale sagen aus.* Berlin, Verlag der Nation, 1970.

Medvedev, Dmitry N. *Silnyie dukhom (Eto bylo pod Rovno).* Moscow: Pravda Publishing, 1951/1989.

Ministry of Foreign Affairs of the U.S.S.R. *Correspondence between the Chairman of the Council of Ministers of the USSR and the Presidents of the USA and the Prime Ministers of Great Britain during the Great Patriotic War of 1941–1945.* 2 Vols. Moscow, U.S.S.R.: Foreign Languages Publishing House, 1957.

Montefiore, Simon Sebag. *Stalin: The Court of the Red Tsar.* New York: Random House, 2003.

Official Kremlin International News Broadcast. "Press Conference with Veterans of the Russian Foreign Intelligence Service." *Federation of American Scientists,* November 18, 2003. https://fas.org/irp/world/russia/teheran43.html.

O'Sullivan, Adrian. *Espionage and Counterintelligence in Occupied Persia (Iran): The Success of the Allied Secret Services, 1941–45*. New York: Palgrave Macmillan, 2015.

———. *Nazi Secret Warfare in Occupied Persia (Iran): The Failure of the German Intelligence Services, 1939–45*. New York: Palgrave Macmillan, 2014.

Paehler, Katrin. *The Third Reich's Intelligence Services: The Career of Walter Schellenberg*. New York: Cambridge University Press, 2017.

Payne, Robert. *The Life and Death of Adolf Hitler*. New York: Praeger Publishers, 1973.

Plutenko, Iurii, and Gevork Vartanian. "Tegeran-43: 'My byli ne takie! . . .'" *Zavtra*, October 31, 2007. https://zavtra.ru/blogs/2007–10–3122.

———. "Tehran-43: Wrecking the Plan to Kill Stalin, Roosevelt and Churchill." *RIA Novosti*, October 16, 2007. https://web.archive.org/web/20120629234011/http://en.rian.ru/analysis/20071016/84122320.html.

Reilly, Michael F. *Reilly of the White House*. New York: Simon & Schuster, 1947.

Rezun, Miron. *The Soviet Union and Iran: Soviet Policy in Iran from the Beginnings of the Pahlavi Dynasty until the Soviet Invasion in 1941*. Geneva: Stijthoff & Noordhoff International Publishers, 1981.

Roll, David L. *The Hopkins Touch: Harry Hopkins and the Forging of the Alliance to Defeat Hitler*. Oxford: Oxford University Press, 2013.

Roosevelt, Franklin D. *"Day of Infamy" Speech: Joint Address to Congress Leading to a Declaration of War Against Japan*. December 8, 1941. SEN 77A-H1, Records of the United States Senate. Record Group 46, National Archives. https://www.archives.gov/historical-docs/day-of-infamy-speech.

Rosenman, Samuel I. *The Public Papers and Addresses of Franklin D. Roosevelt*. 13 vols. New York: Random House, 1938–1950.

Sainsbury, Keith. *The Turning Point: Roosevelt, Stalin, Churchill, and Chiang Kai-shek, 1943: The Moscow, Cairo, and Tehran Conferences*. New York: Oxford University Press, 1985.

Schellenberg, Walter. *Hitler's Secret Service (The Labyrinth)*. Translated by Louis Hagen. New York: Harper & Row, 1971.

Schultz, Colin. "Meet the Woman Who Taste-Tested Hitler's Dinner." *Smithsonian Magazine*, April 29, 2013. https://www.smithsonianmag.com/smart-news/meet-the-woman-who-taste-tested-hitlers-dinner-44682990/.

Scott, James M. "The Untold Story of the Vengeful Japanese Attack after the Doolittle Raid." *Smithsonian Magazine*, April 15, 2015. https://www.smithsonianmag.com/history/untold-story-vengeful-japanese-attack-doolittle-raid-180955001/.

The Security Service, KV 2. Folder 1477–1491. The National Archives, United Kingdom.

Skorzeny, Otto. *My Commando Operations: The Memoirs of Hitler's Most Daring Commando*. Translated by David Johnston. Atglen, PA: Schiffer Publishing, 1995.

———. *Skorzeny's Special Missions: The Memoirs of Hitler's Most Daring Commando*. Minneapolis: Zenith Press, 2011.

Sherwood, Robert E. *Roosevelt and Hopkins: An Intimate History.* New York: Harper and Brothers, 1948.

———. *The White House Papers of Harry L. Hopkins. Vol. 2, January 1942–July 1945.* London: Eyre & Spottiswood, 1949.

Smith, Jean Edward. *FDR.* New York: Random House, 2007.

Smith, Stuart. *Otto Skorzeny: The Devil's Disciple.* New York: Bloomsbury USA, 2018.

Stephan, Robert W. *Stalin's Secret War: Soviet Counterintelligence against the Nazis, 1941–1945.* Lawrence: University Press of Kansas, 1995.

Sudoplatov, Pavel, Anatoli Sudoplatov, Jerrold L. Schecter, and Leona P. Schecter. *Special Tasks: The Memoirs of an Unwanted Witness, a Soviet Spymaster.* Boston: Little, Brown, 1994.

Toland, John. *The Rising Sun: The Decline and Fall of the Japanese Empire, 1936–1945.* New York: Modern Library, 2003.

———. "Triple Jeopardy: The Nazi Plan to Kill WWII Leaders in Tehran." *Sputnik News* (2007), http://sputniknews.com/20070104/94756632.html.

Trial of the Major War Criminals Before the International Military Tribunal, Vols. 4–5. Nuremberg: International Military Tribunal, 1947. The Avalon Project: Documents in Law, History and Diplomacy, Yale Law School's Lillian Goldman Law Library. https://avalon.law.yale.edu/subject_menus/imt.asp#proc.

Tully, Grace. *F.D.R.: My Boss.* Chicago: People's Book Club, 1949.

West, Nigel. *Historical Dictionary of World War II Intelligence.* Lanham, MD: Scarecrow Press, 2007.

———. *Encyclopedia of Political Assassinations.* Lanham, MD: Rowman & Littlefield, 2017.

Wires, Richard. *The Cicero Spy Affair: German Access to British Secrets in World War II.* Westport, CT: Praeger Publishers, 1999.

Yenne, Bill. *Operation Long Jump: Stalin, Roosevelt, Churchill, and the Greatest Assassination Plot in History.* Washington: Regnery History, 2015.

Index

AXIS DOMINATED
EUROPE
Statute Miles

0 50 100   200   300

As of July 1, 1943
Base map as of June 22, 1941,
the day Germany attacked
the Soviet Union